The Oceans

A TREASURY
OF THE SEA WORLD

The Oceans

A TREASURY
OF THE SEA WORLD

EDITED BY

Seon Manley and Gogo Lewis

1967

Doubleday & Company, Inc.

GARDEN CITY, NEW YORK

This book is for the Giannottis
and the Lidas . . .
and the sea.

We are grateful to the authors, agents, and publishers who have given us permission to reprint the following selections:

"The Gray Beginnings" from *The Sea Around Us* by Rachel Carson. Copyright © 1950, 1951, 1961 by Rachel L. Carson. Reprinted by permission of Oxford University Press, Inc.

"Surfing" from *The Cruise of the Snark* by Jack London. Reprinted by permission of Irving Shepard.

"The Maelstrom" from *Unsolved Mysteries of the Sea and Shore* by Edward Rowe Snow. Copyright © 1963 by Edward Rowe Snow. Reprinted by permission of Dodd, Mead & Company, Inc.

"The Riddle of the Ridley" from *The Windward Road* by Archie Carr. Copyright © 1955 by Archie Carr. Reprinted by permission of Alfred A. Knopf, Inc.

"Winter Visitors" from *The Outermost House* by Henry Beston. Copyright 1928, 1949, © 1956 by Henry Beston. Reprinted by permission of Holt, Rinehart and Winston, Inc.

"Battlefield of the Shore" from *Nonsuch: Land of Water* by William Beebe. Copyright 1932 by William Beebe. Reprinted by permission of Elswyth Thane Beebe.

"The Marvel of a Tide" from *The Ocean Island* by Gilbert C. Klingel. Copyright 1940 by Dodd, Mead & Company, Inc. Reprinted by permission of Dodd, Mead & Company, Inc.

"Shark Close-Ups" from *The Silent World* by Captain Jacques-Yves Cousteau with Frédéric Dumas. Copyright 1953 by Harper & Brothers. Reprinted by permission of Harper & Row, Publishers.

"The Palaus and the Best Spearfisherman" from *Lady With a Spear* by Eugenie Clark. Copyright 1953 by Eugenie Clark Konstantinu. Reprinted by permission of Harper & Row, Publishers.

Abridgment of chapters v–vi "Boy Beneath the Sea" from *The Treasure of the Great Reef* by Arthur C. Clarke with Mike Wilson. Copyright © 1964 by Arthur C. Clarke. Reprinted by permission of Harper & Row, Publishers. Permission to reprint also granted by David Higham Associates, Ltd. and Arthur Barker, publisher.

"Batfish" from *Submarine!* by Commander Edward L. Beach, U.S.N. Copyright 1952 by Edward L. Beach. Reprinted by permission of Holt, Rinehart and Winston, Inc.

"In an Open Boat" from *South: The Story of Shackleton's Last Expedition* by Sir Ernest Shackleton. Reprinted by permission of William Heinemann, Ltd., Publishers.

"Typhoon" from *Sea Fights and Shipwrecks* by Hanson W. Baldwin. Copyright © 1938, 1955 by Hanson W. Baldwin. Reprinted by permission of Doubleday & Company, Inc.

"An August Day's Sail" from *Spring Tides* by Samuel Eliot Morison. Copyright © 1965 by Samuel Eliot Morison. Reprinted by permission of Houghton Mifflin Company, Publishers.

We would also like to thank the following persons, agencies, libraries, and museums who contributed to various aspects of this book:

Seth Agnew, Douglas G. Allan, Preston Brown, Robert A. Carter, John Ernst, Fire Island National Seashore, W. C. Givens, Mr. and Mrs. Robert Higden, Phil Hubert, Columbus Iselin, Don Jones, James Jump, Lew King, Ian Moffat, Dr. and Mrs. Robert Cushman Murphy, the Mariners Museum, New York Zoological Society, Office of the Assistant Secretary of Defense, Dr. George Papinski, Ralph Paterline, Carol Rockhold, Robert Rod, Scripps Institute of Oceanography, Joseph Spector, Charles Summer, Dr. George Vineyard, Mr. and Mrs. George Webster, Dr. Virginia Werden, Woods Hole Marine Biological Laboratory, Martin Zwerin.

Illustrations

The marvel of an ebb tide ("The Marvel of a Tide")
  Courtesy of The American Museum of Natural History

A close-up of a blue shark group ("Shark Close-ups")
  Courtesy of The American Museum of Natural History

FOLLOWING PAGE 192

Eugenie Clark spearfishing in the Red Sea ("The Palaus and the Best Spearfisherman")
  From *Lady With a Spear* by Eugenie Clark (Harper, 1953)

This is the gear used by treasure hunters ("Boy Beneath the Sea")
  Courtesy of Scripps Institue of Oceanography

The heroic submarine USS *Batfish* ("Batfish")
  Official US Navy photograph

A contemporary print depicting the mutiny on the whaleship *Globe:* Comstock running Lumbert through the body ("Mutiny!")
  Courtesy of the New York Historical Society, New York City

The execution of Humphries ("Mutiny!")
  Courtesy of the New York Historical Society, New York City

The whaleship *Globe* off the Mulgrave Islands ("Mutiny!")
  Courtesy of the New York Historical Society, New York City

The death of Samuel Comstock ("Mutiny!")
  Courtesy of the New York Historical Society, New York City

Blackbeard boarding a sloop ("Enter Blackbeard the Pirate")
  Courtesy of the Mariners Museum, Newport News, Virginia

The *Cachalot* in which Frank Bullen sailed ("Our First Whale")
  A contemporary print

Moonlight on a frozen Antarctic sea ("In an Open Boat")
  Courtesy of The American Museum of Natural History

Sir Ernest Shackleton, the Antarctic explorer ("In an Open Boat")
  Courtesy of The American Museum of Natural History

Contents

The Sea

The Shore

Underwater

The Sea

The Gray Beginnings

RACHEL CARSON

The ocean dominates our planet. Today the world of inner space—the oceans—is as exciting as the world of outer space. Neither inner nor outer space has yet revealed all of its mysteries, but we live in a great age of exploration, as rich and exciting as the Elizabethan period that opened our modern world. The scientist who discovers, and the writer who interprets, are both adventurers into that world. Here, Rachel Carson, both a scientist and a writer, tells us about the very beginnings of inner space.

And the earth was without form, and void; and darkness was upon the face of the deep. GENESIS

*B*eginnings are apt to be shadowy, and so it is with the beginnings of that great mother of life, the sea. Many people have debated how and when the earth got its ocean, and it is not surprising that their explanations do not always agree. For the plain and inescapable truth is that no one was there to see, and in the absence of eyewitness accounts there is bound to be a certain amount of disagreement. So if I tell here the story of how the young planet Earth acquired an ocean, it must be a story pieced together from many sources and containing whole chapters the details of which we can only imagine. The story is founded on the testimony of the earth's most ancient rocks, which were young when the earth was young; on other evidence written on the face of the earth's satellite, the moon; and on hints contained in the history of the sun and the whole universe of star-filled space. For although no man was there to witness this cosmic birth, the stars and the moon and the rocks were there, and, indeed, had much to do with the fact that there is an ocean.

The events of which I write must have occurred somewhat more than 2 billion years ago. As nearly as science can tell that is the approximate age of the earth, and the ocean must be very nearly as old. It is possible now to discover the age of the rocks that compose the crust of the earth by measuring the rate of decay of the radioactive materials they contain. The oldest rocks found anywhere on earth—in Manitoba—are about 2.3 billion years old. Allowing 100 million years or so for the cooling of the earth's materials to form a rocky crust, we arrive at the supposition that the tempestuous and violent events connected with our planet's birth occurred nearly 2½ billion years ago. But this is only a minimum estimate, for rocks indicating an even greater age may be found at any time.

The new earth, freshly torn from its parent sun, was a ball of whirling gases, intensely hot, rushing through the black spaces of the universe on a path and at a speed controlled by immense forces. Gradually the ball of flaming gases cooled. The gases began to liquefy, and Earth became a molten mass. The materials of this mass eventually became sorted out in a definite pattern: the heaviest in the center, the less heavy surrounding them, and the least heavy forming the outer rim. This is the pattern which persists today—a central sphere of molten iron, very nearly as hot as it was 2 billion years ago, an intermediate sphere of semi-plastic basalt, and a hard outer shell, relatively quite thin and composed of solid basalt and granite.

The outer shell of the young earth must have been a good many millions of years changing from the liquid to the solid state, and it is believed that, before this change was completed, an event of the greatest importance took place—the formation of the moon. The next time you stand on a beach at night, watching the moon's bright path across the water, and conscious of the moon-drawn tides, remember that the moon itself may have been born of a great tidal wave of earthly substance, torn off into space. And remember that if the moon was formed in this fashion, the event may have had much to do with shaping the ocean basins and the continents as we know them.

There were tides in the new earth, long before there was an ocean. In response to the pull of the sun the molten liquids of the earth's whole surface rose in tides that rolled unhindered around the globe and only gradually slackened and diminished as the earthly shell cooled, congealed, and hardened. Those who believe that the moon is a child of earth say that during an early stage of the earth's development something happened that caused this rolling, viscid tide to gather speed and momentum and to rise to unimaginable heights. Apparently the force that created these greatest tides the earth has ever known was the force of resonance, for at this time the period of the solar tides had come to approach, then equal, the period of the free oscillation of the liquid earth. And so every sun tide was given increased momentum by the push of the earth's oscillation, and each of the twice-daily tides was larger than the one before it. Physicists have calculated that, after 500 years of such monstrous, steadily increasing tides, those on the side toward the sun became too high for stability, and a great wave was torn away and hurled into space. But immediately, of course, the newly created satellite became subject to physical laws that sent it spinning in an orbit of its own about the earth.

There are reasons for believing that this event took place after the earth's crust had become slightly hardened, instead of during its partly liquid state. There is to this day a great scar on the surface of the globe. This scar or depression holds the Pacific Ocean. According to some geophysicists, the floor of the Pacific is composed of basalt, the substance of the earth's middle layer, while all other oceans are floored with a thin layer of granite. We immediately wonder what became of the Pacific's granite covering and the most convenient assumption is that it was torn away when the moon was formed. There is supporting evidence. The mean density of the moon is much less than that of the earth (3.3 compared with 5.5), suggesting that the moon took away none of the earth's heavy iron core, but that it is composed only of the granite and some of the basalt of the outer layers.

The birth of the moon probably helped shape other regions of the world ocean besides the Pacific. When part of the crust was torn away, strains must have been set up in the remaining granite envelope. Perhaps the granite mass cracked open on the side opposite the moon scar. Perhaps, as the earth spun on its axis and rushed on its orbit through space, the cracks widened and the masses of granite began to drift apart, moving over a tarry, slowly hardening layer of basalt. Gradually the outer portions of the basalt layer became solid and the wandering continents came to rest, frozen into place with oceans between them. In spite of theories to the contrary, the weight of geologic evidence seems to be that the locations of the major ocean basins and the major continental land masses are today much the same as they have been since a very early period of the earth's history.

But this is to anticipate the story, for when the moon was born there was no ocean. The gradually cooling earth was enveloped in heavy layers of cloud, which contained much of the water of the new planet. For a long time its surface was so hot that no moisture could fall without immediately being reconverted to steam. This dense, perpetually renewed cloud covering must have been thick enough that no rays of sunlight could penetrate it. And so the rough outlines of the continents and the empty ocean basins were sculptured out of the surface of the earth in darkness, in a Stygian world of heated rock and swirling clouds and gloom.

As soon as the earth's crust cooled enough, the rains began to fall. Never have there been such rains since that time. They fell continuously, day and night, days passing into months, into years, into centuries. They poured into the waiting ocean basins, or, falling upon the continental masses, drained away to become sea.

That primeval ocean, growing in bulk as the rains slowly filled its basins, must have been only faintly salt. But the falling rains were the symbol of the dissolution of the continents. From the moment the rains began to fall, the lands began to be worn away and carried to the sea. It is an endless, inexorable process that has never stopped—the dissolving of the rocks, the leaching out of their contained minerals, the carrying of the rock fragments and dissolved minerals to the ocean. And over the eons of time, the sea has grown ever more bitter with the salt of the continents.

In what manner the sea produced the mysterious and wonderful stuff called protoplasm we cannot say. In its warm, dimly lit waters the unknown conditions of temperature and pressure and saltiness must have been the critical ones for the creation of life from non-life. At any rate they produced the result that neither the alchemists with their crucibles nor modern scientists in their laboratories have been able to achieve.

Before the first living cell was created, there may have been many trials and failures. It seems probable that, within the warm saltiness of the primeval sea, certain organic substances were fashioned from carbon dioxide, sulphur, phosphorus, potassium, and calcium. Perhaps these were transition steps from which the complex molecules of protoplasm arose—molecules that somehow acquired the ability to reproduce themselves and begin the endless stream of life. But at present no one is wise enough to be sure.

Those first living things may have been simple microorganisms rather like some of the bacteria we know today—mysterious borderline forms that were not quite plants, not quite animals, barely over the intangible line that separates the non-living from the living. It is doubtful that this first life possessed the substance chlorophyll, with which plants in sunlight transform lifeless chemicals into the living stuff of their tissues. Little sunshine could enter their dim world, penetrating the cloud banks from which fell the endless rains. Probably the sea's first children lived on the organic substances then present in the ocean waters, or, like the iron and sulphur bacteria that exist today, lived directly on inorganic food.

All the while the cloud cover was thinning, the darkness of the nights alternated with palely illumined days, and finally the sun for the first time shone through upon the sea. By this time some of the living things that floated in the sea must have developed the magic of chlorophyll. Now they were able to take the carbon dioxide of the air and the water of the sea and of these elements, in sunlight, build the organic substances they needed for life. So the first true plants came into being.

Another group of organisms, lacking the chlorophyll but needing organic food, found they could make a way of life for themselves by devouring the plants. So the first animals arose, and from that day to this, every animal in the world has followed the habit it learned in the ancient seas and depends, directly or through complex food chains, on the plants for food and life.

As the years passed, and the centuries, and the millions of years, the stream of life grew more and more complex. From simple, one-celled creatures, others that were aggregations of specialized cells arose, and then creatures with organs for feeding, digesting, breathing, reproducing. Sponges grew on the rocky bottom of the sea's edge and coral animals built their habitations in warm, clear waters. Jellyfish swam and drifted in the sea. Worms evolved, and starfish, and hard-shelled creatures with many-jointed legs. The plants, too, progressed, from the microscopic algae to branched and curiously fruiting seaweeds that swayed with the tides and were plucked from the coastal rocks by the surf and cast adrift.

During all this time the continents had no life. There was little to induce living things to come ashore, forsaking their all-providing, all-embracing mother sea. The lands must have been bleak and hostile beyond the power of words to describe. Imagine a whole continent of naked rock, across which no covering mantle of green had been drawn—a continent without soil, for there were no land plants to aid in its formation and bind it to the rocks with their roots. Imagine a land of stone, a silent land, except for the sound of the rains and winds that swept across it. For there was no living voice, and nothing moved over its surface except the shadows of the clouds.

Meanwhile, the gradual cooling of the planet, which had first given the earth it's hard granite crust, was progressing into its deeper layers; and as the interior slowly cooled and contracted, it drew away from the outer shell. This shell, accommodating itself to the shrinking sphere within it, fell into folds and wrinkles—the earth's first mountain ranges.

Geologists tell us that there must have been at least two periods of mountain building (often called "revolutions") in that dim period, so long ago that the rocks have no record of it, so long ago that the mountains themselves have long since been worn away. Then there came a third great period of upheaval and readjustment of the earth's crust, about a billion years ago, but of all its majestic mountains the only reminders today are the Laurentian hills of eastern Canada, and a great shield of granite over the flat country around Hudson Bay.

The epochs of mountain building only served to speed up the processes of erosion by which the continents were worn down and their crumbling rock and contained minerals returned to the sea. The uplifted masses of the mountains were prey to the bitter cold of the upper atmosphere and under the attacks of frost and snow and ice the rocks cracked and crumbled away. The rains beat with greater violence upon the slopes of the hills and carried away the substance of the mountains in torrential streams. There was still no plant covering to modify and resist the power of the rains.

And in the sea, life continued to evolve. The earliest forms have left no fossils by which we can identify them. Probably they were soft-bodied, with no hard parts that could be preserved. Then, too, the rock layers formed in those early days have since been so altered by enormous heat and pressure, under the foldings of the earth's crust, that any fossils they might have contained would have been destroyed.

For the past 500 million years, however, the rocks have preserved the fossil record. By the dawn of the Cambrian period, when the history of living things was first inscribed on rock pages, life in the sea had progressed so far that all the main groups of backboneless or invertebrate animals had been developed. But there were no animals with backbones, no insects or spiders, and still no plant or animal had been evolved that was capable of venturing onto the forbidding land. So for more than three-fourths of geologic time the continents were desolate and uninhabited, while the sea prepared the life that was later to invade them and make them habitable. Meanwhile, with violent tremblings of the earth and with the fire and smoke of roaring volcanoes, mountains rose and wore away, glaciers moved to and fro over the earth, and the sea crept over the continents and again receded.

It was not until Silurian time, some 350 million years ago, that the first pioneer of land life crept out on the shore. It was an arthropod, one of the great tribe that later produced crabs and lobsters and insects. It must have been something like a modern scorpion, but, unlike its descendants, it never wholly severed the ties that united it to the sea. It lived a strange life, half-terrestrial, half-aquatic, something like that of the ghost crabs that speed along the beaches today, now and then dashing into the surf to moisten their gills.

Fish, tapered of body and stream-molded by the press of running waters, were evolving in Silurian rivers. In times of drought, in the drying pools and lagoons, the shortage of oxygen forced them to develop swim bladders for the storage of air. One form developed an air-breathing lung and by its aid could live buried in the mud for long periods.

It is very doubtful that the animals alone would have succeeded in colonizing the land, for only the plants had the power to bring about the first amelioration of its harsh conditions. They helped make soil of the crumbling rocks, they held back the soil from the rains that would have swept it away, and little by little they softened and subdued the bare rock, the lifeless desert. We know very little about the first land plants, but they must have been closely related to some of the larger seaweeds that had learned to live in the coastal shallows, developing strengthened stems and grasping, rootlike holdfasts to resist the drag and pull of the waves. Perhaps it was in some coastal lowlands, periodically drained and flooded, that some such plants found it possible to survive, though separated from the sea. This also seems to have taken place in the Silurian period.

The mountains that had been thrown up by the Laurentian revolution gradually wore away, and as the sediments were washed from their summits and deposited on the lowlands, great areas of the continents sank under the load. The seas crept out of their basins and spread over the lands. Life fared well and was exceedingly abundant in those shallow, sunlit seas. But with the later retreat of the ocean water into the deeper basins, many creatures must have been left stranded in shallow, landlocked bays. Some of these animals found means to survive on land. The lakes, the shores of the rivers, and the coastal swamps of those days were the testing grounds in which plants and animals either became adapted to the new conditions or perished.

As the lands rose and the seas receded, a strange fishlike creature emerged on the land, and over the thousands of years its fins became legs, and instead of gills it developed lungs. In the Devonian sandstone this first amphibian left its footprint.

On land and sea the stream of life poured on. New forms evolved; some old ones declined and disappeared. On land the mosses and the ferns and the seed plants developed. The reptiles for a time dominated the earth, gigantic, grotesque, and terrifying. Birds learned to live and move in the ocean of air. The first small mammals lurked inconspicuously in hidden crannies of the earth as though in fear of the reptiles.

When they went ashore the animals that took up a land life carried with them a part of the sea in their bodies, a heritage which they passed on to their children and which even today links each land animal with its origin in the ancient sea. Fish, amphibian, and reptile, warm-blooded bird and mammal—each of us carries in our veins a salty stream in which the elements sodium, potassium, and calcium are combined in almost the same proportions as in sea water. This is our inheritance from the day, untold millions of years ago, when a remote ancestor, having progressed from the one-celled to the many-celled stage, first developed a circulatory system in which the fluid was merely the water of the sea. In the same way, our lime-hardened skeletons are a heritage from the calcium-rich ocean of Cambrian time. Even the protoplasm that streams within each cell of our bodies has the chemical structure impressed upon all living matter when the first simple creatures were brought forth in the ancient sea. And as life itself began in the sea, so each of us begins his individual life in a miniature ocean within his mother's womb, and in the stages of his embryonic development repeats the steps by which his race evolved, from gill-breathing inhabitants of a water world to creatures able to live on land.

Some of the land animals later returned to the ocean. After perhaps 50 million years of land life, a number of reptiles entered the sea in Mesozoic time. They were huge and formidable creatures. Some had oarlike limbs by which they rowed through the water; some were web-footed, with long, serpentine necks. These grotesque monsters disappeared millions of years ago, but we remember them when we come upon a large sea turtle swimming many miles at sea, its barnacle-encrusted shell eloquent of its marine life. Much later, perhaps no more than 50 million years ago, some of the mammals, too, abandoned a land life for the ocean. Their descendants are the sea lions, seals, sea elephants, and whales of today.

Among the land mammals there was a race of creatures that took to an arboreal existence. Their hands underwent remarkable development, becoming skilled in manipulating and examining objects, and along with this skill came a superior brain power that compensated for what these comparatively small mammals lacked in strength. At last, perhaps somewhere in the vast interior of Asia, they descended from the trees and became again terrestrial. The past million years have seen their transformation into beings with the body and brain and the mystical spirit of man.

Eventually man, too, found his way back to the sea. Standing on its shores, he must have looked out upon it with wonder and curiosity, compounded with an unconscious recognition of his lineage. He could not physically re-enter the ocean as the seals and whales had done. But over the centuries, with all the skill and ingenuity and reasoning powers of his mind, he has sought to explore and investigate even its most remote parts, so that he might re-enter it mentally and imaginatively.

He fashioned boats to venture out on its surface. Later he found ways to descend to the shallow parts of its floor, carrying with him the air that, as a land mammal long unaccustomed to aquatic life, he needed to breathe. Moving in fascination over the deep sea he could not enter, he found ways to probe its depths, he let down nets to capture its life, he invented mechanical eyes and ears that could re-create for his senses a world long lost, but a world that, in the deepest part of his subconscious mind, he had never wholly forgotten.

And yet he has returned to his mother sea only on her own terms. He cannot control or change the ocean as, in his brief tenancy of earth, he has subdued and plundered the continents. In the artificial world of his cities and towns, he often forgets the true nature of his planet and the long vistas of its history, in which the existence of the race of men has occupied a mere moment of time. The sense of all these things comes to him most clearly in the course of a long ocean voyage, when he watches day after day the receding rim of the horizon, ridged and furrowed by waves; when at night he becomes aware of the earth's rotation as the stars pass overhead; or when, alone in this world of water and sky, he feels the loneliness of his earth in space. And then, as never on land, he knows the truth that his world is a water world, a planet dominated by its covering mantle of ocean, in which the continents are but transient intrusions of land above the surface of the all-encircling sea.

Surfing

JACK LONDON

At the same time that the scientists are acquiring greater knowledge of the oceans, everyday adventurers are acquiring a more intimate relationship with the world's waters. Surfing, which had its origins in Hawaii where it was the royal game of the ancient Hawaiian kings, is now a world-wide sport.

John Griffith London, known to the reading world as Jack London, went to sea at the age of seventeen. The Pacific was his school—from the Bering Sea to the South Seas. As London shipped from port to port in the South Seas, he recorded in wonder the world around him. He discovered surfing on the beach of Waikiki in Hawaii.

He would sit close to the ocean and feel, he said, "microscopically small." Like all young men, he could not sit forever. He had to try to vanquish the waves.

Get in and wrestle with the sea; wing your heels with the skill and power that reside in you; bit the sea's breakers, master them, and ride upon their backs as a king should. JACK LONDON

A wave is a communicated agitation. The water that composes the body of a wave does not move. If it did, when a stone is thrown into a pond and the ripples spread away in an ever widening circle, there would appear at the centre an ever increasing hole. No, the water that composes the body of a wave is stationary. Thus, you may watch a particular portion of the ocean's surface and you will see the same water rise and fall a thousand times to the agitation communicated by a thousand successive waves. Now imagine this communicated agitation moving shoreward. As the bottom shoals, the lower portion of the wave strikes land first and is stopped. But water is fluid, and the upper portion has not struck anything, wherefore it keeps on communicating its agitation, keeps on going. And when the top of the wave keeps on going, while the bottom of it lags behind, something is bound to happen. The bottom of the wave drops out from under and the top of the wave falls over, forward, and down, curling and cresting and roaring as it does so. It is the bottom of a wave striking against the top of the land that is the cause of all surfs.

But the transformation from a smooth undulation to a breaker is not abrupt except where the bottom shoals abruptly. Say the bottom shoals gradually for from a quarter of a mile to a mile, then an equal distance will be occupied by the transformation. Such a bottom is that off the beach of Waikiki, and it produces a splendid surf-riding surf. One leaps upon the back of a breaker just as it begins to break, and stays on it as it continues to break all the way in to shore.

And now to the particular physics of surf-riding. Get out on a flat board, six feet long, two feet wide, and roughly oval in shape. Lie down upon it like a small boy on a coaster and paddle with your hands out to deep water, where the waves begin to crest. Lie out there quietly on the board. Sea after sea breaks before, behind, and under and over you, and rushes in to shore, leaving you behind. When a wave crests, it gets steeper. Imagine yourself, on your board, on the face of that steep slope. If it stood still, you would slide down just as a boy slides down a hill on his coaster. "But," you object, "the wave doesn't stand still." Very true, but the water composing the wave stands still, and there you have the secret. If ever you start sliding down the face of that wave, you'll keep on sliding and you'll never reach the bottom. Please don't laugh. The face of that wave may be only six feet, yet you can slide down it a quarter of a mile, or half a mile, and not reach the bottom. For, see, since a wave is only a communicated agitation or impetus, and since the water that composes a wave is changing every instant, new water is rising into the wave as fast as the wave travels. You slide down this new water, and yet remain in your old position on the wave, sliding down the still newer water that is rising and forming the wave. You slide precisely as fast as the wave travels. If it travels fifteen miles an hour, you slide fifteen miles an hour. Between you and shore stretches a quarter of mile of water. As the wave travels, this water obligingly heaps itself into the wave, gravity does the rest, and down you go, sliding the whole length of it. If you still cherish the notion, while sliding, that the water is moving with you, thrust your arms into it and attempt to paddle; you will find that you have to be remarkably quick to get a stroke, for that water is dropping astern just as fast as you are rushing ahead.

And now for another phase of the physics of surf-riding. All rules have their exceptions. It is true that the water in a wave does not travel forward. But there is what may be called the send of the sea. The water in the overtopping crest does move forward, as you will speedily realize if you are slapped in the face by it, or if you are caught under it and are pounded by one mighty blow down under the surface panting and gasping for half a minute. The water in the top of a wave rests upon the water in the bottom of the wave. But when the bottom of the wave strikes the land, it stops, while the top goes on. It no longer has the bottom of the wave to hold it up. Where was solid water beneath it, is now air, and for the first time it feels the grip of gravity, and down it falls, at the same time being torn asunder from the lagging bottom of the wave and flung forward. And it is because of this that riding a surf-board is something more than a mere placid sliding down a hill. In truth, one is caught up and hurled shoreward as by some Titan's hand.

I deserted the cool shade, put on a swimming suit, and got hold of a surf-board. It was too small a board. But I didn't know, and nobody told me. I joined some little Kanaka boys in shallow water, where the breakers were well spent and small—a regular kindergarten school. I watched the little Kanaka boys. When a likely-looking breaker came along, they flopped upon their stomachs on their boards, kicked like mad with their feet, and rode the breakers in to the beach. I tried to emulate them. I watched them, tried to do everything that they did, and failed utterly. The breaker swept past, and I was not on it. I tried again and again. I kicked twice as madly as they did, and failed. Half a dozen would be around. We would all leap on our boards in front of a good breaker.

Away our feet would churn like the stern-wheels of river steamboats, and away the little rascals would scoot while I remained in disgrace behind.

I tried for a solid hour, and not one wave could I persuade to boost me shoreward. And then arrived a friend, Alexander Hume Ford, a globe trotter by profession, bent ever on the pursuit of sensation. And he had found it at Waikiki. Heading for Australia, he had stopped off for a week to find out if there were any thrills in surf-riding, and he had become wedded to it. He had been at it every day for a month and could not yet see any symptoms of the fascination lessening on him. He spoke with authority.

"Get off that board," he said. "Chuck it away at once. Look at the way you're trying to ride it. If ever the nose of that board hits bottom, you'll be disembowelled. Here, take my board. It's a man's size."

I am always humble when confronted by knowledge. Ford knew. He showed me how properly to mount his board. Then he waited for a good breaker, gave me a shove at the right moment, and started me in. Ah, delicious moment when I felt that breaker grip and fling me. On I dashed, a hundred and fifty feet, and subsided with the breaker on the sand. From that moment I was lost. I waded back to Ford with his board. It was a large one, several inches thick, and weighed all of seventy-five pounds. He gave me advice, much of it. He had had no one to teach him, and all that he had laboriously learned in several weeks he communicated to me in half an hour. I really learned by proxy. And inside of half an hour I was able to start myself and ride in. I did it time after time, and Ford applauded and advised. For instance, he told me to get just so far forward on the board and no farther. But I must have got some farther, for as I came charging in to land, that miserable board poked its nose down to bottom, stopped abruptly, and turned a somersault, at the same time violently severing our relations. I was tossed through the air like a chip and buried ignominiously under the downfalling breaker. And I realized that if it hadn't been for Ford, I'd have been disembowelled. That particular risk is part of the sport, Ford says. Maybe he'll have it happen to him before he leaves

Waikiki, and then, I feel confident, his yearning for sensation will be satisfied for a time.

When all is said and done, it is my steadfast belief that homicide is worse than suicide, especially if, in the former case, it is a woman. Ford saved me from being a homicide. "Imagine your legs are a rudder," he said. "Hold them close together, and steer with them." A few minutes later I came charging in on a comber. As I neared the beach, there, in the water, up to her waist, dead in front of me, appeared a woman. How was I to stop that comber on whose back I was? It looked like a dead woman. The board weighed seventy-five pounds, I weighed a hundred and sixty-five. The added weight had a velocity of fifteen miles per hour. The board and I constituted a projectile. I leave it to the physicists to figure out the force of the impact upon that poor, tender woman. And then I remembered my guardian angel, Ford. "Steer with your legs!" rang through my brain. I steered with my legs, I steered sharply, abruptly, with all my legs and with all my might. The board sheered around broadside on the crest. Many things happened simultaneously. The wave gave me a passing buffet, a light tap as the taps of waves go, but a tap sufficient to knock me off the board and smash me down through the rushing water to bottom, with which I came in violent collision and upon which I was rolled over and over. I got my head out for a breath of air and then gained my feet. There stood the woman before me. I felt like a hero. I had saved her life. And she laughed at me. It was not hysteria. She had never dreamed of her danger. Anyway, I solaced myself, it was not I but Ford that saved her, and I didn't have to feel like a hero. And besides, that leg-steering was great. In a few minutes more of practice I was able to thread my way in and out past several bathers and to remain on top my breaker instead of going under it.

"Tomorrow," Ford said, "I am going to take you out into the blue water."

I looked seaward where he pointed, and saw the great smoking combers that made the breakers I had been riding look like ripples. I don't know what I might have said had I not recollected just then that I was one of a kingly species. So all that I did say was, "All right, I'll tackle them tomorrow."

The water that rolls in on Waikiki Beach is just the same as the water that laves the shores of all the Hawaiian Islands; and in ways, especially from the swimmer's standpoint, it is wonderful water. It is cool enough to be comfortable, while it is warm enough to permit a swimmer to stay in all day without experiencing a chill. Under the sun or the stars, at high noon or at midnight, in midwinter or in midsummer, it does not matter when, it is always the same temperature—not too warm, not too cold, just right. It is wonderful water, salt as old ocean itself, pure and crystal-clear. When the nature of the water is considered, it is not so remarkable after all that the Kanakas are one of the most expert of swimming races.

So it was, next morning, when Ford came along, that I plunged into the wonderful water for a swim of indeterminate length. Astride of our surf-boards, or, rather, flat down upon them on our stomachs, we paddled out through the kindergarten where the little Kanaka boys were at play. Soon we were out in deep water where the big smokers came roaring in. The mere struggle with them, facing them and paddling seaward over them and through them, was sport enough in itself. One had to have his wits about him, for it was a battle in which mighty blows were struck, on one side, and in which cunning was used on the other side—a struggle between insensate force and intelligence. I soon learned a bit. When a breaker curled over my head, for a swift instant I could see the light of day through its emerald body; then down would go my head, and I would clutch the board with all my strength. Then would come the blow, and to the onlooker on shore I would be blotted out. In reality the board and I have passed through the crest and emerged in the respite of the other side. I should not recommend those smashing blows to an invalid or delicate person. There is weight behind them, and the impact of the driven water is like a sand-blast. Sometimes one passes through half a dozen combers in quick succession, and it is just about that time that he is liable to discover new merits in the stable land and new reasons for being on shore.

Out there in the midst of such a succession of big smoky ones, a third man was added to our party, one Freeth. Shaking the water from my eyes as I emerged from one

wave and peered ahead to see what the next one looked like,
I saw him tearing in on the back of it, standing upright on his
board, carelessly poised, a young god bronzed with sunburn.
We went through the wave on the back of which he rode.
Ford called to him. He turned an airspring from his wave,
rescued his board from its maw, paddled over to us and joined
Ford in showing me things. One thing in particular I learned
from Freeth, namely, how to encounter the occasional breaker
of exceptional size that rolled in. Such breakers were really
ferocious, and it was unsafe to meet them on top of the board.
But Freeth showed me, so that whenever I saw one of that
caliber rolling down on me, I slid off the rear end of the board
and dropped down beneath the surface, my arms over my
head and holding the board. Thus, if the wave ripped the
board out of my hands and tried to strike me with it (a
common trick of such waves), there would be a cushion of
water a foot or more in depth, between my head and the
blow. When the wave passed, I climbed upon the board and
paddled on. Many men have been terribly injured, I learn,
by being struck by their boards.

The whole method of surf-riding and surf-fighting, I learned,
is one of non-resistance. Dodge the blow that is struck at you.
Dive through the wave that is trying to slap you in the face.
Sink down, feet first, deep under the surface, and let the big
smoker that is trying to smash you go by far overhead. Never be
rigid. Relax. Yield yourself to the waters that are ripping and
tearing at you. When the undertow catches you and drags you
seaward along the bottom, don't struggle against it. If you do,
you are liable to be drowned, for it is stronger than you. Yield
yourself to that undertow. Swim with it, not against it, and you
will find the pressure removed. And, swimming with it, fooling
it so that it does not hold you, swim upward at the same time.
It will be no trouble at all to reach the surface.

The man who wants to learn surf-riding must be a strong
swimmer, and he must be used to going under the water.
After that, fair strength and common-sense are all that is
required. The force of the big comber is rather unexpected.
There are mix-ups in which board and rider are torn apart
and separated by several hundred feet. The surf-rider must
take care of himself. No matter how many riders swim out

with him, he cannot depend upon any of them for aid. The fancied security I had in the presence of Ford and Freeth made me forget that it was my first swim out in deep water among the big ones. I recollected, however, and rather suddenly, for a big wave came in, and away went the two men on its back all the way to shore. I could have been drowned a dozen different ways before they got back to me.

One slides down the face of a breaker on his surf-board, but he has to get started to sliding. Board and rider must be moving shoreward at a good rate before the wave overtakes them. When you see the wave coming that you want to ride in, you turn tail to it and paddle shoreward with all your strength, using what is called the windmill stroke. This is a sort of spurt performed immediately in front of the wave. If the board is going fast enough, the wave accelerates it, and the board begins its quarter-of-a-mile slide.

I shall never forget the first big wave I caught out there in the deep water. I saw it coming, turned my back on it and paddled for dear life. Faster and faster my board went, till it seemed my arms would drop off. What was happening behind me I could not tell. One cannot look behind and paddle the windmill stroke. I heard the crest of the wave hissing and churning, and then my board was lifted and flung forward. I scarcely knew what happened the first half-minute. Though I kept my eyes open, I could not see anything, for I was buried in the rushing white of the crest. But I did not mind. I was chiefly conscious of ecstatic bliss at having caught the wave. At the end of the half-minute, however, I began to see things, and to breathe. I saw that three feet of the nose of my board was clear out of water and riding on the air. I shifted my weight forward, and made the nose come down. Then I lay, quite at rest in the midst of the wild movement, and watched the shore and the bathers on the beach grow distinct.

The Great Storm

LAFCADIO HEARN

Storms and the oceans are inseparable. The great body of water which is the Gulf of Mexico has often been a storm center. Its storms slam over the Texas-Louisiana border and often devastate Louisiana itself. Not too long ago such a storm, moving at over 100 miles per hour, with the tides rising at 1½ feet per hour, and waves 4 to 5 feet high, lashed the coast of Louisiana. In two days more than five hundred people lost their lives. The estimate of the damage caused by that famous hurricane, known by the name of Audrey, was $200,000,000.

Hurricanes form over tropical oceans, the winds always blowing counterclockwise around a center called the eye. Anybody who has been in a hurricane knows the agonizing feeling of suspense, anguish, fear, and a kind of terrible excitement that can batter the body even more than the wind does. Lafcadio Hearn, who spent a long time observing the people and places of Louisiana, has written one of the most extraordinary verbal portraits of a hurricane ever to be set on paper. Listen to it rage as it comes out of the Gulf of Mexico.

*O*ne great noon, when the blue abyss of day seemed to yawn over the world more deeply than ever before, a sudden change touched the quicksilver smoothness of the waters—the swaying shadow of a vast motion. First the whole sea-circle appeared to rise up bodily at the sky; the horizon-curve lifted to a straight line; the line darkened and approached—a monstrous wrinkle, an immeasurable fold of green water, moving swift as a cloud-shadow pursued by sunlight. But it had looked formidable only by startling contrast with the previous placidity of the open: it was scarcely two feet high;—it curled slowly as it neared the beach, and combed itself out in sheets of wooly foam with a low, rich roll of whispered thunder. Swift in pursuit another followed—a third—a feebler fourth; then the sea only swayed a little, and stilled again. Minutes passed, and the immeasurable heaving recommenced—one, two, three, four . . . seven long swells this time;—and the Gulf smoothed itself once more. Irregularly the phenomenon continued to repeat itself, each time with heavier billowing and briefer intervals of quiet—until at last the whole sea grew restless and shifted color and flickered green;—the swells became shorter and changed form. Then from horizon to shore ran one uninterrupted heaving—one vast green swarming of snaky shapes, rolling in to hiss and flatten upon the sand. Yet no single cirrus-speck revealed itself through all the violet heights: there was no wind!—you might have fancied the sea had been upheaved from beneath. . . .

And indeed the fancy of a seismic origin for a windless surge would not appear in these latitudes to be utterly without foundation. On the fairest days a southeast breeze may bear you an odor singular enough to startle you from sleep—a strong, sharp smell as of fish-oil; and gazing at the sea you might be still more startled at the sudden apparition of great oleaginous patches spreading over the water, sheeting over the swells. That is, if you had never heard of the mysterious submarine oil-wells, the volcanic fountains, unexplored, that well up with the eternal pulsing of the Gulf Stream. . . .

But the pleasure-seekers of Last Island knew there must have been a "great blow" somewhere that day. Still the sea swelled; and a splendid surf made the evening bath delightful. Then, just at sundown, a beautiful cloud-bridge grew up and arched the sky with a single span of cottony pink vapor, that changed and deepened color with the dying of the iridescent day. And the cloud-bridge approached, stretched, strained, and swung round at last to make way for the coming of the gale— even as the light bridges that traverse the dreamy Têche swing open when luggermen sound through their conch-shells the long, bellowing signal of approach.

Then the wind began to blow, with the passing of July. It blew from the northeast, clear, cool. It blew in enormous sighs, dying away at regular intervals, as if pausing to draw breath. All night it blew; and in each pause could be heard the answering moan of the rising surf—as if the rhythm of the sea moulded itself after the rhythm of the air—as if the waving of the water responded precisely to the waving of the wind—a billow for every puff, a surge for every sigh.

The August morning broke in a bright sky;—the breeze still came cool and clear from the northeast. The waves were running now at a sharp angle to the shore: they began to carry fleeces, an innumerable flock of vague green shapes, wind-driven to be despoiled of their ghostly wool. Far as the eye could follow the line of the beach, all the slope was white with the great shearing of them. Clouds came, flew as in a panic against the face of the sun, and passed. All that day and through the night and into the morning again the breeze continued from the northeast, blowing like an equinoctial gale. . . .

Then day by day the vast breath freshened steadily, and the waters heightened. A week later sea-bathing had become perilous: colossal breakers were herding in, like moving leviathan-backs, twice the height of a man. Still the gale grew, and the billowing waxed mightier, and faster and faster overhead flew the tatters of torn cloud. The gray morning of the 9th wanly lighted a surf that appalled the best swimmers: the sea was one wild agony of foam, the gale was rending off the heads of the waves and veiling the horizon with a fog of salt spray. Shadowless and gray the day remained; there were mad bursts of lashing rain. Evening brought with it a sinister apparition, looming through a cloud-rent in the west—a scarlet sun in a green sky. His sanguine disk, enormously magnified, seemed barred like the body of a belted planet. A moment, and the crimson spectre vanished; and the moonless night came.

Then the Wind grew weird. It ceased being a breath; it became a Voice moaning across the world—hooting—uttering nightmare sounds—*Whoo!—whoo!—whoo!*—and with each stupendous owl-cry the mooing of the waters seemed to deepen, more and more abysmally, through all the hours of darkness. From the northwest the breakers of the bay began to roll high over the sandy slope, into the salines;—the village bayou broadened to a bellowing flood. . . . So the tumult swelled and the turmoil heightened until morning—a morning of gray gloom

and whistling rain. Rain of bursting clouds and rain of wind-
blown brine from the great spuming agony of the sea.

The steamer *Star* was due from Saint Mary's that fearful
morning. Could she come? No one really believed it—no one.
And nevertheless men struggled to the roaring beach to look for
her, because hope is stronger than reason. . . .

Even to-day, in these Creole islands, the advent of the
steamer is the great event of the week. There are no telegraph
lines, no telephones: the mail-packet is the only trustworthy
medium of communication with the outer world, bringing
friends, news, letters. The magic of steam has placed New
Orleans nearer to New York than to the Timbaliers, nearer to
Washington than to Wine Island, nearer to Chicago than to
Barataria Bay. And even during the deepest sleep of waves
and winds there will come betimes to sojourners in this unfamiliar archipelago a feeling of lonesomeness that is a fear, a
feeling of isolation from the world of men—totally unlike that
sense of solitude which haunts one in the silence of mountain-
heights, or amid the eternal tumult of lofty granitic coasts:
a sense of helpless insecurity. The land seems but an undulation
of the sea-bed: its highest ridges do not rise more than the
height of a man above the salines on either side;—the salines
themselves lie almost level with the level of the flood-tides;—
the tides are variable, treacherous, mysterious. But when all
around and above these ever-changing shores the twin vast-
nesses of heaven and sea begin to utter the tremendous
revelation of themselves as infinite forces in contention, then
indeed this sense of separation from humanity appals. . . .
Perhaps it was such a feeling which forced men, on the tenth
day of August, eighteen hundred and fifty-six, to hope against
hope for the coming of the *Star,* and to strain their eyes
towards far-off Terrebonne. "It was a wind you could lie down
on," said my friend the pilot.

. . . "Great God!" shrieked a voice above the shouting of the
storm—*"she is coming!"* . . . It was true. Down the Atchafalaya,
and thence through strange mazes of bayou, lakelet, and pass,
by a rear route familiar only to the best of pilots, the frail
river-craft had toiled into Caillou Bay, running close to the
main shore;—and now she was heading right for the island,
with the wind aft, over the monstrous sea. On she came,

swaying, rocking, plunging—with a great whiteness wrapping her about like a cloud, and moving with her moving—a tempest-whirl of spray;—ghost-white and like a ghost she came, for her smokestacks exhaled no visible smoke—the wind devoured it! The excitement on shore became wild;—men shouted themselves hoarse; women laughed and cried. Every telescope and opera-glass was directed upon the coming apparition; all wondered how the pilot kept his feet; all marveled at the madness of the captain.

But Captain Abraham Smith was not mad. A veteran American sailor, he had learned to know the great Gulf as scholars know deep books by heart: he knew the birthplace of its tempests, the mystery of its tides, the omens of its hurricanes. While lying at Brashear City he felt the storm had not yet reached its highest, vaguely foresaw a mighty peril, and resolved to wait no longer for a lull. "Boys," he said, "we've got to take her out in spite of Hell!" And they "took her out." Through all the peril, his men stayed by him and obeyed him. By mid-morning the wind had deepened to a roar—lowering sometimes to a rumble, sometimes bursting upon the ears like a measureless and deafening crash. Then the captain knew the *Star* was running a race with Death. "She'll win it," he muttered;—"she'll stand it. . . . Perhaps they'll have need of me to-night."

She won! With a sonorous steam-chant of triumph the brave little vessel rode at last into the bayou, and anchored hard by her accustomed resting-place, in full view of the hotel, though not near enough to shore to lower her gang-plank. . . . But she had sung her swan-song. Gathering in from the northeast, the waters of the bay were already marbling over the salines and half across the island; and still the wind increased its paroxysmal power.

Cottages began to rock. Some slid away from the solid props upon which they rested. A chimney tumbled. Shutters were wrenched off; verandas demolished. Light roofs lifted, dropped again, and flapped into ruin. Trees bent their heads to the earth. And still the storm grew louder and blacker with every passing hour.

The *Star* rose with the rising of the waters, dragging her anchor. Two more anchors were put out, and still she dragged

—dragged in with the flood—twisting, shuddering, careening in her agony. Evening fell; the sand began to move with the wind, stinging faces like a continuous fire of fine shot; and frenzied blasts came to buffet the steamer forward, sideward. Then one of her hog-chains parted with a clang like the boom of a big bell. Then another! . . . Then the captain bade his men to cut away all her upper works, clean to the deck. Overboard into the seething went her stacks, her pilot-house, her cabins—and whirled away. And the naked hull of the *Star*, still dragging her three anchors, labored on through the darkness, nearer and nearer to the immense silhouette of the hotel, whose hundred windows were now all aflame. The vast timber building seemed to defy the storm. The wind, roaring round its broad verandas—hissing through every crevice with the sound and force of steam—appeared to waste its rage. And in the half-lull between two terrible gusts there came to the captain's ears a sound that seemed strange in that night of multitudinous terrors . . . a sound of music!

. . . Almost every evening throughout the season there had been dancing in the great hall;—there was dancing that night also. The population of the hotel had been augmented by the advent of families from other parts of the island, who found their summer cottages insecure places of shelter: there were nearly four hundred guests assembled. Perhaps it was for this reason that the entertainment had been prepared upon a grander plan than usual, that it assumed the form of a fashionable ball. And all those pleasure-seekers—representing the wealth and beauty of the Creole parishes—whether from Ascension or Assumption, Saint Mary's or Saint Landry's, Iberville or Terrebonne, whether inhabitants of the multi-colored and many-balconied Creole quarter of the quaint metropolis, or dwellers in the dreamy paradises of the Têche—mingled joyously, knowing each other, feeling in some sort akin—whether affiliated by blood, connaturalized by caste, or simply interassociated by traditional sympathies of class sentiment and class interest. Perhaps in the more than ordinary merriment of that evening something of nervous exaltation might have been discerned—something like a feverish resolve to oppose apprehension with gayety, to combat uneasiness by diversion. But the hours passed in mirthfulness; the first general feeling of depression began to weigh less and less upon the guests; they had found reason to confide in the solidity of the massive building; there were no positive terrors, no outspoken fears; and the new conviction of all had found expression in the words of the host himself—*"Il n'y a rien de mieux à faire que de s'amuser!"* Of what avail to lament the prospective devastation of cane-fields—to discuss the possible ruin of crops? Better to seek solace in choreographic harmonies, in the rhythm of gracious motion and of perfect melody, than hearken to the discords of the wild orchestra of storms;—wiser to admire the grace of Parisian toilettes, the eddy of trailing robes with its fairy-foam of lace, the ivorine loveliness of glossy shoulders and jewelled throats, the glimmering of satin-slippered feet—than to watch the raging of the flood without, or the flying of the wrack. . . .

So the music and the mirth went on: they made joy for themselves—those elegant guests;—they jested and sipped rich wines;—they pledged, and hoped, and loved, and promised, with never a thought of the morrow, on the night of the tenth of August, eighteen hundred and fifty-six. Observant parents were there, planning for the future bliss of their nearest and dearest;—mothers and fathers of handsome lads, lithe and elegant as young pines, and fresh from the polish of foreign university training;—mothers and fathers of splendid girls whose simplest attitudes were witcheries. Young cheeks flushed, young hearts fluttered with an emotion more puissant than the excitement of the dance;—young eyes betrayed the happy secret discreeter lips would have preserved. Slave-servants circled through the aristocratic press, bearing dainties and wines, praying permission to pass in terms at once humble and officious—always in the excellent French which well-trained house-servants were taught to use on such occasions.

. . . Night wore on: still the shining floor palpitated to the feet of the dancers; still the piano-forte pealed, and still the violins sang—and the sound of their singing shrilled through the darkness, in gaps of the gale, to the ears of Captain Smith, as he strove to keep his footing on the spray-drenched deck of the *Star*.

"A dance!" he muttered—"a dance! If that wind whips round

south, there'll be another dance! . . . But I guess the *Star* will
stay." . . .

Half an hour might have passed; still the lights flamed
calmly, and the violins trilled, and the perfumed whirl went
on. . . . And suddenly the wind veered!

Again the *Star* reeled, and shuddered, and turned, and
began to drag all her anchors. But she now dragged away
from the great building and its lights—away from the voluptuous
thunder of the grand piano—even at that moment outpouring
the great joy of Weber's melody orchestrated by Berlioz:
"*L'Invitation à la Valse*"—with its marvelous musical swing!

"Waltzing!" cried the captain. "God help them!—God help
us all now! . . . *The Wind waltzes tonight, with the Sea for
his partner!*" . . .

O the stupendous Valse-Tourbillon! O the mighty Dancer!
One—two—three! From northeast to east, from east to southeast,
from southeast to south: then from the south he came, whirling
the Sea in his arms . . .

. . . Some one shrieked in the midst of the revels;—some girl
who found her pretty slippers wet. What could it be! Thin
streams of water were spreading over the level planking—curling about the feet of the dancers. . . . What could it be? All
the land had begun to quake, even as, but a moment before,
the polished floor was trembling to the pressure of circling
steps;—all the building shook now; every beam uttered its
groan. What could it be? . . .

There was a clamor, a panic, a rush to the windy night.
Infinite darkness above and beyond; but the lantern-beams
danced far out over an unbroken circle of heaving and swirling
black water. Stealthily, swiftly, the measureless sea-flood was
rising.

"*Monsieurs—mesdames, ce n'est rien.* Nothing serious, ladies,
I assure you. . . . *Mais nous en avons vu bien souvent, les
inondations comme celle-ci; ça passe vite!* The water will go
down in a few hours, ladies;—it never rises higher than this;
il n'y a pas le moindre danger, je vous dis! Allons! il n'y a—My
God! what is that?" . . .

For a moment there was a ghastly hush of voices. And
through that hush there burst upon the ears of all a fearful

and unfamiliar sound, as of a colossal cannonade—rolling up from the south, with volleying lightnings. Vastly and swiftly, nearer and nearer it came—a ponderous and unbroken thunder roll, terrible as the long muttering of an earthquake.

The nearest mainland—across mad Caillou Bay to the sea-marshes—lay twelve miles north; west, by the Gulf, the nearest solid ground was twenty miles distant. There were boats, yes!—but the stoutest swimmer might never reach them now! . . .

Then rose a frightful cry—the hoarse, hideous, indescribable cry of hopeless fear—the despairing animal-cry man utters when suddenly brought face to face with Nothingness, without preparation, without consolation, without possibility of respite. . . . *Sauve qui peut!* Some wrenched down the doors; some clung to the heavy banquet-tables, to the sofas, to the billiard-tables:—during one terrible instant—against fruitless heroisms, against futile generosities—raged all the frenzy of selfishness, all the brutalities of panic. And then—then came, thundering through the blackness, the giant swells, boom on boom! . . . One crash!—the huge frame building rocks like a cradle, see-saws, crackles. What are human shrieks now?—the tornado is shrieking! Another!—chandeliers splinter; lights are dashed out; a sweeping cataract hurls in: the immense hall rises—oscillates—twirls as upon a pivot—crepitates—crumbles into ruin. Crash again!—the swirling wreck dissolves into the wallowing of another monster billow; and a hundred cottages overturn, spin in sudden eddies; quiver, disjoint and melt into the seething. . . . So the hurricane passed—tearing off the heads of the prodigious waves, to hurl them a hundred feet in air—heaping up the ocean against the land—upturning the woods. Bays and passes were swollen to abysses; rivers regorged; the sea-marshes were changed to raging wastes of water. Before New Orleans the flood of the mile-broad Mississippi rose six feet above highest water-mark. One hundred and ten miles away, Donaldsonville trembled at the towering tide of the Lafourche. Lakes strove to burst their boundaries. Far-off river steamers tugged wildly at their cables—shivering like tethered creatures that hear by night the approaching howl of destroyers. Smoke-stacks were hurled overboard, pilot-houses torn away, cabins blown to fragments.

And over roaring Kaimbuck Pass—over the agony of Caillou

Bay—the billowing tide rushed unresisted from the Gulf—tearing and swallowing the land in its course—ploughing out deep-sea channels where sleek herds had been grazing but a few hours before—rending islands in twain—and ever bearing with it, through the night, enormous vortex of wreck and vast wan drift of corpses. . . .

But the *Star* remained. And Captain Abraham Smith, with a long, good rope about his waist, dashed again and again into that awful surging to snatch victims from death—clutching at passing hands, heads, garments, in the cataract-sweep of the seas—saving, aiding, cheering, though blinded by spray and battered by drifting wreck, until his strength failed in the unequal struggle at last, and his men drew him aboard senseless, with some beautiful half-drowned girl safe in his arms. But well-nigh twoscore souls had been rescued by him; and the *Star* stayed on through it all.

Long years after, the weed-grown ribs of her graceful skeleton could still be seen curving up from the sand-dunes of Last Island, in valiant witness of how well she stayed.

The Maelstrom

EDWARD ROWE SNOW

The oceans have many mysteries. The Sargossa Sea, the horse latitudes, the Maelstrom—all of these sailors feared. But the most alarming was the Maelstrom, which was immortalized in a story by Edgar Allan Poe. Here Edward Rowe Snow, "the best chronicler of the days of sail alive today," as the New York Times says, tells what little is known about that great marine mystery.

*T*he Maelstrom, a very dangerous whirlpool on the coast of Norway, is on the 68th degree of latitude, in the province of Nordland and the district of Lofoden, near the island of Moskoe, from which it also takes the name Moskoe-ström. Its violence and roarings can be heard at a great distance and without any intermission except every sixth hour, at the turn of high and low water, when it seems to be at a standstill. During this short interval the fishermen can venture in. The terrible twisting of the waters soon returns, however, and no matter how calm the sea may be, the whirlpool gradually increases with such a draft and vortex as to engulf whatever comes within its sphere of action. Ships and men may be caught in the whirlpool and kept underwater for some hours. Fragments of the ship, splintered by rocks, then appear, but bodies are rarely seen again.

Many residents of the area imagine that there is an abyss penetrating the globe, which a writer called Kircher named the Gulf of Bothnia. But after the most exacting research of the area possible to carry out, it was decided that an abyss going deep into the globe is not possible. This and three other vortices among the Faeroe Islands have no other cause than the collision of waves rising and falling at the flux and reflux against a ridge of rocks and shelves which confine the water so that it precipitates itself like a cataract; and thus the higher the flood rises the deeper the fall must be. The natural result of this is a whirlpool, or vortex, with a terrible suction.

But what has been pulled under remains no longer at the bottom than the ebb lasts. The suction then ceases, and the rising flood tide removes all traces of it and permits whatever had been sunk to make its gradual appearance again.

The following is an account of the Maelstrom written more than a century ago by M. Jonas Ramus:

The mountain of Helseggen, in Lofoden, lies a league from the stream called Moskoe-ström, from the island Moskoe, which is in the middle of it, together with several nearby isles, as Ambaaren, half a quarter of a league northward, Iflesen, Hocholm, Kieldholm, Suarven, and Buckholm.

Betwixt Lofoden and Moskoe the depth of the water is between thirty-six and forty fathoms; but on the other side, toward Ver, the depth decreases, so as not to afford a convenient passage for a vessel without the risk of splitting on the rocks, which happens even in the calmest weather; when it is flood the stream runs up the country between Lofoden and Moskoe with a boisterous rapidity; but the roar of its impetuous ebb to the sea is scarce equalled by the loudest and most dreadful cataracts; the noise being heard several leagues off, and the vortices or pits are of such an extent and depth that if a ship comes within its attraction it is inevitably absorbed and carried down to the bottom, and there beat to pieces against the rocks; and when the water relaxes, the fragments thereof are thrown up again.

But these intervals of tranquillity are only at the turn of the ebb and flood, and calm weather; and last but a quarter of an hour, its violence gradually returning. When the stream is most boisterous, and its fury heightened by a storm, it is dangerous to come within a mile of it. Boats, ships, and yachts have been carried away.

It likewise happens frequently that whales come too near the stream and are overpowered by its violence; and then it is impossible to describe their howlings and bellowings in their fruitless struggles to disengage themselves. A bear once attempting to swim from Lofoden to Moskoe, with a design of preying upon the sheep at pasture in the island, afforded the life spectacle to the people; the stream caught him and bore him down, whilst he roared terribly, so as to be heard on shore.

Large stocks of firs and pine trees, after being absorbed by the current, rise again, broken and torn to such a degree as if bristles grew on them. This plainly shows the bottom to consist of craggy rocks, among which they are whirled to and fro. In the year 1645, early in the morning of Sexagesima Sunday, it raged with such noise and impetuosity that on the island of Moskoe the very stones of the houses fell to the ground.

An unidentified American captain gives the following description:

I had occasion some years since to navigate a ship from the North Cape to Drontheim, nearly all the way between the islands or rocks and the main. On inquiring of my Norwegian pilot about the practicability of running near the whirlpool, he told me that with a good breeze it could be approached near enough for examination without danger, and I at once determined to satisfy myself.

I had been seated but a few moments, when my ship entered the dish of the whirlpool. The velocity of the water altered her course three points toward the center, although she was going three knots through the water. This alarmed me extremely for a moment. I thought destruction was inevitable. She, however, answered her helm sweetly, and we ran along the edge, the waters foaming round us in every form, while she was dancing gaily over them.

The sensations I experienced are difficult to describe. Imagine to yourselves an immense circle running round, of a diameter of one and a half miles, the velocity increasing as it approximates toward the center, and gradually changing its dark blue color to white—foaming, tumbling, rushing to its vortex, very much concave, as much so as the water in a tunnel when half run out; the noise, too, hissing, roaring, dashing all pressing on the mind at once, presented the most awful, grand, and solemn sight I ever experienced. We were near it about eighteen minutes, and in sight of it two hours. It is evidently a sub-terranean passage. From its magnitude, I should not doubt that instant destruction would be the fate of a dozen of our largest ships, were they drawn in at the same moment. The pilot says that several vessels have been sucked down.

One resident of Norway, Peter Arneson, almost lost his life when caught on the very edge of the Maelstrom in the year 1834. Because of his experience, he later claimed, his hair went from jet black to snow white in six hours.

Aboard a schooner-rigged smack of seventy tons, he and his two brothers, Fredrik and Niels, found fishing in the general vicinity of the Moskoe-ström extremely lucrative, but, of course, they had to be very careful not to be caught in the terrible vortex. Aboard the fishing smack they often caught more in a single day than others could in an entire week.

On July 20, 1834, the three men started out from their anchorage early that morning in a gentle breeze, which blew from the southwest. A good load of fish was soon aboard. Suddenly, when the men were starting for home just a short time after two o'clock, a fresh wind hit their starboard quarter and soon increased to hurricane strength. They could do noth-ing against it. Then a strange sight was seen in the heavens, a copper-colored cloud.

The cloud came at them with terrible velocity, and in less than a minute a new storm hit them. It was soon so dark that they could not see each other a few feet away. Both masts went by the board, and when the mainmast broke off, the youngest brother, Niels, was lost in the sea. The boat had a flush deck, with a small hatch in the bow, but the hatch had been battened down, and that saved the two survivors.

The gale swept them into that terrible area where the Maelstrom is located. Peter's older brother, Fredrik, was the first to realize what was happening.

"Moskoe-ström, Moskoe-ström!" he shrieked, and Peter heard him even above the roar of the storm. Peter said later that he began to shake from head to foot as he realized they were heading right for the terrifying vortex. Desperately figuring their chances, Peter estimated that they would be driven by the gale to the whirlpool at the time of its slack, and there was a possible chance of survival. Suddenly, in the sky, the heavens brightened, and a full moon burst out from behind a retreating cloud. It was a terrible scene which the moon lighted up, and Peter glanced at his watch, which said seven o'clock.

Then brother Fredrik shouted, "Listen!" and Peter heard the roaring whirl of the Maelstrom. His watch had run down, it was behind the time of slack, and they were doomed, for the Maelstrom was in full fury!

Now about a fifth of a mile dead ahead, the Maelstrom was far greater in intensity than on an average day. The hurricane had whipped up the vortex into unbelievable turmoil, and the whirlpool no more resembled its usual awesomeness than it did a millpond.

The roaring noise of the water was drowned out by a strange shrill shriek, and Peter knew that they were on the very edge of the surf which is the outer fringe of the Maelstrom. Peter thought that another moment would carry them down into the depths, but for some reason the craft stayed on the extreme edge minute after minute. The boat did not sink into the water at all, but seemed to skim in the manner of a stone skipping across the surface. Her starboard or right side was next to the whirl itself.

Feeling that he was doomed to perish in the whirlpool, a strange calmness came over Peter, and he began to think that in the presence of such a spectacle he had no right to consider his own life. He actually thought of the exploration of the Maelstrom itself, and the idea struck him that he and his brother would find out its secret, although perishing in the attempt.

Around and around the fringe of the whirlpool the schooner went, until more than a full hour had elapsed. In the stern Fredrik clung to a small empty water cask. He now left the cask, went forward, and attached his hands to an iron ring embedded in the deck.

Suddenly the schooner gave a lurch, and rushed headlong down over the edge, entering the Maelstrom itself. Peter uttered a short prayer, and then opened his eyes. Moments later the strange feeling of falling through a void passed, and Peter looked out on a scene of wonderful but terrible beauty.

Balanced halfway down the sloping side of the vortex, the

schooner seemed to be kept by the terrifying speed of the
whirlpool from going lower. Round and round the vessel went,
and every so often the rays of the full moon hit the tiny craft,
balanced precariously on the towering walls of the Maelstrom.

As the mad journey continued, Peter noticed that the smack
was now on an even keel. Nevertheless, because of the forty-
five-degree angle of the whirlpool itself, the craft appeared to
be on her beam ends. He glanced every so often toward the
bottom of the deep gulf, but the heavy mist or spray prevented him from seeing far down. In spite of the night time,
there was a magnificent rainbow. Peter decided that the mist
was the result of the mighty sides of the whirlpool coming together, smashing and churning as they collided.

Gradually Peter came to notice other objects on the side of
the whirlpool; timbers, trees, shattered remains of ships,
boxes, crates, barrels, chairs, and tables. As he watched, it
seemed to him that he was not a participant in what was
going on, but merely a witness. One by one the objects were
sucked down into the lower part of the funnel and disappeared. Suddenly the great wreck of a Dutch merchant ship,
which had been at a lower level, was caught in the suction
and went down.

Peter began to develop an idea. He recalled the material he
had seen thrown up on the shore at Lofoden, having been
pulled down and then thrown back by the Moskoe-ström. Most
of the objects had been shattered in unusual ways, but some
were not disfigured at all. Peter wondered if some did not
reach the bottom before the turn of the tide, could it be possible that they might reach the level of the ocean again in
undamaged condition?

He noticed that barrels or cylinder-shaped objects offered
much more resistance than those which were larger and flatter.
He decided he might have a chance to survive if he lashed
himself to the water cask, cut it free, and jumped overboard.
He attracted his brother's attention by signs, pointing to the
floating barrels that came near, suggesting that it was the only
way to save himself. Fredrik refused. Resigning his brother to
his fate, Peter leaped with the barrel into the Maelstrom.

About an hour afterward, while Peter had stayed with
the barrel, the schooner had gone down and down. Finally it

was far below. Then, as Peter watched with overwhelming emotion, the craft sank headlong into the spray and vanished. Some time later the Maelstrom began to flatten out. As the funnel became less and less steep, the whirlpool seemed to slow up in speed and became less violent. By degrees the froth and the rainbow disappeared, the bottom of the gulf slowly rose, and the wind went down. Peter noticed that the moon was about to set in full view of the shores of Lofoden, above the spot where the pool of the Moskoe-ström had been. It was the hour of slack—but the sea still heaved in mountainous waves from the effects of the hurricane.

Peter and the barrel were eventually blown across Ström Channel into the fishing grounds, where he sighted a vessel. Drawing near, Peter was discovered by the fishermen, who rescued him. For a long time Peter was speechless from the memory of the horror through which he had just passed. Although he knew the fishermen as his daily companions, his ordeal had changed him so much that they did not recognize him. Raven black the day before, his hair now was as white as snow, and his entire countenance had aged twenty years!

The story told above was used by Boston-born Edgar Allan Poe in his masterful short story, *A Descent into the Maelstrom*, the material for which he is said to have obtained during his interview with a Norwegian seaman on the wharves of Baltimore. Whether or not that seaman was the original Peter Arneson, the sole survivor of that terrible experience, we shall never know.

The Shore

The Riddle of the Ridley

ARCHIE CARR

Every ocean and sea has a shoreline, and on that shore are found food, wonder, and mystery. The great sea turtles of the Caribbean supplied food for the pirates of long ago (and for tables today), wonder for all who have ever seen them on the tropical beaches, and mystery for every biologist. Archie Carr, Professor of Biological Sciences at the University of Florida, has pursued with all the dedication of a marine Sherlock Holmes the mystery of their migrations and the riddle of their habits.

The twelve-foot pole flew a high arc and struck true over the skidding shadow. It plunged quarter-down and stopped short against the hard shell of the turtle. Then it fell free and floated to the top.

"Missed him," I said. I should have known better. It was Jonah Thompson who threw the iron.

But how does anyone hit a target like that? The bow of the little launch was bucking and shying in a cross-channel chop. A gusty breeze kept throwing the surface of the bay into crowds of tight wrinkles that raced by and shot back the light in confused reflections. The water was milky white to start with, and the turtle was thirty feet out and a yard down and dodging like a rabbit. It was like trying to hit a scared pig from the bed of a truck lurching across a plowed field. Only the pig would be out in plain view, while the turtle was a dim blur in the cloudy water.

"He's carrying the iron," Jonah said. Then I saw the line snaking out of the bucket in the bow.

"How do you do it?" I said.

"I'm sixty-five and I started early. It's worse with green turtles; they run like a seagull. This here's a ridley."

He clawed in the pole with a boat hook. He took up the smoothly paying line and slowly closed both hands on it. The tension pulled us around a few points, and then a flipper broke water fifty feet out in front. Very carefully Jonah began to take in line, and the boat and the surfaced turtle drew together. When the gap closed he handed the tight line to his boy and deftly dropped a loop of rope over one of the flailing flippers. Then he heaved, and the turtle slid over the gunwale and fell back-down on deck, where it scraped and thrashed for purchase on the smooth planks.

"Stay clear of him," Jonah said. "He's mad. Ridleys is always mad."

I poked a rope end at the turtle's face. It seized the knot and crunched and then flew into a long frenzy of flopping and pounding about the deck.

"You can't keep a ridley on its back. Only a few hours. They're crazy. They break their hearts."

That was how I got to know the Atlantic Ridley. That was how the great ridley mystery began for me.

It is the sea that holds the great mysteries. There is still much to be learned in the land, to be sure, but it is the third dimension of the oceans that hides the answers to broad elemental problems of natural history. Somewhere out there young salmon lose themselves, and the Pribilof seals go there when they leave the rocks where they were born. Through chance concordance of cryptic forces, the Red Tide brews up and sporadically drifts in to the rich littoral of Florida, killing thousands of fishes, sending the tourists scurrying to flee the stink, and then sweeping away again, unchecked and uncomprehended. As long as man has had the wit to wonder, he must have puzzled over the new eels in his pasture pond; and being told they come from the sea where their parents went to spawn them is as preposterous as some theory of astrophysics. When J. L. B. Smith found a cœlacanth fish fifteen years ago, it was a living fossil, as stirring a discovery to a biologist, and quite as great a probing of the past, as finding a dinosaur would be. Who can trace the way of the great blue marlin or of Rhineodon, the whale shark, or tell anything worth hearing about the oarfish or the giant squid, or even say for sure where the homely mullet spawns its millions or where the gleaming hordes of tarpon come from?

And who can tell what the ridley is?

It was eighteen years ago when Jonah Thompson pulled in that first ridley out at Sandy Key in Florida Bay. I was there because of a letter from my friend Stew Springer, who is a gifted naturalist, versed in all sorts of seacraft. He was running a shark fishery at Islamorada on the upper Florida Keys at the time. He wrote to me to complain about a kind of turtle his fishermen brought in for shark bait. It was an evil-natured turtle, he said, flat and gray, with a big head and short, broad shell. Unlike the docile greens, which lie for weeks backdown on a ship's deck, or the formidable but philosophic loggerheads, this species made an unrestful, even dangerous, boatfellow. It snapped and fought, Stew said, from the moment it fell over the gunwale, biting the air and slapping its feet till it burned itself out from rage and frustration. The people on the keys called it ridley, and Stew said he could not even find the name—much less any information on it—in any of the books.

Neither could I. From the description I decided that Stew must be talking about a species that was first described some sixty years ago as *Lepidochelys kempi*, the specific name being taken from that of Richard Kemp of Key West, who sent the type specimen to Samuel Garman at the Museum of Comparative Zoology at Harvard. Practically nothing was known about the natural history of Kemp's turtle. Most people were unable to distinguish it from the loggerhead, and many even doubted that there really was such a thing. A scattering of herpetologists had published records of its occurrence or comments on its osteology, but the great majority of reptile students had never even seen one and the general attitude was that Kemp's turtle was a somehow inferior, if not altogether spurious form, not worthy of scholarly sweat. But Stew had a different opinion, and I had great respect for his perspicacity; I decided to go down and see his hotheaded sea turtle in the flesh. I suppose that one reason for my steadfast affection for ridleys is the memory of that trip to the keys.

My wife went with me. We were young then, and the keys were not yet real estate. A few outsiders were beginning to nose

around, but most of the people living there were Conches—
descendants of the original English-Bahamian stock, the wreck-
ers and turtlers of a hundred and two hundred years ago. You
could still catch all the fish you wanted without a charter boat.
The reefs were next to virgin, and the grouper and muttonfish
would rise to a strip of your shirt tail; and even the mangrove
snappers were still naïve. Around any pass or coral head you
could cover the bottom of your dinghy with yellowtails or
heap a particolored cargo of porkfish, queen triggers, rock
hinds, and Spanish hogfish; or if rough weather sent you home
you could always take back at least a mess of grunts to go
with your grits. The grunts ran two sizes bigger then, and
their mouths were more flaming scarlet; and they tasted far,
far better.

If it was not something to eat but adrenaline in the blood
you were after, you only had to drag a lure for a barracuda in
the channel, or commune with the Bahía Honda tarpon train,
or creep about the marl flats till you saw the tilted shadows of
bonefish, foraging in their primitive peace; and if you made a
proper approach you might hook one of these. After that your
life would not be quite the same.

Over and above any mysteries of natural history they held,
the keys were wonderful in those days. The overseas highway had just been built, but there was yet hardly a trickle of
the stream that would one day make the islands a suburb of
Miami. You could hardly notice it, but you knew it would
come.

You knew the lovely bay would one day buzz with kickers,
and the beaches be littered with people and their leavings, and
the sunsets be dulled by neon. Among the first things to go
would be the old crocodile in her hole too near the highway; and everywhere the fish would grow scarce or cynical.
Even the ancient silvered logs of mahogany and princewood
would be snaked off to cabinet shops and the gemlike tree snails
snatched from the Jamaica dogwood limbs in the dim hammocks.

The lay and figure of the islands would not change. The
indigo of the Gulf Stream would always lap the eastern rim of
the arc, and inside, it would confine the incredible spectrum of
the bay and its hot marl waters, swirled and banded with

every shade from turquoise to green and milky jade. The thousand little mangrove-bordered islets would be there, and the big black niggerhead sponges; and new vast jewfish would move in to take the places of the ones the fishermen horsed out from among the piling at the old ferry slip.

Some things would last. But the year Margie and I went down to see Stew's ridleys, the keys were so fair and un-plagued that we resented the existence of the road that led us there. No one else is so innately opposed to the more overt signs of human progress as a naturalist—especially a young one; and I remember well how bitterly we wished the keys might be left forever to the sun and wind, to the white-crowned pigeons and red coons and little key deer, and to a few quiet people with names like Lowe and Thompson and Sweeting. And to us, of course.

I remember Margie asked me if I would really be so callous as to deny to my fellow man the joy of conch soup; and I said I damn sure would—because there was only a certain amount of conch soup in the world, while the fellow man had no limits to his abundance. And now, these short two decades later, you can go lusting the length of the archipelago and never find a spoonful of conch soup anywhere. The conches are gone—unless you live there and know the little secret caches—like the stone crabs, and the easy fishing.

But the ridleys are still there and we must get around to them.

We had hardly thrown our things on the bed in one of Stew's cabins when he herded us out again and into a launch with two Matacumbe men, a Mr. Jonah Thompson and his grown son, who looked just like him. Mr. Thompson had lost one side of his buttocks in the '35 hurricane—the one when the glass fell to 26.35 and a two-hundred-mile wind slammed a twelve-foot wall of water across the low islands, shattering and carrying away everything in its path. The official list num-bered eight hundred dead, mostly from the camp of bonus-marching veterans of World War I who were living in tents on Lower Matacumbe, but everyone knows the counting stopped too soon. The survivors were mostly natives, who weathered the raving wind and seas in small, flush-deck boats heavily an-chored among dense mangroves. The driving water wrecked a

locomotive on the railroad and carried huge masses of re-
inforced concrete twenty miles to the tip of the mainland, but
some of the people in the little boats got by.

Jonah Thompson got by, but he lost half of his buttocks
when a flying timber nearly cut him in two. The injury would
have made an invalid of an average man, but Jonah quickly
dominated it and soon regained his place as the best boatman
on the upper keys. He could handle an iron better than any
man of any color I ever saw. He knew weather and water and
fish and, what was most important of all, he knew turtles.

And so, when he contemplated the irate ridley he had just
pulled up on deck and said: "Some say these ridleys is cross-
breeds," I took notice and urged him on.

"We don't know where they lay," he said. "All the rest come
up on the beaches one time or other, but you never see the
ridleys there. We all say they are made when a loggerhead
pairs with a green." He mumbled something else in an embarrassed sort of way. I thought I heard him right, but I didn't
think my wife did.

"We think they're so damn mean owing to them not getting
to coot none," was what I believe he said.

"What did he say?" asked Margie.

"Shut up," I said.

"Did he say they are mean because they don't make love?"

"That was the gist of it."

"Isn't that anthropomorphic?" Margie asked, in an unpleasant way.

"Could be," I said. I could see nothing wrong with the man's
reasoning, provided he was right about the ridley's not breeding; but this assumption I did not like, and still don't.

It bothered me that the ridley should be such a distinctive
and original-looking creature, with his traits his own and nothing about him that seemed intermediate between the other
species. A mule is clearly a mixture of the ass that sired him
and the mare that bore him, but a ridley is his own kind
of animal. I nodded over Jonah Thompson's theory, but I resolved then to get the straight of it somehow.

As I said, that was a long time ago, and I have made very
little progress. Indeed, the ridley mystery has grown rather
than shrunk, and I am farther from a solution than I seemed

then. The answer is so elusive that I have come to regard the ridley as the most mysterious air-breathing animal in North America.

First of all, there is the unimportant but vexing question of the creature's name. Ridley! What kind of name is it anyway, and where did it come from? I've traced it all along the coast from Fernandina to Key West and out to Pensacola and people only look vague or grieved when I ask about the name. To most people it's like asking why they call a mackerel a mackerel, or a dog a dog. Once in a while I run into somebody who knows the ridley as "mulatto" or "mule-turtle," in reference to its supposed hybrid origin; but most places the name is ridley, and not a soul knows why. Maybe one out of a couple of dozen fishermen pronounce it "ridler"; and it may be that this form represents an earlier stage in the etymology of the term, but it seems impossible to confirm this. Anyway, compared to other things we don't know about the ridley, the question of its name is a bagatelle; and our ignorance here is exasperating, but not necessarily demoralizing.

A more unsettling eccentricity is the animal's range—the territory in which it has been found to occur. All the other sea turtles—trunkback, green, loggerhead, and hawksbill—occupy pretty much the same area, each being found in the Atlantic, the Caribbean, the Pacific, and the Indian Ocean. Moreover, while the representative of each of these species in the Indo-Pacific is isolated by land or by great expanses of cold water from its counterpart in the Atlantic-Caribbean, the populations are remarkably similar. In fact, if you go to Colón, on the Caribbean side of Panama, and catch a green turtle, haul him across the Isthmus to Panama City, and compare him point for point with a green from the Pacific, you have to look very close indeed to see any difference at all. It is the same with a great number of other marine animals, both vertebrate and invertebrate, on the two sides of the Isthmus: they are separated by thousands of miles of alien territory but they nevertheless show very little of the divergence that such isolation usually brings. This is especially striking when you consider that the emergence of the isthmus that cut off the Caribbean animals from their eastern Pacific kin took place at least thirty million years ago.

The ridley partly fits this pattern; that is, there is an Atlantic ridley and a very similar one in the eastern Pacific. They are numerous only in the warmer parts of their ranges, and are apparently not in contact around the tips of either Cape Horn or the Cape of Good Hope, except perhaps as occasional, current-borne flotsam. But here the orthodoxy of the ridley stops. For some utterly unaccountable reason it is not found in the Bahamas or Bermuda, where all the rest are, or have been, abundant; and most peculiar of all, it is absent from the Caribbean.

It is not a simple matter to get a clear picture of the range of the ridley. You don't just go out and catch sea turtles on an afternoon collecting trip, and there are no really good sea-turtle collections in any of the world's museums.

Before Mr. Kinsey became preoccupied with sex, he worked on insects. At one time he wanted to learn all he could about a certain group of tiny wasps that make galls on twigs. In his spare time he went out and drove along the roads and stopped at hundreds of places where he collected the animals he was after. He caught seventeen thousand of them, and when he wrote a monograph on this material, it was a classic. This is the way to do a problem in animal distribution; but you can't do it with sea turtles.

Counting specimens I have begged or bought from fishermen or seen being butchered in fish houses, and the collections of the Museum of Comparative Zoology, the American Museum of Natural History, and the British Museum, I have managed to look at about a hundred ridleys in eighteen years. Add to what these show the small amount of information that has been published and the carefully sifted oral reports of fishermen, and there is still not a great deal to work with. But it is enough to give the outlines of the ridley story, and to show that it is a strange one.

There are two centers of abundance of ridleys: the Gulf coast of Florida from the Suwannee Delta to Florida Bay and the east coast from about St. Augustine to Melbourne. On the east coast, ridleys are best known by trawlers who work some distance off shore, perhaps indicating that even this far south the animals are being swept northward by the Florida Current —the headwaters of the Gulf Stream. I know a fisherman at

Canaveral who claims to have caught a thousand ridleys during twenty years of fishing there. On the Gulf coast they are taken along with the green turtles that support the small turtle fisheries there, and are frequently sold with the greens to buyers who never know the difference. There they are caught in nets set across small channels among the flats, and like the young greens, they appear to be at home there. A single setting of a net will sometimes yield two or three of each species, while loggerheads are almost never taken.

Outside of Florida, ridleys occur all along the Gulf coast to Texas. At the Mexican border our information peters out; nobody knows what happens to the range of the ridley from there on. The few published articles on Mexican sea turtles mention the other four kinds, but not the ridley. On the Atlantic coast it seems to me that the distribution of the ridley is no true "range" in the zoo-geographic sense—an expanse of territory that an animal occupies or voluntarily moves across—but is a one-way, passive dispersal by the Florida Current and the Gulf Stream; an exodus with no return. Expatriate ridleys drift with the current with little more control over their ultimate fate than the plankton there. The ones near the edges may be able to move out into the coastal waters, reach shore, and live there more or less conveniently; but those deep within the stream go on. Where the Florida Current picks up its supply of ridleys is not known, for reasons that I shall reveal presently; but there can be little doubt that it is the northward sweep of this current just off the eastern shore that accounts for the occurrence in North Carolina and New York Harbor and Martha's Vineyard. Little as we know about ridleys, we can be sure they are not born in those places. They are carried there.

And they do not stop in Massachusetts. The Gulf Stream goes on, and they go with it. How they are amusing themselves all this time is hard to say, but they ride the great global drift out into the cold North Atlantic, where it travels its new easterly course at a reduced speed but glides on over the tail of the Grand Banks, pushes aside the arctic icebergs, and splits at last against western Europe, making it barely possible for human beings to stand the English climate, and stranding ridleys on such shores as Ireland, Cornwall, the Scilly Isles, southern France, and the Azores.

The range of the ridley, thus, is not an expanse of ocean or a strip of shore. Mostly it is the Gulf Stream. Ridleys are part of a vast planetary swirl that starts when the equatorial current and the easterly trades push water through the Yucatán Channel and pile it up in the Gulf of Mexico. The surface there rises six to eighteen inches higher than the Atlantic level and breeds the head that drives warm water clockwise around the eastern Gulf and nozzles it out through the Straits of Florida as the Florida Current. This soon meets the Antilles Current, and the two now form the "Gulf Stream" in the new strict sense, and this moves northward with an initial speed of about three knots. Somewhere along the line ridleys are fed into this system, to drift downstream to England through three thousand slow miles.

It would be wrong to give the impression that ridleys are of common occurrence in Europe. I recently looked at six English ridleys in the collection of the British Museum, which is the best sea-turtle collection in the world, and those six represent all the European specimens in that museum. These may represent half of all the English ridleys that have fallen into the hands of naturalists. Ridleys, and sea turtles of all kinds, are very rare in European waters. But even so, I wonder how many ridleys had to begin the voyage in America for each of the six that lodged at last in the British Museum!

Two features of the British waifs must be of some sort of significance in the cryptic life history of the animal: they are all small—none over eight inches long and one only four— and they have all washed up during the months from October to December. I suppose the small size merely means that baby turtles are swept away more easily than big ones; but the meaning of the seasonal occurrence of the strandings is unexplained.

If we suppose that the point of injection of ridleys into the Gulf Stream system is somewhere about the tip of the Florida peninsula—and the slim evidence that seems to support this assumption will come out shortly—then the trip to Europe might take as much as a year or even more. It seems unlikely that even a turtle could survive this period with no food at all.

So, even though the ridley is characteristically a bottom feeder —a crusher of crabs and mollusks—we must conclude that it finds some sort of fare in the Gulf Stream.

It must have occurred to you some time back that the sensible way to go about finding out where ridleys get into the Gulf Stream would be to locate the beaches where the young hatch out. That makes sense, certainly. The only trouble is, the beaches can't be found.

In fact, I can't find any evidence that ridleys breed at all; at least, by any of the accepted methods. I am still just about where Jonah Thompson's folk theory left me. As far as I can determine, nobody ever saw a pair of ridleys courting or copulating. People are constantly catching and butchering sea turtles and looking about inside them for eggs, but no female ridley has ever turned up pregnant—not even with the beadlike, yellow eggs that other female turtles carry for most of every year. No ridley has ever been seen on a nesting beach, and no hatchling has been found. The smallest ridley known is a four-inch specimen that washed up in England. This one was at least several months old. A newly hatched one should be little more than an inch long, because the loggerhead, a turtle two or three times the size of the ridley at maturity, is only slightly more than an inch long at birth. Not only that, all hatchling turtles have a soft umbilical scar, marking the place where they were attached to the yolk in the egg; and at the tip of the snout there is a sharp spine called an egg tooth that the little turtle uses in freeing itself from the shell. Turtles retain these signs of infancy for several weeks after hatching. No little ridley has ever been seen with them.

When Kemp sent the ridley to Harvard in 1880 he said: "We know that they come out on the beach to lay in the months of December, January and February, but cannot tell how often or how many eggs." I don't think he knew any such thing. When I made my first visit to Springer's shark camp on the keys, I went armed with this observation; and since it seemed a bizarre reversal of the usual nesting schedule, I went to some effort to authenticate it. I had no success at all. I talked with people who knew ridleys all the way from Homestead to Key West and none had ever heard of a turtle nesting in the wintertime or had seen a ridley nest or egg or baby at any time. Since then I have heard the same story from something over 160 of the most knowledgeable fishermen I could find between Cape Hatteras and the mouth of the Mississippi. I have dissected every mature ridley I could get and have cross-questioned the men who slaughter turtles for the market, and I have begun to feel the real weight of the enigma.

When the turtlers and fishermen are pressed to account for the facts of the case, they tell three different stories. Most of them agree with Jonah Thompson that the creature does no breeding on its own but is produced when two other species hybridize. The comment of an old pod at St. Lucie Inlet was the sort of thing you hear:

"This yer ridley don't raise. He's a crossbreed you get when a loggerhead mounts a green—and a loggerhead will mount anything down to a stick of wood when he's in season. This yer ridley don't have no young 'uns. He's at the end of the line, like a mule."

A minority among the people I talk to say that ridleys breed all right—bound to; everything does; but they do it somewhere 'way off, outside our field of responsibility. On some remote shore of the Caribbean, maybe, where they have yet to be observed by sapient man. Sapient gringo, anyway.

This kind of talk used to reassure me. It was something to fall back on when the thought of a parentless, childless animal weighed me down. It was no disgrace not knowing where the brute bred if it happened in some far corner of the Caribbean. The Caribbean is a big place, and I knew its shore only in a couple of spots. Ridleys were unknown in those spots, but this proved nothing at all.

Imagine my state of mind, then, when I had completed a carefully spaced series of visits all the way around the Caribbean and had found no sign either of ridleys or of people who knew them, anywhere in a dozen countries and islands. I went out with turtle-hunters and looked at turtles in crawls, and at shells on trash heaps, and at stuffed turtles on museum shelves. I walked some of the finest turtle beaches in the hemisphere. I saw a lot of things, but no ridleys. Everywhere I went the people knew four kinds of sea turtles, and none of them was the ridley.

This was a body blow. It threw the whole problem back into the Gulf of Mexico—into my lap. My ignorance became embarrassing again.

The third explanation I commonly hear is the opinion of a still smaller group that the ridley is out there each June laying, along with the other species, in the same places and at the same time. I have heard this seriously proposed by responsible parties five times. That is, five times people have named definite stretches of beach on which they believed ridleys laid. Four of these stories fizzled out under cross-questioning, proving to have been based either on pure hearsay or on erroneous identification of the turtle involved. In one case only, the battering system of interrogation I have developed through the years was unable to find the weakness in a man's claim that he had seen a ridley lay on a certain beach; and we parted at deadlock—he clinging to his memory of one lone ridley in moonlight twenty-five years old, and I sure without any proof at all that he was off his rocker.

I will admit that there is a slight possibility that each June ridleys lumber up at first full moon and dig their nests on the shoulders of State Road A1A, like the loggerheads; but I rest no easier for it.

That, then, is the riddle of the ridley: a big, edible, shorewater beast, abundant and well known to everybody along the east-Gulf littoral and around the tip of Florida, is swept up the Atlantic coast by the Florida Current and the Gulf Stream, through some whimsey never crossing to the eastern side of the current and being unknown in the Bahamas and in Bermuda. The drifting migrants trickle out of the stream into coastal waters as far north as Massachusetts, straggle across to Europe, and very rarely stick with the deflected drift as far as the Azores and probably farther. Nowhere in this vast territory has any hint of reproductive activity been seen.

What do you make of it? I used to think the solution would one day fall into my lap, but I believe this no longer. It will have to be worked for, and the campaign will require drive and imagination and patience. It will probably resolve itself into a systematic ransacking of ideas and places on a purely trial-and-error basis. It will not be settled on week-end field trips, and there is nothing to take into the laboratory. The solution will very likely turn out to be absurdly simple and obvious, once we get hold of it; but meantime it is a tough and nagging mystery.

While waiting for something else to happen, it is interesting, if not really profitable, to take stock of the information at hand and see what can be done with it. Most of the laws of science, as we call them, have started out as theories; and theories are just figments of a disciplined imagination—until they can be proved. The scientific way to formulate a theory is to examine every possible explanation for your facts that presents itself, however outrageous it may seem at the time. Some of the craziest notions turn out to be the best.

In the case of the ridley mystery, then, we have to weigh without bias all the trial solutions at hand, whether conceived by unlettered menhaden hands or by sadistic colleagues, or by my own troubled mind. We must list these and evaluate each in its turn and then make an objective choice; and this will then be the current, tentative answer to the riddle of the ridley. It will probably be wrong, but it will be the best we can do.

Of all the explanations that suggest themselves, the simplest is that the ridley just doesn't reproduce, but arises by spontaneous generation. This is the most direct answer, in view of what we know, and in olden times it would have been accepted as the only reasonable solution. But nowadays biologists are pretty insistent that everything alive must have at least one parent, and this sets limits to our imagination.

As a variant of that idea, we might toy with this one, which has been suggested to me independently by several acquaintances, some of whom at least are perfectly sane. May not the ridley once have been able to reproduce its kind, but have suddenly lost the ability—have become sterile through some sudden racial mishap? In such a case, the ridleys we see today would be the last members of a line on its way toward extinction. It is hard to put your finger on the defect in this effort, but it seems a bit fey and irresponsible. Quite frankly, I get no real comfort out of the notion and mention it at all only to be scientific.

We just about have to start from the assumption that the animal breeds—somehow, somewhere. It must be, then, that it is the place or the manner of the breeding that bewilders. There must be something about where or how little ridleys come about that it is just a bit beyond the scope of our imagining.

Maybe, for instance, this turtle lays no eggs, but bears its young alive, on the high seas, as a sea snake does. It is certainly conceivable, and it excuses our failure to find nests and eggs ashore. But don't forget the lack of pregnant females. You have to get just as pregnant to bear live young as to lay eggs. And not only that, an eggless turtle is too far out of character. Turtles are unwaveringly conservative. A live-bearing turtle would be almost as exciting as an egg-laying dog. No matter where they live—on dry land, in fresh water, or in the sea—all known turtles inflexibly dig holes and lay white-shelled eggs in them; and they have been doing this since the Cretaceous.

Suppose, then, that the ridley abides by the conventions of its kind and lays eggs, but lays them in the water—lays buoyant eggs so far from land that the young stop being young before we ever get to see them. If the laying place is very far away, maybe it takes the females a long time to get there, and we see them only when they are not carrying eggs. This is a variation of the preceding theory and a slight improvement on it, but is unacceptable on the same grounds. It just seems like too much of an innovation for a turtle suddenly to make, after fifty million years of making hardly any innovations at all. Besides, prolonged wetting with salt water kills the embryos in the eggs of other reptiles and other sea turtles, and we would have to propose a brand-new and very ingenious kind of egg for our theoretical pelagic ridley.

Perhaps, instead of a strange *way* of breeding, it is a strange *time* of breeding that has thrown us off. Maybe the laying season is very short or very oddly scheduled and restricted in time. Maybe they lay only on New Year's Eve or Twelfth Night, or on the shortest night or coldest night of the year. All the other Atlantic sea turtles have a laying season of several weeks in late spring and early summer; but the ridley may lay in midwinter when turtle-hunters are doing something else. Why not? Well, mainly because it again brings us up against the failure of the females to turn up pregnant. And not

only that, even in the dead of winter there is traffic on most
Florida beaches—people driving, hotrodding, surf fishing, courting, catching coquinas, even swimming. It is impossible to
believe that winter turtle tracks, or tracks laid at any time
however unlikely, could simply have escaped notice. This was
Kemp's theory, you remember, but I think he was just repeating idle talk.

Next we might try the possibility that the ridleys in the
United States originate somewhere else and either migrate
into the Gulf of Mexico or are carried there by currents. This
looks good at first, because there are the currents to do the
job—currents that could, and almost surely do, bring ridleys
clear across the Atlantic from Africa to the Antilles and very
probably into the Gulf of Mexico. But if you look closely at
the foreign ridley colonies that could lose turtles into these
currents, you see that the ridley population in the Gulf could
not possibly be derived this way. In the first place the Gulf
form is too abundant to qualify as an accumulation of
accidental waifs; and even more conclusive, there is a simple
but constant difference between the ridleys in the Gulf and
those in West Africa and on the Pacific coast of South
America, which are the only stocks adjacent to the currents
that bring foreign drift into Florida waters. All extra-Floridian
ridleys everywhere in the world have two to six more scales in
the upper shell than our Gulf ridley does. If we suppose that all
those in the Gulf were brought in by the Equatorial Current,
then we have to believe that each of them stopped over
somewhere along the way and had its shell remodeled. It is
possible that an occasional Gulf ridley does come into American waters on the Equatorial Current; but if so it is surely one
that began its voyage three years before when it was swept
away by the Florida Current and survived the world-wide
circuit to return at last to its native waters. Any African
ridley that turned up in the Gulf would be easily recognized
as such. There is, thus, little point in looking to the ocean
currents for a solution to the puzzle.

Why not just take it easy and accept the popular notion
that the ridley is a hybrid after all, and, like many hybrids,
sterile? This is what most of the fishermen and turtle-hunters
believe, as I have said, and you can even read it in the

Riverside Natural History. Mostly the responsibility for furnishing us with ridleys is laid to a loggerhead father and a green-turtle mother, but sometimes you hear the sexes switched. A few say the *mésalliance* involves a loggerhead and a hawksbill, and rarely you may be told that it is a hawksbill and a green.

This is where the pressure is, and where my skepticism has lost me friends and made me out, in the eyes of men I respected, a plain damn fool. Nearly everything we know, and everything we don't know, about this animal makes it easy to say it is a half-breed, with no more personal continuity than a medieval choirboy, or a mule.

As I have said before, there are also ridleys in the Pacific. And in the Pacific the males chase the females about, and catch them, and they mate, and the females go ashore and dig holes in the sand and lay round, white eggs in them. The eggs hatch and release baby ridleys with egg teeth and umbilical scars, like any other new turtle.

Now, what earthy sense would it make for the ridley to be a hybrid in one part of his range and a separate species in another—to do his own breeding at Acapulco but rely on other kinds of turtles to do it for him at Tampa? It is a distressing thought. In fact, it is untenable.

As I have pointed out, the Atlantic and Pacific ridleys are separated by a great deal of territory and are not exactly alike. But they are very nearly alike, and far more like each other than like any other kind of turtle. In fact, the only differences I have been able to make out are the extra scales in the shell of the Pacific form and sometimes a slightly greener color; and maybe a few trifling disparities in proportions. Certainly nothing that would lead a person with bat brains to believe that a ridley begot one of them and a loggerhead the other.

The problem would be simple if we didn't know about the Pacific ridley. My friends around the fish houses don't know about the Pacific ridley. They are at peace. I am not. It's what a Ph.D. in biology gets you. . . . The ridley breeds, like anybody else.

The same objections that make the hybrid idea unsatisfactory seem also to throw out the possibility that the ridley is some sort of sport—an occasional freak occurring among normal offspring of one of the other kinds of turtles, the loggerhead, for instance. Here again the almost identical Pacific ridley, with its orthodox breeding habits, stares us in the face and makes the sport theory seem just a shade too easy. It is possible, but only very feebly so.

Now, what can be said to the people who suggest that the nests have just been overlooked—that ridleys nest right along with the other turtles, at the same time and in the same places, and have simply escaped notice by a person competent to distinguish between them and the other species?

Well, as far as I'm concerned those are fighting words. Maybe my own hundreds of hours of unproductive beach-walking, and those of my zoological friends and correspondents, are not a valid test. But how about the lifetimes spent without seeing ridleys by professionals like Joe Saklin and Tony Lowe and Paco Ortega, and by the band of my consultants among the illegal east-coast turtle-hunters? These men spend three months of every year patrolling the beaches in turtle buggies—cut-down cars with oversized tires—dodging the far-spaced conservation officers and turning turtles by the yearly hundreds. They have always done this and they keep doing it at growing risk—slowly growing risk—because a few commercial bakers have learned what Savannah and Charleston house-wives always knew about the keeping qualities turtle eggs give cakes, and will pay fantastic prices for them; and because the shoddier jooks and barbecue joints along the Dixie Highway like to cut their fifty-cent-a-pound hamburger meat with twenty-five-cent loggerhead. These men don't hunt turtles for fun. They are tough and practical. I know a game warden whom they threw into the sea just to show how tough they are. They know their business. They know ridleys and know the beaches and what goes on there during the long summer nights, and it is wonderful what goes on there, but it is not the nesting of ridleys. All these men have told me that ridleys never come ashore. By not moralizing on their ways, I have made friends among these poachers, and if a ridley ever comes up on one of the good mainland beaches in the turtle season, I bet I hear about it within hours.

But suppose she should not come ashore on one of the good turtle beaches. There is a lot of coast between Tampico

The ocean floor looked like this in "The Gray Beginnings." This is a recon-
struction of a Devonian sea floor. Center, a frilled cephalopod attacking a
trilobite; left, a large crinoid, and below it a spiny trilobite; right, other
trilobites, shells, and seaweed. (The Devonian period started 320 million
years ago and lasted for 55 million years says Rachel Carson in "The Gray
Beginnings.") *Courtesy of New York State Museum and Science Service.*

The Hawaiian surf where Jack London discovered surfing—"the sport of kings."

Mobile hurricane clouds over the Gulf of Mexico, the kind that Lafcadio Hearn watched just before "The Great Storm."

"The Maelstrom," the dangerous whirlpool off the coast of Norway, was such a fascinating natural phenomenon that it was used to illustrate one of the early geography books. This old woodcut is from Olney's *A Practical System of Modern Geography*.

The mysterious ridley turtle of the Caribbean, whose habits have led Archie Carr to feats of sleuthing worthy of a Sherlock Holmes. *Courtesy of Marineland of Florida.*

These gulls are "Winter Visitors" on the snow of the beach.

Newly laid eggs of flyingfish in sargassum weed which William Beebe found in the "Battlefield of the Shore." (Greatly enlarged photograph)

The shipwrecks that Thoreau encountered sometimes went through these dramatic evolutions: first, the free-sailing ship . . .

. . . then, the wreck . . .

. . . and finally, the hulk in the sand.

The marvel of an ebb tide.

A close-up of a blue shark group.

and Beaufort, and there are still some unpatrolled, unbathed-on segments of shore not even shown as sand on maps. And as long as this is true, we can never be sure but that we have missed what we were after simply because we have not looked in the right place. Till every one of the unsearched beaches has been walked with ridleys in mind we can never be sure they do not nest on some rarely visited little island or cluster of keys or short, broken strand somewhere on the coast of the southeastern United States.

This, I believe, is the theory we must choose. It best fits the known facts and introduces the fewest wild assumptions. It is distasteful, because it proposes the laborious ransacking of every scrap of sand along hundreds of miles of coast. It seems unlikely, because no other turtle anywhere is so fanatically finicky in choosing a breeding ground as this explanation would imply. But the ridley has shown its disregard for tradition in other ways, remember. In spite of the drawbacks, this hypothesis seems the best of the lot.

So I guess we must go looking for a small, isolated stretch of shore as the answer to the ridley mystery. It must be some improbable place right under our noses. Cape Sable may occur to you, or Dry Tortugas, but it will not be so easy as that. People have been turning turtles on those shores for too many years. I believe it can't be any of the good turtle territory on the east coast—the strip from Palm Beach up to Melbourne: it is too well known, too continuously visited. It is not Sanibel or Bonita Beach or Naples, and it almost surely is none of the islands along the bend of the Panhandle. It barely might be outside Florida—one of the Sea Islands of Georgia or South Carolina, or some place the Mexicans have somehow missed between Vera Cruz and Brownsville. But I doubt this; and I doubt that it is anywhere in all the island chain from Grand Bahama to Turks and Caicos.

As long as we believed the zoologists who kept quoting one another about there being ridleys in the Caribbean, we could just say, well, hell, the ridley must breed down there somewhere. But now there's no comfort there, for me at least. In all the poking about that I'm going to tell you of in chapters to come, the ridley mystery was right there with me. Stirred up as I may seem over other matters—over the green

turtles I was mainly after down there, over the endless odd
detours and distractions I relate—the one most exciting thing I
found in all my wandering was no ridleys in the Caribbean.

What remains to be done, then, is slow, piecemeal searching.
And before I look anywhere else I am going back to Florida
Bay—to the shallow, island-set sea between the cape and the
upper keys. There are dozens of little islands there like Sandy
Key, and they have been little visited by naturalists with eyes
open for ridley sign. The shores there are mostly mangrove
thickets, where no turtle could nest; but in some the mangrove
fringe is broken by sand; and while the strips of beach are
short and narrow, they may be all the ridley needs. The bay
is handy to both the Florida Current, which must be the
agent that feeds the waifs into the Gulf Stream, and to the
coastal waters of the peninsula of Florida, where ridleys are
more abundant than anywhere else. It is at least possible that
the natural secretiveness of sea-turtle hatchlings keeps baby
ridleys out of sight, and that some local, seasonal migration
of the egg-heavy females hides them from view. All this seems
unlikely, but it is the most possible solution at hand.

So I guess I should have stayed on there in the bay to
look for the answer, where Jonah Thompson threw the iron
so long ago. Perhaps all the Atlantic ridleys everywhere come
from down there where the first one was, in the hot, white
water with the sea cows and bonefish and the last crocodiles.
Maybe the long questing will come full circle there on some
first full moon of summer, and the riddle of the ridley will
end where it began.

Winter Visitors

HENRY BESTON

The ocean and its shore change with the seasons. What of the beach and sea in winter? Henry Beston was able to plot the path of winter at the beach as he sat each day writing on a kitchen table in a little room that overlooked the North Atlantic.

The result was The Outermost House, *a book that became world famous. Here are the "winter visitors" that Beston could see from his lonely window.*

During the winter the world of the dunes and the great beach was entirely my own, and I lived at the Fo'castle as undisturbed as Crusoe on his island. Man disappeared from the world of nature in which I lived almost as if he, too, were a kind of migratory bird. It is true that I could see the houses of Eastham village on the uplands across the marsh, and the passing ships and fishing boats, but these were the works of man rather than man himself. By the middle of February the sight of an unknown someone walking on the beach near the Fo'castle would have been a historical event. Should any ask how I endured this isolation in so wild a place and in the depth of winter, I can only answer that I enjoyed every moment to the full. To be able to see and study undisturbed the processes of nature—I like better the old Biblical phrase "mighty works"—is an opportunity for which any man might well feel reverent gratitude, and here at last, in this silence and isolation of winter, a whole region was mine whose innermost natural life might shape itself to its ancient courses without the hindrance and interferences of man. No one came to kill, no one came to explore, no one even came to see.

Earth, ocean, and sky, the triune unity of this coast, pursued each one their vast and mingled purposes as untroubled by man as a planet on its course about the sun.

It is not good to be too much alone, even as it is unwise to be always with and in a crowd, but, solitary as I was, I had few opportunities for moods or to "lose and neglect the creeping hours of time." From the moment that I rose in the morning and threw open my door looking toward the sea to the moment when the spurt of a match sounded in the evening quiet of my solitary house, there was always something to do, something to observe, something to record, something to study, something to put aside in a corner of the mind. There was the ocean in all weathers and at all tides, now gray and lonely and veiled in winter rain, now sun-bright, coldly green, and marbled with dissolving foam; there was the marsh with its great congresses, its little companies, its wandering groups, and little family gatherings of winter birds; there was the glory of the winter sky rolling out of the ocean over and across the dunes, constellation by constellation, lonely star by star. To see the night sky in all its divinity of beauty, the world beneath it should be lovely, too, else the great picture is split in halves which no mind can ever really weld into a unity of reverence. I think the nights on which I felt most alone (if I paused to indulge myself in such an emotion) were the nights when southeasterly rains were at work in the dark, immense world outside my door dissolving in rain and fog such ice and snow as lingered on after a snowfall or a cold spell had become history. On such southeasterly nights, the fog lay thick on marsh and ocean, the distant lights of Eastham vanished in a universal dark, and on the invisible beach below the dune, great breakers born of fog swell and the wind rolled up the sands with the slow, mournful pace of stately victims destined to immolation, and toppled over, each one, in a heavy, awesome roar that faded to silence before a fellow victim followed on out of the darkness on the sea. Only one sense impression lingered to remind me of the vanished world of man, and that the long, long complaints and melancholy bellowings of vessels feeling their way about miles offshore.

But I was not entirely alone. My friends the coast guards at Nauset Station, patrolling the beach every night and in all weathers, often came in to see how I was faring, to hand me on a letter, or to tell me the news of the Cape. My pleasure in such visits was very real, and between half after seven and eight o'clock I always hoped for a step. When one has not spoken to another human being for twenty-four hours, a little conversation is pleasant exercise, though to the speaker the simplest phrases, even the simple idiom, "Come in," may take on a quaint air of being breathless and voluble. Sometimes no one came, and I spent the evening by my fire reading quietly, going over my notes, and wondering who it was who walked the beach.

It is not easy to live alone, for man is a gregarious creature; especially in his youth, powerful instincts offer battle to such a way of life, and in utter solitude odd things may happen to the mind. I lived as a solitary, yes, but I made no pretense of acting the conventional hermit of the pious tract and the Eighteenth Century romance. With my weekly trips to Orleans to buy fresh bread and butter, my frequent visits to the Overlook, and my conversations with the men on night patrol, a mediæval anchorite would have probably regarded me as a dweller in the market place. It was not this touch with my fellows, however, which alone sustained me. Dwelling thus upon the dunes, I lived in the midst of an abundance of natural life which manifested itself every hour of the day, and from being thus surrounded, thus enclosed within a great whirl of what one may call the life force, I felt that I drew a secret and sustaining energy. There were times, on the threshold of spring, when the force seemed as real as heat from the sun. A skeptic may smile and ask me to come to his laboratory and demonstrate; he may talk as he will of the secret workings of my own isolated and uninfluenced flesh and blood, but I think that those who have lived in nature, and tried to open their doors rather than close them on her energies, will understand well enough what I mean. Life is as much a force in the universe as electricity or gravitational pull, and the presence of life sustains life. Individuals may destroy individuals, but the life force may mingle with the individual life as a billow of fire may mingle for a moment with a candle flame.

But now I must begin to tell of the birds who are wintering

on the coast, of the exchange of species which takes place here, and of how all manage to live.

As I walk the beach on a bright and blustery January morning, my first impression is one of space, beauty, and loneliness. The summer bird life of the beach has completely disappeared, and at the moment of which I tell, not a single beach bird or sea bird, not even a resident gull, is to be seen on the beach along all these empty miles. I walk, and no terns come swooping down at me out of the dunes, scolding me for my intrusion on their immense and ancient privacy; no sandpipers rise at my approach, wheel over the inner breakers, and settle down again a hundred yards ahead. Summer residents and autumn migrants of the beach, sandpipers, plovers, yellowlegs, "knots," and sanderlings, all have gone south with the sun and are now to be found anywhere from the Carolinas south to Patagonia. The familiar sanderlings—it is of *Crocethia alba* that I write—lingered surprisingly late; they seemed almost as numerous in October as in August, there were plenty to be seen in November, but in December flocks were rare, and by Christmas, there were only a few strays and cripples left behind.

New Year's Day, on the deserted beach, I surprised a little flock of ruddy turnstones, *Arenaria interpres morinella,* who took wing on my approach and flew south close along the seaward face of the dunes. I shall always remember this picture as one of the most beautiful touches of color I have ever seen in nature, for the three dominant colors of this bird—who is a little larger than the semipalmated sandpiper—are black, white, and glowing chestnut red; and these colors are interestingly displayed in patches and bold stripes seen at their best when the bird is flying. The great dunes behind them and the long vista of the beach were cold silver overlaid with that faint, loveliest violet which is the overtone color of the coast.

As I watched these decorative birds flying away ahead of me into that vast ocean world, I began thinking of how little has ever been written or said about the loveliness of our North Atlantic birds. There are plenty of books about them, there are a world of kind people who cherish and love them as birds, but there is a lack of printed material and discussion celebrating their qualities of beauty. Such aesthetic appreciation of our shore birds as we have had seems to have reached that showy and unfortunate creature, the wood duck, *Aix sponsa,* and been permanently overcome. Now, the turnstone is a lovely little bird, the least tern is another; the king eider is a magnificent creature, and there are many more whose beauty deserves comment and attention. A second notion, too, came into my head as I saw the turnstones fly away—that no one really knows a bird until he has seen it in flight. Since my year upon the dunes, spent in a world of magnificent fliers, I have been tempted to believe that the relation of the living bird with its wings folded to the living bird in flight is almost that of the living bird to the same bird stuffed. In certain cases, the difference between the bird on the wing and the bird at rest is so great that one might be watching two different creatures. Not only do colors and new arrangements of colors appear in flight, there is also a revelation of personality. Study your birds on the ground as you will, but once you have thus observed them and studied their loveliness, do not be afraid to clap your hands and send them off into the air. They will take no real alarm and will soon forgive you. Watch birds flying.

The tide is going out, and the breakers are shallowing to chiding curls of foam along the edge of the ebb. Gone are the thin-footed, light-winged peoples, the industrious waders, the busy pickup, runabout, and scurry-along folk. South, south with the sun, along bright beaches and across wide bays, south with the sun along the edge of a continent, with heaven knows what ancient mysteries stirring in their tiny minds and what ancient instincts waking in their veins. As I think of the tropical lands to which these birds have flown, I remember walking one night along a tropical beach in Central America. It was late at night, no one was about, the warm, endless, pouring wind shook a sound like rain out of endlessly agitated palms, and a magnificent full moon sailed through the wind over an ocean and a surf that might have been a liquid and greener moonlight. Suddenly, a flock of little birds rose up on the beach from nowhere, wheeled, fell off a little with the wind, and then disappeared completely into the turbulent splendor. I wonder now if you were by any chance Cape Cod sandpipers, little birds!

But now to return to the North Atlantic, the Eastham dunes, and the exchange of species I mentioned earlier in the chapter. As the smaller birds have flown south to their tropics, birds from the arctic north, following the same migrational impulse of the ebbing year, have moved south along the New England coast, and found in the open, deserted Cape a region which is to them a Florida. These birds are the arctic sea ducks, many of them big, heavy, powerful birds, all of them built to stand icy water and icy weather, all of them enclosed in a water-tight pack of feathers which is almost a kind of feather fur. These ducks belong to the sub-family *Fuligulinæ,* the people of the outermost waters, but there are still other arctic visitors, auks, murres, and even guillemots. The region which these birds prefer is the region south of Cape Cod, where the currents of warmer water swirl over the great south shoals. I have for neighbors the three varieties of "scoters," or more familiarly and wrongly "coots," the black-winged coot *Oidemia americana,* the white-winged coot *Oidemia deglandi,* the skunk coot, *Oidemia perspicillata;* I have scaups or blue-billed widgeons, *Marila marila,* dipper ducks, *Charitonetta albeola,* old squaws, *Harelda hyemalis,* eiders, *Somateria dresseri,* king eiders, *Somateria spectabilis,* and others. It is possible that, before the coming of the white man, the number of these winter outer-sea birds in the Cape Cod region exceeded that of the summer birds, but now, alas! the shotgun and the killer had their fun, the winter peoples have been wasted away, and some even exterminated. Today, the summer birds outnumber their winter kin.

A new danger, moreover, now threatens the birds at sea. An irreducible residue of crude oil, called by refiners "slop," remains in stills after oil distillation, and this is pumped into southbound tankers and emptied far offshore. This wretched pollution floats over large areas, and the birds alight in it and get it on their feathers. They inevitably die. Just how they perish is still something of a question. Some die of cold, for the gluey oil so mats and swabs the thick arctic feathering that creases open through it to the skin above the vitals; others die of hunger as well. Captain George Nickerson of Nauset tells me that he saw an oil-covered eider trying to dive for food off Monomoy, and that the bird was unable to plunge. I am glad to be able to write that the situation is better than it was. Five years ago, the shores of Monomoy peninsula were strewn with hundreds, even thousands, of dead sea fowl, for the tankers pumped out slop as they were passing the shoals—into the very waters, indeed, on which the birds have lived since time began! Today oil is more the chance fate of the unfortunate individual. But let us hope that all such pollution will presently end.

My beach is empty, but not the ocean beyond. Between the coast guard station and Nauset Light, a "raft" of skunk coots is spending the winter. Patches of white on the forehead and the hind neck of the glossy black head of the male are responsible for this local name. The birds sit in the ocean, just seaward of the surf—the coast guardsmen say there is a shallow close by and shellfish—and the whole raft rises and falls unconcernedly as the swells roll under it. Sometimes a bird will dive through the oncoming ridge of a breaker and emerge casually on the other side; sometimes a bird will stand up in the water, flap its wings, and settle down again unconcernedly. There are perhaps thirty birds in this flock. In Thoreau's time, these rafts of coots formed a flock which was practically continuous the whole length of the outer Cape, but today such rafts, though not at all rare, are but occasional.

Standing at the door of my house, I watch these winter birds pass and repass, flying well offshore. Now a company of a hundred or more old squaws pass, now a tribe of one of the scoter folk; now a pair of eiders come to rest in the ocean directly in front of the Fo'castle.

These birds practically never come ashore during the winter. They eat, sleep, live, and meet together at sea. When you see a sea duck on the beach, you can be sure something is the matter with him, so runs a saying of the Cape which I had from Captain Nickerson. The only way in which I can observe these winter folk is by using a good glass or by catching a specimen who has got into some kind of trouble and taken refuge on the beach. All these creatures are at a great disadvantage when ashore, and have a world of difficulty trying to launch themselves into the air; they make unwieldy jump after jump, the auks being practically unable to rise at all upon their wings. It was thrilling to walk the beach, and catch sight of a bird sitting solitary on the sands. What might it be? What had led it ashore? Could I possibly catch it and give it a careful looking over? The keynote of my strategy lay in the attempt to prevent the birds from getting back into the water, so between them and the surf I would rush—for the birds would begin to move down the slope to the surf the instant they saw or heard or felt me—and I soon learned that a brisk countercharge was worth all the ruse and the patient stalking in the world. Then began a furious game of tag, the alarmed bird skittering all over the beach, being gradually driven by me toward the dunes, till I maneuvered him into the angle between the beach and the sandy wall.

My first prisoners were three unhappy little auks, *Alle alle*, who had dipped themselves in oil somewhere on their way down from the arctic—odd little browny-black and white birds about the size of a pigeon, who stood up on queer little auk feet, faced me, and beat little bent wings with a penguin look to them; indeed, the bird has much of an Adelie penguin air. On the Cape, these auks are known as "pine knots"—a term said to be derived from the creature's tough compactness —or as "dovekies." They have always been "aukies" to me. At the Fo'castle I gave them a generous corner floored with newspaper and walled in with boards and a chair. I tried to clean off what I could of the oil; I gave them what I could find of sea victuals, but all in vain; they would not eat, and I let them go just as soon as I saw that I could not possibly help them and that Nature had best deal with the problem in her own way.

When they stood up almost perpendicularly and tried to walk about on their little legs set far aft—they are *pygopodes*— it was much as if an acrobat, standing on his head, were trying to patter about, using the length between his elbow and his finger tips as feet. These little birds used both wings and feet when trying to escape me on the beach. They ran and *rowed* the sand with their wings; the verb gives the precise motion. Moreover, what had taken place was beautifully marked upon the *tabula rasa* of the sand—little webbed feet running in a close chain, wing tips nicking the sand once in each stroke. Coming south from their distant arctic, these little auks do not fly above the ocean as do the more advanced birds; they "skitter" along just over the surface of the waves and keep well out to sea, even well out of sight of land.

One aukie I caught at night. I was on the beach walking north to meet the man coming south from Nauset, and, as I flashed my searchlight to see who the surfman might be, I saw an aukie coming toward me, fluttering along the very edge of surf, all sticky and a-glisten with fuel oil. Strange little fragment of life on the edge of that mysterious immensity! I picked him up; he struggled and then kept still, and I carried him back to the Fo'castle. The bird was small enough to be carried in one hand, and as I held him, his duck feet rested on my palm and his head and neck emerged from the fork between my thumb and index finger. At the Fo'castle he opened his beak, "chattered" with it (there is no word for that motion without sound), transformed his short neck into a surprisingly long one, and looked at me with a kind of "all is well but anything may be expected" expression in his eyes. Every now and then he rather solemnly winked, showing the delicate tan-colored feathering on his lid. I put him in a corner by himself, and when I went to bed he had given up trying to pick himself free of the oil with his pointed, sparrowy bill, and was standing in his corner of shadow, facing the angle of the walls, for all the world like a small boy who has been naughty at school. The next morning I let him go at his own insistent request.

I found a razor-billed auk, *Alca torda*, cornered him, looked him over while he threatened me with a bill held open and motionless, and then left him to his own devices. I did the same with a Brünnich's murre, and I might have had an eider, too, had I wanted one, for Alvin Newcomb, surfman No. 1 at Nauset, captured a male one night while on north patrol. The eider, however, is a huge bird, and I was not quite prepared to turn the Fo'castle into a kind of ocean hen yard. So the eider at Nauset, after having most unconcernedly listened to the station radio for a little while, was returned that same evening to the North Atlantic. I had one chance at a rare bird. On the first day of the great northeast storm, as I was wandering about at noontime through the sleet, I found in the mouth of a cut the body of a murre. The bird had been dead but a short time, for it was still limp when I picked it up, and as I held it I could even feel a faint vanishing warmth in its exhausted flesh. This bird was the rarer murre, *Uria troile troile,* he of the sharper beak whom men have almost erased from the list of living things. It had apparently died of being caught and battered about for long hours by the gale. After the storm, I tried to find the creature again, but the tide and the storm had poured through the cut and swept everything before them into a confusion of sand and ruin.

These ocean peoples live on such little fish as they can seize; they pick up shellfish on shallow areas; they eat certain marine growths. Some have a taste for the local mussel, *Mytilus edulis.* Unless the winter is an exceptionally severe one, the birds seem to fare well enough. Many stay late, and May is usually at hand before the long lines of scoters fly north again under the command of their feathered admirals. Such is the history of the migrant seafarers of the Cape. A word remains to be said about the residents and the migrants in the marsh.

About the middle of December, I began to see that an amusing game of cross purposes was being played by the sea birds and the land birds of the region west of the dunes. Food becoming scarce upon the uplands, crows, bobwhites, and starlings began to take an interest in the sea and the salt meadows, while gulls took to exploring the moors and to sitting in the top branches of inland pines. One wise old gull once discovered that there was good fare to be had in Mr. Joe Cobb's chicken yard just off the western rim of the great marsh, and every morning this sagacious creature would separate himself from the thousands milling about over the cold tides and flutter down among the hens. There he would forage about, picking up grain like a barnyard fowl till he had dulled the edge of his hunger. I doubt if gulls ever do more. After visiting the chicken yard regularly for several winters, the bird disappeared one spring and was never seen again. He had probably lived out the span of his days.

I pause here to wonder at how little we know of the life span of wild animals. Only cases of exceptionally long life or short life seem to attract the attention of man. I can open any good bird book and find a most careful, a most detailed study of the physical selves and habits of birds, but of their probable length of life, never a word. Such material would be exceedingly difficult to secure, and perhaps the suggestion is folly, but there are times when one wishes that this nelgected side of animal existence might have more attention.

During the summer, I never saw starlings on the marsh, but now that winter is here they leave the uplands by the coast guard station, and venture out along the dunes. These flights of exploration are very rare. I have seen the birds flying over the salt meadows, I have seen them light on the ridgepole of a gunning camp, but I have never once encountered them on the outer beach. With crows, it is a different story. The birds will investigate anything promising, and during the summer I found crows on the beach on four or five different occasions, these visits being made, for the most part, early in the morning.

Chancing to look toward the marsh one warm October afternoon, I witnessed a battle between two gulls and a young crow for the possession of some marine titbit the crow had picked up on the flats; it was a picturesque contest, for the great silvery wings of the gulls beat down and enclosed the crow till he resembled a junior demon in some old lithograph of the war in heaven. Eventually one of the gulls seized on the coveted morsel, flew off a bit, and gulped it down, leaving the crow and the other gull to "consider" like the cow in the old song. Winter and necessity now make the crow something of a beach comber. The birds cross over to the beach at low tide on mild days, forage about warily, and return to their uplands the instant they no longer have the beach all to themselves. A flight of gulls will send them cawing home, their great somber wings beating the ocean air. Even on this immense and lonely beach, they remain the wariest of creatures, and if I wish to see what they are up to, I have to use ten times the care in stalking them that I would have to use in stalking any casual sea bird. I have to creep through cuts and valleys in the dunes and worm my way over cold sand that drinks the warmth and life out of the flesh. I usually find them picking at a fish flung out of the breakers perhaps a day or two before—picking industriously and solemnly.

Once in a while, a covey of shore larks will cross the dunes and alight on the beach in the lee and the afternoon shadow of the sand bank. They fly very low, the whole group rising and falling with the rise and fall of the hills and hollows, a habit that gives their flights a picturesque and amusing roller-coaster quality. Once having settled down on the outer side of the dunes, the birds keep well up on the beach and never seem to venture close to ocean.

This same shore lark, *Otocoris alpestris*, is perhaps the bird I encounter most frequently during the winter months. This season they are here by the thousand; indeed, they are so thick that I scarce can walk behind the dunes without putting up a flock of these alert, brownish, fugitive creatures. Their kingdom lies to the west of the dunes, in the salt-hay fields and intermingled marsh areas which extend between the dunes and the creek running more or less parallel to the sand bar. Coming from Greenland and Labrador, these birds reach the Eastham meadows in October and November, and all winter long they forage and run about in the dead bristles of the hay. Their only note here is a rather sad little *"tseep, tseep,"* which they utter as they skim the grass in alarm, but it is said that they have an interesting song during their breeding season in springtime Labrador.

It is early on a pleasant winter afternoon, and I am returning to the Fo'castle through the meadows, my staff in my hand and a load of groceries in a knapsack on my back. The preceding day brought snow flurries to us out of the northwest, and there are patches of snow on the hay fields and the marshes, and, on the dunes, nests of snow held up off the ground by wiry spears of beach grass bent over and tangled into a cup. Such little pictures as this last are often to be seen on the winter dunes; I pause to enjoy them, for they have the quality and delicacy of Japanese painting. There is a blueness in the air, a blue coldness on the moors, and across the sky to the south, a pale streamer of cloud smoking from its upper edge. Every now and then, I see ahead of me a round, blackish spot in the thin snow; these are the cast-off shells of horseshoe crabs, from whose thin tegument the snow has melted. A flock of nervous shore larks, hidden under an old mowing machine, emerge running, take to their wings, and, flying south a fifty yards, suddenly drop and disappear into the grass. Hesitating on the half-alert, a little flock of bobwhites, occasional invaders of this stubble, watch me pass, and then continue feeding. To the west, from the marsh, I hear the various cries of gulls, the mewing note, the call, and that queer sound which is almost a guttural bark. Afternoon shadows are gathering in the cuts of the dunes, blue shadows and cold, and there is a fine sea tang in the air.

It is low tide, and the herring gulls, *Larus argentatus*, are feeding on the flats and gravel banks. As I watch them through a glass, they seem as untroubled as fowls on an inland farm. Their talkative groups and gatherings have a domestic look. The gull population of the Cape is really one people, for, though separate gull congregations live in various bays and marshes, the mass of the birds seem to hear of any new food supply and flock as one to the feast. So accustomed to man have they grown, and so fearless, that they will follow in his very footsteps for a chance to scavenge food; I have seen the great birds walking round clammers who threw broken clams to them as they might throw scraps of meat to kittens. In hungry seasons the clammer may hear a flapping just behind and discover that a gull has just made off with a clam from his pail. They follow the eelers, too, and on the ice of the Eastham salt pond you may chance to see a pair of gulls disputing an eel which the eelers have thrown away; one will have it by the tail, the other by the head, and both tug with insistence and increasing bad temper. The victory in this primitive battle goes either to the strongest gull or to the fastest swallower.

An unhurried observation of the marsh, especially a study of its lesser creeks and concealed pools, reveals hundreds of ducks. To identify and classify these birds is a next to impossible task, for they are very suspicious and have chosen their winter quarters with a sound instinct for defensive strategy. The great majority of these birds are undoubtedly black duck, *Anas rubripes*, the most wary and suspicious of all wintering birds. All day long, back and forth over the dunes between the marsh and the ocean, these ducks are ever flying; by twos and threes and little flocks they go, and those who go out to sea fly so far out that the eye loses them in the vastness of ocean. I like to walk in the marsh early in the evening, keeping out as far as I can toward the creeks. The ducks hear me and begin a questioning quacking. I hear them talk and take alarm; other ducks, far off, take up the alert; sometimes wings whistle by in the darkness. The sound of a pair of "whistler" ducks on the wing is a lovely, mysterious sound at such a time. It is a sound made with wings, a clear, sibilant note which increases as the birds draw near, and dies away in the distance like a faint and whistling sigh.

One March evening, just as sundown was fading into night, the whole sky chanced to be overspread with cloud, all save a golden channel in the west between the cloud floor and the earth. It was very still, very peaceful on my solitary dune. The whole earth was dark, dark as a shallow cup lifted to a solemnity of silence and cloud. I heard a familiar sound. Turning toward the marsh, I saw a flock of geese flying over the meadows along the rift of dying, golden light, their great wings beating with a slow and solemn beauty, their musical, bell-like cry filling the lonely levels and the dark. Is there a nobler wild clamor in all the world? I listened to the sound till it died away and the birds had disappeared into darkness, and then heard a quiet sea chiding a little at the turn of tide. Presently, I began to feel a little cold, and returned to the Fo'castle, and threw some fresh wood on the fire.

Battlefield of the Shore

WILLIAM BEEBE

Charles William Beebe, the dean of deep-sea explorers, made a famous undersea journey in a bathysphere that is now part of marine history. He always pointed out, however, that great adventures were close at hand—on the very seashore along which anyone can walk. The shore is a true battlefield; the life of the shore is constantly brought to terms with the rhythm and temper of the oceans. Here Beebe describes such a battlefield on an island in the Bermudas.

*T*he edges and rims of things are much more exciting than the things themselves. This is true even of man's handiwork when he works for the love of the working—witness the glorious, cosmic-horizon, china rims of Ming tissue bowls.

As long as the planet Earth was covered by the waters these were monotonous and comparatively safe. But with the appearance of the first dry land, shores began to be. Up to this time fish and other sea creatures could enjoy their three planes of watery space, they could swim up, down and around, and when the active air made the surface unpleasant, they simply dived to calm.

All was changed with the coming of a shore. The stand-patters, to be sure, merely swam away from it, and to the flyingfishes, if there were flyingfish then, the shore meant nothing, for they must ever rise from and fall into the sea.

But out of hoi polloi, from protozoa to fish, there was, as please God there always will be, a moiety—a small glorious band disturbed by a blind, divine discontent, by unconsciously progressive guts, who gathered from far and near, and began an unending assault on this primeval shore, this new, amazing rim of things. From that first dry land—shall we say a thousand million years ago—up to the present moment (which as I write goes to join the billion years) this contest has never ceased for a moment.

The thought comes to me that to keep from writing as a rank outsider, I should plunge into and pass through this battlefield unprepared, on the impulse of the moment. So I go.

I have just returned from my pragmatic experiment and I would not exchange the experience for anything. Just as the creatures of old had to make their first attack with their sea-evolved equipment, so it seemed fair for me to rise from my desk and walk straight down to the shore without preparation. This was not as drastic a performance as it sounds, quite unlike jumping off a high bridge in full evening dress for a bet, for on Nonsuch my costume consists of three articles of clothing—a woolen shirt, khaki shorts, and a pair of canvas sneakers.

As I rose from my table I could hear the surf booming on the rocks at the foot of the hillside of cedars. The day was sheer brilliant sunshine, hot and with very little breeze, but from some disturbance far to the south the rollers were piling in. I walked comfortably on the mat of soft needles and in the shade of dense foliage—I was a land mammal and this was my native habitat. Even so, the eons of years had left me only partly adapted to these haunts; if I looked intently at the sun I should be blinded, if I exposed my skin unwisely, the result would be an intolerable burn. Yet there were delicate adaptations for assurance of safety, such as the protective ochraceous tawny (by Ridgeway's Color Key!) of my skin at present.

I reached the last of the stunted cedars and walked among weeds—goldenrod and sea-lavender. Then I came to the end of the soil and the beginning of the naked rocks. The most casual onlooker could tell that I was getting beyond my natural environment, for I had to desert the upright bipedal locomotion of a Lord of Creation and clamber down on all fours. I had already passed beyond the permanent home of any true terrestrial animal, but here and there in sheltered hollows, where a handful of soil and débris had lodged, sturdy little sea-oxeyes fought for enough rain and sun to counteract the choking brine. Two feet below and to the left of the last of these green pioneers appeared a tiny basin of water. It was

slimy and exceedingly hot, and a few drops on my tongue in-
dicated a saturated salt solution. At times of storm or any
high surf, such as five days ago, this cup was replenished by
flying drops, and between storms slowly evaporated. It was
lined with a dense, yellow-green nap of algae—as true seaweed
as the sargassum a thousand miles from shore. I let myself
down and stood with one hand on the silvery green foliage of
the ox-eye, cousin of thistles, daisies, and goldenrod, and with
my other I plucked tufts of seaweed, so close in physical space
have the plants of sea and land approached.

I found an easier descent and climbed painfully over the
needle sharp points, rough carved by the acids of the water
and sharpened by the emery of shifting sand and wind. A
projecting pinnacle gave suddenly and I tore my shirt and the
skin within. As I approached the great curving, green surges
my enthusiasm for a direct undeviating path became moderated,
and crab-wise I sidled into a deep, narrow canyon floored with
sand. At the moment I dropped to the welcome softness, a
curling, roaring mass of foam and green shreds of water tore
around a bend, undermined my footing as if it had been
quicksand, and I was flung to my knees. I staggered upright,
turned to offer my side to the wash, and instantly was buried
in a smother of flying spume from the opposite direction, thrown
back from the impact on the rocks. Nose, eyes, ears were filled
with the stinging sand-roiled salt water and I climbed several
feet up the sharp points to get my breath. The smashing blow
and the rebound had come too quickly to be avoided, and the
first round belonged quite conclusively to the sea.

Still preferring the sand-floored gully to a precarious, barbed-
wire descent from a rock, I retraced my steps to the head of
the narrow gorge and began anew, gripping the roughnesses as
I walked knee-deep through the swirling half-sand, half-water.
At every step I passed the tight-clinging, vacuumed limpets,
winkles, and chitons, and here and there clusters of small
black mussels, anchored firmly in sheltered hollows. Close overhead swooped a pair of creaking tropicbirds, wheeling and
circling in raucous protest at my too close approach to their
young, undetectable, except to the sense of smell, at the end
of some long, meandering tunnel.

I reached my cover safely, peered around it and instantly

darted back, and tried to become a limpet, crab and mussel at once. It was no use. I was only a human being, quite out of place. My clothing kept catching on corners and I was again knocked off my feet. This time, like white mice and other higher terrestrial mammals, I had learned by trial and error, and did not fight against the backwash, but allowed it to sweep me around the corner in full view of the open sea. Another mighty roller was headed in, and met the backwash, and the two, after leaping high in air, sank rather quietly and quickly, leaving me limp and looking much like a drowned rat, braced with all my muscles against an impact which did not materialize. As result of this I pitched seawards and was rolled partly over, my side scraping against a submarine cross-cut saw of sorts. A lull ensued, so long that a dozen little fish came and dashed about excitedly, apparently wrought to highest pitch by the presence of my life blood diffused through the water.

I marched unsteadily onward and found a partly submerged reef just before the next wave came, and with its undertow I struck out strongly from shore. Twice I was carried back almost to the rocks a few yards farther east, then I reached the outer zone where the rollers only rose and fell, and the only unpleasant thing was the choppiness of the water. This slapped, slapped in my face, until I turned over and sculled with my hands.

A minute passed and I was considering returning, when I felt a rather sharp blow on the top of my head. This was quite new to my sea experience and I righted myself with utmost speed. There, staring with large, frightened eyes into mine, was a full-plumaged young tropicbird. I reached out toward it and it flapped helplessly a few times. It was evidently too water-logged to rise. This explained the daring swoops of the parent birds close over my head ever since I had reached the beach. Twice I swam with all my might toward the bird, but it avoided me easily. Its tail was raised and spread like the rays of a heraldic sun, but it gave forth no sound. Seeing the uselessness of further pursuit I turned and struck out for home. For the fraction of a second I had a sinking of the heart—the tide and what breeze there was, were against me, and the undertow was apparent if I lowered my feet even a little. The panic passed and in spite of my dragging clothes and shoes I knew I could certainly make it. So my mood changed to the appreciation of how completely I had made my point: The difficulty of adjustment, or in my case, readjustment to a strange element. Certain offshoots of my ancestors—whales, dolphins and seacows—had successfully achieved a return to aquatic life. Here however was a tropicbird, essentially a being of the air, and a mammal of the land, both in trouble of sorts, due to maladjustment. I sculled and got my breath, and found myself at the outer line of foam. I had no trouble at first in getting in, once I secured a good grip on the rocks, but farther on a second bit of stone gave way and down I rolled, half buried in the smother before I could scramble a few feet higher. Here I made two brief stops, once to dig in as the water broke over me, and again when I reached a wide pool, freshened by every tide and full of the brave little gobies who had fought and won this great fight. When well out of the waves, I sat and got my breath back again, examined my wounds and wrung out my clothes, gradually assuming again the characteristics of a member of the terrestrial fauna of the globe.

I looked out at the young tropicbird bobbing up and down and realized that after all I was even more sharply set off from the creatures of the sea than my habiliments and unaquatic, inadequate limbs suggested—for my difficulty in getting inshore again, my temporary panic were due to my altruistic attempts to save the bird from what, sooner or later, must have been certain death. And this was a mental attribute which would never have worried any oceanic being trying in past ages to go terra firma.

In my laboratory I threw away my cheap, watersoaked watch and unlimbered another, dried my rust-proof knife, hung up my leather belt in the sun, and sent out a man in a boat to salvage the young tropicbird.

I am anxious to get down to the affairs of the creatures who are waging their shore conflict, but I keep wishing that someone would first write a most wonderful essay—a veritable saga—of this area from the point of view of the elements—the physics and chemistry of this most active, dynamic, pseudo-vital zone.

Here we have a gas, a liquid, and a solid forever having it out, with force, movement, sound, victories and defeats, all of which would pass as organic in a hundred particulars.

The shore being what it is, a place unique, dramatic, of the greatest interest, it should not have to depend on any simile, however apt, any metaphor despite its appropriateness. Yet such is human frailty, with such mental difficulty can we set apart man's quarrels and nature's competitions, that the strife on the seashore for new opportunities, increased advantages in life, can be considered only in phraseology of warfare and battle. Once we yield to this temptation, the superficial resemblances become amazing.

From my desk I look down the south hillside of Nonsuch, over the solid ranks of goldenrod and between the gnarled cedar trunks to the heaving green waters. There is no scream of shells overhead but an almost continuous roar of the surf in my ears, not to be distinguished in memory from the sound of distant guns, as they came, night after night, to Verdun, to Furcy and to Dunkirk. As I look I see fountains of spray shoot up into the air, like the return of material things to their native elements after a direct hit with HE. The shore is almost as bare of vegetation as were the fields about Douaumont, and the gradual approach of the tide, foot after foot, yard after yard, is the perfect parallel of a creeping barrage.

Now that we have labored our simile we might strive to realize the lack of changes in our shore-line since Cain killed Abel or the first apeman showed signs of progress toward humanity by fashioning a club and braining his neighbor.

Evolution is going on everywhere, but usually so quietly that we are not conscious of it. The turbulent warfare of elements and life on the seashore is so tempestuous that we cannot forget it. We may cut down trees and dig ourselves into cities on land, or we may travel in only slight peril of our lives from shore to shore across the ocean. But when all the wildernesses have been tamed, all the deserts made to grow food and clothing, cradles and coffins, the open shore-line will still be a wild place. Wharves and jetties and breakwaters may last for a time, but sooner or later, wind and wave will lift together and reduce them to sand and rust and splinters.

Let us take our stand on a cliff a few yards above the sea,

with rocks to our right and a sandy beach to the left. We have here, on southeastern Nonsuch, a typical sample of the tens of thousands of miles of narrow shore ribbon which mosaics the surface of the globe. In the far north, to be sure, the water at times pretends to be solid like the real land, but that only means pushing the shore for a time farther out.

To have pass in review a résumé, a panorama of the daily and nightly rhythm of the meeting place of air, water and land, we should begin our watch at high tide, and if it is the time of the new moon the waters will be pulled to their maximum. On the beach the rollers break high, and the foam slithers up to the very foliage of the hardy shock troops of land plants. Sargassum weed is tossed about, great furrows are worn in the sand, visible momentarily, as an interval longer than usual between two waves sends the sand and water far out. Off the rocks the breakers sweep landward in low mounds, hardly perceptible at first; then rise higher and higher, finally curving in an endless length of crescent. For a terrible moment this hangs in midair before the tons of water crash down—splintering into an infinitude of drops and thinning the air into an agonizing vacuum which instantly is released in an explosion of sound—liquid on the shifting sands and a solid deep roar against the sounding board of the cliffs.

The wide zone between low and high tide marks is now all water and filled with watery beings. Great emerald and rufus, yard-long parrotfish are close inshore, wallowing on their sides, browsing among the waving banners of seaweed; I see a goat-fish now and then sand-tapping for what-there-is for goatfish. Strange crabs and crayfish creep behind the incoming surges—camp followers picking here and there at stray corpses of things.

Six hours later everything is changed. The wind has gone down and the water—far out at lowest tide mark—laps against the rocks and slithers gently over a few inches of sand. Recalling conditions a quarter of a day before, there comes to mind the tricky arrangement I have seen in the store windows of a circular aquarium filled with swinging goldfish surrounding a space in which canaries fly about, so that to the eye of the onlooker fish and birds seem inextricably mingled in the same medium. Where sergeant-majors and parrotfish and wrasse wandered and browsed, turnstones, sandpipers, catbirds and sparrows now hop and fly and chase beach-fleas, a pair of silver-spotted butterflies flutter low over the sand, flies hover about the dead seaweed, a skink darts among the crevices and I myself creep down to the water's very edge. The fish have been forced back by the pull of the moon and in their place are representatives of the four great groups of land animals—insects, reptiles, birds and mammals.

I can find no words adequately to tell what this shift of creatures means to me but it has something in it of the deep significance of evolution, of the impersonal, inevitable rhythm of the inorganic, compared with the malleable adaptiveness of organic life. The point is wholly lost unless the entire phenomenon is considered simultaneously,—fish-crab-fly-sparrow-lizard-man-sand-rocks-water-air-moon; then we have it for a moment. It is almost immediately lost again, and our restless weakling minds reassume their myopic casualness, and we see only a fish, a wave, a bird, or a beach.

In war there are two major methods of attack, a frontal assault by sheer force, or a lateral movement, usually concealed as much as possible, which ultimately will develop into an attempt on the flank or even on the rear.

Let us go back sufficient millions of years to when most of the important groups of animals have become established in the sea and imagine the more adventurous spirits among them approaching this new thing—a shore. Most of the creatures, being Babbitts, or John Smiths or good middle-class peasants of the great marine democracies, never heard of the shore, or if they became conscious of it through what passed for movies in the Cambrian or wireless in the Ordovician, they shivered and gave thanks that they did not have to leave their abyssal hearths for any such new-fangled resorts. The gloriously discontented aforementioned few, however, began their attack and to this day are still continuing it.

Their early success proved to be their ultimate failure to achieve land life. Their story is comparable with an expedition which sets out to explore a swamp-surrounded desert, and the members of which become so skilled in conquering the difficulties of swamp that they expire in the heat of the desert's sun.

The floating population of the incoming tide is of indirect but of great importance to our shore zone. No tide ever goes out that it does not leave at least one stranded and wrecked jelly-fish on the sand. Of all aquatic beings this is the most wholly unadapted to a life in any other element. We see one of these beautiful creatures throbbing slowly through the water—a round transparent or translucent sun, with disk, vein-like channels, tentacles, poison darts, eye-spots, nerves, mouth, stomach, eggs—every mechanism of life, and an hour later a thin, glairy, glistening film on the sand is all that is left. That we are three-fourths water is marvel enough, but the living, active, successful race of jellies is only one half of one per cent animal matter.

The thought of a jellyfish coming ashore and running on the sand or scampering up the rocks on the tips of its tentacles is worthy of a place only in a fantasy of Dunsany. A still wilder and more fantastic tale could be written of a jelly which, envious of a shore life and aware of its own watery quintessence, regards the success of the fast-rooted seaweeds and thereafter deposits eggs which hatch and sprout into comely plants whose fruit is piles of infant jelly saucers. Only in this case, the tale, censored of anthropomorphic allusion, is a scientific truth. A jelly can never learn anything of static seashore life, but its mother and its daughter—hydroids we call them—might tell it much about the rhythmic swing, back and forth, of waves crashing in, and all that has to do with tides.

Early in the shore assault, the impetuous shock troops having won an advanced position dug themselves into such concrete bomb-proofs that they have never been able to get out—either to advance or retreat, and there they are today, splendid examples of over-specialization. And not one group but many have thus fallen and taken root by the wayside. Next to jellies, sea anemones would seem to be the most susceptible to unusual outer obstacles, yet here and there on the rocks I find colonies of these wine-colored blobs of hardened jelly, whose resistance to injury from the elements, compared with jellyfish, is as rubber to cobwebs.

Advance scouts of crustaceans have won to success, such as crabs and pill-bugs, but barnacles are shut-ins, forever cribbed and confined between tides. As an eskimo can fish through the floor of his igloo if built on the ice, so barnacles at times of flood reach out through the roof of their marble wigwams and hook in passing bits of food.

The great race of snails has won a step farther on. After hatching they find some quiet place, and set up a lime kiln and devote themselves to architecture. By subtle alchemy of glands they spin magic imitation rocks from the invisible water, and mould them on the potter's wheel of their own bodies. Then the limpets and the chitons wage their life war, and advance over the rocks like a battalion of diminutive tanks,—taking shelter in a vacuum-rooted immobility under stress of waves, and moving slowly about when hungry. Even the mussels, apparently moored for life by a nexus of silken cables, can cut those farther aft, and throw out fresh ones forward and to starboard, and so warp themselves slowly toward the promised land. We might go on through the whole animal kingdom, and find still more exciting units in the front-line trenches. And always we must credit these pioneers with having solved in this maelstrom zone all the primary problems of existence—the finding and securing of a foothold, sufficient oxygen in water or air, safety from enemies, access to and ability to woo a mate, and nursery sanctuary for their offspring.

Tidepools are both a source of help and an added scene of difficulties. When the tide goes out they remain as a welcome oasis—for them tides do not exist. But when a warrior from the sea puts his trust in them he finds his troubles multiplied— the sun pours down and heats the water beyond all bearing, or the rain changes them from salt to brackish, and from brackish to fresh. Or if they are very high upon the rocks they become stagnant between spring tides.

Tidepools raise false hopes which end all progress. For fish like gobies they have always been a welcome halfway house of rest—a littoral dâk bungalow—but so pleasant withal that these and other fish have lingered in them too long. They are inured to fresh water, to excess of heat, to stagnancy, but to maintain themselves they have sacrificed their nether paired fins to the fashioning of a vacuum cup, and thus ended all hope of future legs. So however we may rightly admire the amazing adaptations and nice adjustments of the shore folk to their difficult haunts of life, yet we see that if life on land was their goal they are all failures, and we see no answer to our own evolution. In their own field, however, let us continue to think of them as supreme, as absolute victors, and not forget the thousands and thousands of other attempts which failed and were blotted from our knowledge.

What about the flank or rear attack which we mentioned? While the brilliant courageous campaigns were going on along the sea front, there were, in ages past, side lagoons, salt marshes and mud holes scattered in bays and hinterlands of the shore. Mud-loving fish wallowed and slithered their way through the slime and shallow water, consolidating first of all lung-like structures which could use the oxygen of the air. Then, pottering about and continually lifting their heads to gulp air, their fins assumed more and more the nature of feet, and soon they were rather amphibian than fish. Some as usual became too good amphibians, and hence the frogs and toads of today, with their fishy tadpoles and their necessity for dampness or water. And side-tracked, there was no more hope—amphibians they were and amphibians they must always remain.

But other inconspicuous chaps stuck to the safe, middle way, and hence—we have reptiles and birds and ourselves. The real missing links are gone forever—reptiles were too reptilian, and birds were too avian to carry through. And after all the smugness of our ancestral line—with its slow, watchful waiting, and wading through safe and sane slime, and keeping to the unexciting, sure path marked Up and Onward or Excelsior—some of them I am sure named Eric or Bertie or Reginald—I go back to the clean, smashing waves and I see the limpets and hydroids and crabs, and I look into the bright knowing eyes of the gobies and we feel something in common. I again recall what Colonel Theodore Roosevelt said to me many years ago, "If I were the last of my race I would rather be a sabre-toothed tiger than a field mouse," and I hope in my heart I am not a typical middle-liner. There is something that transcends comfort and contentment, safety and sanity. I would rather be a goby than a salamander.

The Shipwreck

HENRY DAVID THOREAU

Shipwrecks and the oceans once went together as did the shore-lines and seas. In the last century you could walk any beach and find the debris of a ship that had come to grief. Henry David Thoreau, the great American naturalist, walked the beaches a century ago. The reviewers predicted that his story of those walking tours would last well over a century. Those predictions came true. Thoreau's observations of the oceans and beaches are still as fresh as sea air.

*C*ape Cod is the bared and bended arm of Massachusetts: the shoulder is at Buzzard's Bay; the elbow, or crazy-bone, at Cape Mallebarre; the wrist at Truro; and the sandy fist at Provincetown,—behind which the State stands on her guard, with her back to the Green Mountains, and her feet planted on the floor of the ocean, like an athlete protecting her Bay, —boxing with northeast storms, and, ever and anon, heaving up her Atlantic adversary from the lap of earth,—ready to thrust forward her other fist, which keeps guard the while upon her breast at Cape Ann.

On studying the map, I saw that there must be an uninterrupted beach on the east or outside of the forearm of the Cape, more than thirty miles from the general line of the coast, which would afford a good sea view, but that, on account of an opening in the beach, forming the entrance to Nauset Harbor, in Orleans, I must strike it in Eastham, if I approached it by land, and probably I could walk thence straight to Race Point, about twenty-eight miles, and not meet with any obstruction.

We left Concord, Massachusetts, on Tuesday, October 9, 1849. On reaching Boston, we found that the Provincetown steamer, which should have got in the day before, had not yet arrived, on account of a violent storm; and, as we noticed in the streets a handbill headed, "Death! one hundred and forty-five lives lost at Cohasset," we decided to go by way of Cohasset. We found many Irish in the cars, going to identify bodies and to sympathize with the survivors, and also to attend the funeral which was to take place in the afternoon;— and when we arrived at Cohasset, it appeared that nearly all the passengers were bound for the beach, which was about a mile distant, and many other persons were flocking in from the neighboring country. There were several hundreds of them streaming off over Cohasset common in that direction, some on foot and some in wagons,—and among them were some sportsmen in their hunting-jackets, with their guns, and game-bags, and dogs.

As we passed the graveyard we saw a large hole, like a cellar, freshly dug there, and, just before reaching the shore, by a pleasantly winding and rocky road, we met several hay-riggings and farm-wagons coming away toward the meeting-house, each loaded with three large, rough deal boxes. We did not need to ask what was in them. The owners of the wagons were made the undertakers. Many horses in carriages were fastened to the fences near the shore, and, for a mile or more, up and down, the beach was covered with people looking out for bodies, and examining the fragments of the wreck. There was a small island called Brook Island, with a hut on it, lying just off the shore. This is said to be the rockiest shore in Massachusetts, from Nantasket to Scituate,—hard sienitic rocks, which the waves have laid bare, but have not been able to crumble. It has been the scene of many a shipwreck.

The brig St. John, from Galway, Ireland, laden with emigrants, was wrecked on Sunday morning; it was now Tuesday morning, and the sea was still breaking violently on the rocks. There were eighteen or twenty of the same large boxes that I have mentioned, lying on a green hillside, a few rods from the water, and surrounded by a crowd. The bodies which had been recovered, twenty-seven or -eight in all, had been collected there. Some were rapidly nailing down the lids, others were carting the boxes away, and others were lifting the lids, which were yet loose, and peeping under the cloths, for each body, with such rags as still adhered to it, was covered loosely with a white sheet. I witnessed no signs of grief, but there was a sober dispatch of business which was affecting. One man was seeking to identify a particular body, and one undertaker or carpenter was calling to another to know in what box a certain child was put.

I saw many marble feet and matted heads as the cloths were raised, and one livid, swollen, and mangled body of a drowned girl,—who probably had intended to go out to service in some American family,—to which some rags still adhered, with a string, half concealed by the flesh, about its swollen neck; the coiled-up wreck of a human hulk, gashed by the rocks or fishes, so that the bone and muscle were exposed, but quite bloodless,—merely red and white,—with wide-open and staring eyes, yet lustreless, dead-lights; or like the cabin windows of a stranded vessel, filled with sand. Sometimes there were two or more children, or a parent and child, in the same box, and on the lid would perhaps be written with red chalk, "Bridget such-a-one, and sister's child."

The surrounding sward was covered with bits of sails and clothing. I have since heard, from one who lives by this beach, that a woman who had come over before, but had left her infant behind for her sister to bring, came and looked into these boxes, and saw in one—probably the same whose superscription I have quoted—her child in her sister's arms, as if the sister had meant to be found thus; and within three days after, the mother died from the effect of that sight.

We turned from this and walked along the rocky shore. In the first cove were strewn what seemed the fragments of a vessel, in small pieces mixed with sand and seaweed, and great quantities of feathers; but it looked so old and rusty, that I at first took it to be some old wreck which had lain there many years. I even thought of Captain Kidd, and that the feathers were those which sea-fowl had cast there; and perhaps there might be some tradition about it in the neighborhood. I asked a sailor if that was the St. John. He said it was. I asked him where she struck. He pointed to a rock in front of us, a mile from the shore, called the Grampus Rock, and added,—

"You can see a part of her now sticking up; it looks like a small boat."

I saw it. It was thought to be held by the chain-cables and the anchors. I asked if the bodies which I saw were all that were drowned.

"Not a quarter of them," said he.

"Where are the rest?"

"Most of them right underneath that piece you see."

It appeared to us that there was enough rubbish to make the wreck of a large vessel in this cove alone, and that it would take many days to cart it off. It was several feet deep, and here and there was a bonnet or a jacket on it. In the very midst of the crowd about this wreck, there were men with carts busily collecting the seaweed which the storm had cast up, and conveying it beyond the reach of the tide, though they were often obliged to separate fragments of clothing from it, and they might at any moment have found a human body under it. Drown who might, they did not forget that this weed was a valuable manure. This shipwreck had not produced a visible vibration in the fabric of society.

About a mile south we could see, rising above the rocks, the masts of the British brig which the St. John had endeavored to follow, which had slipped her cables, and, by good luck, run into the mouth of Cohasset Harbor. A little further along the shore we saw a man's clothes on a rock; further, a woman's scarf, a gown, a straw bonnet, the brig's caboose, and one of her masts high and dry, broken into several pieces. In another rocky cove, several rods from the water, and behind rocks twenty feet high, lay a part of one side of the vessel, still hanging together. It was, perhaps, forty feet long, by fourteen wide.

I was even more surprised at the power of the waves, exhibited on this shattered fragment, than I had been at the sight of the smaller fragments before. The largest timbers and iron braces were broken superfluously, and I saw that no material could withstand the power of the waves; that iron must go to pieces in such a case, and an iron vessel would be cracked up like an egg-shell on the rocks. Some of these timbers, however, were so rotten that I could almost thrust my umbrella through them. They told us that some were saved on this piece, and also showed where the sea had heaved it into this cove which was now dry. When I saw where it had come in, and in what condition, I wondered that any had been saved on it.

A little further on a crowd of men was collected around the mate of the St. John, who was telling his story. He was a slim-looking youth, who spoke of the captain as the master, and seemed a little excited. He was saying that when they jumped into the boat, she filled, and, the vessel lurching, the weight of the water in the boat caused the painter to break, and so they were separated. Whereat one man came away, saying,—

"Well, I don't see but he tells a straight story enough. You see, the weight of the water in the boat broke the painter. A boat full of water is very heavy,"—and so on, in a loud and impertinently earnest tone, as if he had a bet depending on it, but had no humane interest in the matter. Another, a large man, stood near by upon a rock, gazing into the sea, and chewing large quids of tobacco, as if that habit were forever confirmed with him.

"Come," says another to his companion, "let's be off. We've seen the whole of it. It's no use to stay to the funeral."

Further, we saw one standing upon a rock, who, we were told, was one that was saved. He was a sober-looking man, dressed in a jacket and gray pantaloons, with his hands in the pockets. I asked him a few questions, which he answered; but he seemed unwilling to talk about it, and soon walked away. By his side stood one of the life-boat men, in an oil-cloth jacket, who told us how they went to the relief of the British brig, thinking that the boat of the St. John, which they passed on the way, held all her crew,—for the waves prevented their seeing those who were on the vessel, though they might have saved some had they known there were any there. A little further was the flag of the St. John spread on a rock to dry, and held down by stones at the corners. This frail, but essential and significant portion of the vessel, which had so long been the sport of the winds, was sure to reach the shore. There were one or two houses visible from these rocks, in which were some of the survivors recovering from the shock which their bodies and minds had sustained. One was not expected to live.

We kept on down the shore as far as a promontory called Whitehead, that we might see more of the Cohasset Rocks. In a little cove, within half a mile, there were an old man and his son collecting, with their team, the seaweed which that fatal storm had cast up, as serenely employed as if there had never been a wreck in the world, though they were within sight of the Grampus Rock, on which the St. John had struck. The old man had heard that there was a wreck and knew most of the particulars, but he said that he had not been up there since it happened. It was the wrecked weed that concerned him most, rock-weed, kelp, and seaweed, as he named them, which he carted to his barnyard; and those bodies were to him but other weeds which the tide cast up, but which were of no use to him. We afterwards came to the life-boat in its harbor, waiting for another emergency,—and in the afternoon we saw the funeral procession at a distance, at the head of which walked the captain with the other survivors.

Underwater

The Marvel of a Tide

GILBERT C. KLINGEL

Tides are the signatures of the seas. Primitive man wondered at them when he first stood beside the ocean, and throughout history man's explorations, battles, and food supplies have often been dependent upon the tides. They are one of the wonders of the world, and they can play strange tricks. Gilbert C. Klingel was once shipwrecked on the island of Inagua in the Bahamas because of a tide; he knows its nature.

*A*ll living, when looked upon in a large sense, is a tide. Ebb and flow is one of the inevitable characteristics of existence. The growths of nations and their declines, the boiling sweep of conquests and their recessions, the rise and fall of cultures are manifestations of the turn of tides in the affairs of men. The Dark Ages and the Renaissance that followed were opposite halves of a single flow of energy just as the devastation of the hordes commanded by Chepe Noyon had its counterpart in the brilliance of the court of Kublai Khan. Only time pours ceaselessly in one direction; but even the march of the hours leaves behind a trail of risings and fallings, of comings and goings. The geologic eras bear bountiful evidence of the fluctuations of existence. Great waves of life washed up on the shores of eternity and fell back again; the extinct dinosaurs and amphibians, the fossils of armored fish and the billions of long buried trilobites are proof of this. Even individual lives are only tides in miniature; birth, growth and swelling maturity, decline and dissolution are separate phases in this phenomenon.

I have often wondered if the ancient and very primitive

religions which recognized the existence of Selene, the goddess of the moon, did not have as their origin an instinctive recognition of the immense power of that satellite over the ceaseless pulsing of the tide-controlled sea. The phases of the moon and the correlation of the creeping of the waters into bays and lagoons could hardly have escaped the attention of early man, who was highly conscious of natural phenomena and who was just becoming aware of a sense of power and articulation. The moon worships date far into the recesses of unrecorded history. Many of the primitive peoples of today to whom the printed page is an inexplicable mystery have a keen appreciation of the relationship of the tide to that orb and regulate their activities accordingly.

The flowing of a tide to anyone familiar with the sea, and with the least grain of perception, is an impelling and inspiring event. The tides of time are discernible only from a distance, but the surging and falling of a sea tide is a potent and tangible happening. Perhaps the inexorable character of a tide is its impressive quality, but I think the emotional response to the occurrence goes deeper than that. The newly formed embryo of a human being bearing its telltale marks of ancient gill clefts harks back to the time when our ancestors, no matter how far removed, strove and battled fin and tail with the tide. If you have never leaned over a ship's rail and watched the soft swirl and eddy of the tide-urged water flowing past a rudder you cannot fully appreciate what I mean. If you have, and were at all aware, you will know that the sight of a moving tide is a stimulating experience.

Here at my typewriter, far from the flow of moving water, the feel of a tide is a difficult emotion to catch and imprison on a sheet of paper. If a tide boomed and crashed like the surf it would not be so hard. But a tide is *silent;* it cannot be heard except faintly when interrupted by a rudder or a ship's bow; it cannot be smelled nor touched. A tide is best seen though it is more readily *sensed* than visualized. Its very vastness makes it difficult to grasp. In my mind's eye I see barren sand bars lying idle in the sun with fiddler crabs moving about, or boats lying on their bellies in the sand; I picture seaweeds trailing toward the mouth of a river or whirlpools eddying about a buoy and I say "this is a tide." But it is not. These are only small manifestations of a tide. A complete tide is a stupendous awakening, a gargantuan breathing of the whole ocean, or a monstrous wave running the circuit of the earth extending from pole to pole. It is a swelling giant that sends millions of creeping fingers into the hollows of the land, bringing life to those hollows and as regularly withdrawing it again. A tide is the pulsing bosom of our planet. The Norsemen grasped the idea better than we when they believed it to be the breathing of the earth-serpent, Iörmungander, a monster so enormous that it encircled the globe and held its tail in its mouth to make room for that appendage.

> *"Beneath the lashings of his tail*
> *Seas, mountain high, swelled on the land."*

It was a tide that wrecked me on Inagua when I thought all danger from the ocean was past, and it was to the tide that I turned for one of the most entertaining days I spent on that island. Near Mathewtown, toward the south and in the direction of the opening of the Windward Passage, the coast of Inagua makes a last turn before sweeping away in a long spit toward the desolate frozen sand dunes of the weather side of the island. At the last point of the turn the rock cliffs by the settlement crumble away, and a little beyond, the interminable arcs of the barrier reef take up their existence and fling away toward the infinite horizon. Here the full force of the tide, sweeping in twice a day from the wastes of the Atlantic Ocean and from the turbulent deeps of the blue Caribbean, meets in a boiling mass of currents and counter-currents. When all the remainder of the coast was calm and smooth this point was flecked with foam and with the peculiar lapping waves of tide-rips. This was the final meeting place of east and west where the debris and flotsam of two oceans mingled before being swept into the blue depths or piled on the high white beach which was already littered with the fragments of a hundred thousand sea tragedies.

The diving at this rendezvous of the seas promised to be good, so I lugged the heavy helmet with its hose and line down to a little shelf on the very edge of the breakers. Instead of diving from a boat I decided to crawl from dry land to the depths on foot, so that I might experience the full sensation of the transition from dry to wet and examine the structure of the cliff wall and its life on the way. A small oblique opening in

the sloping rock made an easy entering wedge without making
it necessary to battle the full force of the surf. In addition,
the opening was well padded with algae on its upper slopes
and was reasonably free of the ubiquitous spiny sea urchins.

With a tremendous heave I hoisted the eighty-pound helmet
on my head and settled it on my shoulders. It was so top-
heavy that I staggered and nearly fell. The native boy that I
hired for the task, started the pump, and, like a drunken man,
I felt my way across the padded algae and stepped into the
first gradient of the slope. The foam whirled slightly about my
knees and then about my hips. In a second I had advanced
to my shoulders and the intolerable weight was suddenly lifted.
Once more I assumed control of my feet. I paused a moment
at eye height gazing at the strange sight of a world divided
in half and enjoying the unusual perspective of being exactly at
the level of the water. Most impressive was the definiteness of
the division; above was dry air and sunshine, all the familiar
sights, flowers and white clouds; below was a strange blue
cosmos of tumbled rocks, vague shadows and dancing bubbles.
The surface was as rigid a barrier for most life as if it had
been made of hard metal instead of the light-transmitting, yet
opaque, film that it appeared from beneath.

The amount of life that clung to the film itself was surprising.
On the upper side it was dusted with yellow grains of pollen
drifted from the bushes on shore, and with down and winged
seeds that had floated too far on the trades. There were also a
few dead bugs, the frayed and broken wings of a butterfly,
and some beetle elytra, little else. For the land creatures the
top of the sea was death and failure. But a mere fraction of
an inch beneath, the reverse was true; the under film was a
marine maternity ward. For clinging to the burnished ceiling
was a host of just-created things: baby fishes scarcely a quarter
of an inch in length, transparent as glass and as helpless as the
current-swirled plankton; microscopic lacy crustaceans aglow
with jets of iridescent color; round globular pelagic eggs with
long filaments and dark specks of nuclei; small blobs of pulsat-
ing jellies just released from their rock-dwelling, hydroid-like,
animal-flower parents; and other myriads too small to be
identifiable to the naked eye but made apparent by the rays of
sunlight they caught and refracted. This final yard of open

sea before the beginning of dry land was a veritable hatchery of sea-life.

Swiftly I dropped into the wedge and entered the frothing line of bubbles. These hurled about in all directions and I had to seize a rock to keep from being smashed against the sheer wall. The waves retreated and came plunging in again forcing me to cling tightly, digging in toes and fingers like one of the Grapsus crabs against the swirling retreat. Six times I crouched against the onslaughts before there came a lull and I was able to step lightly into space and float downwards to a ledge eight or nine feet below. I had hardly landed when the seventh wave came in and I had to fall on my knees to keep a firm hold. Once more there came a period of quiet and again I jumped, pausing momentarily on a round mound of meandrina before I gave a final seven-league step and landed thirty feet below the surface on the level white sand at the base of the cliff that was the foundation of Inagua.

Catching my balance and my breath I looked about. Seaward a smooth plain of dazzling white sand leveled off into a blue immensity, dipping slightly at the point where it went out of vision. To the right the southwesternmost crags of the island lay piled in gigantic fashion, torn loose in great blocks by some heavy force. On the left a similar but smaller bluff jutted out into the azure world. Like the first it was scarred and pitted, festooned with a tremendous mass of living objects. Long fronds of exceedingly lacy algae alternately drooped listlessly, then flung skyward as the advancing pulse of a wave hit and rushed upward, deflected by the stone. Looking at the combers from below I was interested to observe that it was the wave form that moved, not the water itself; the great bulk of blue liquid seemed to throb forward slightly but always came back to its original station. I ascertained this by watching some floating bumpers that hung close to the watery ceiling. Only in the last few yards did the inverted wave-mounds fling themselves in their entirety at the cliff. In the open the wave shapes advanced ceaselessly; their power seemed to be transmitted from particle to particle, but the particles remained in their relative positions. Were this not so the destruction that would be wreaked on the land would be so tremendous that the islands and the continents would be quickly eaten away.

In order to take in the entire vista of the base of an island
resting on its bed of sand I moved forward towards the open
plain and stepped from the shelter of the twin bluffs. Instantly, and unexpectedly, I was met by a blast of water that
threw me off my feet, rolling and twisting on my side over the
smooth sand bottom. My helmet filled with bitter salt water.
I gasped for breath and fought to stand erect. With a jerk I
came to the end of the light rope that I was trailing between
my fingers, then was startled to find myself yanked off my
feet, and streamed out on the end of the line like a rag in the
breeze. Fortunately my flight into open water brought me erect
again and with a final splash the liquid subsided in the helmet
so that I was able to catch my breath once more. The savage
current caught my lightly balanced body, swooped it in a great
arc nearly to the surface, swirled me towards the shore
where it slackened and let me drop again on the sand.

Then I became aware that beyond the shelter of the crags
a great assortment of objects was floating by at a dizzy rate.
I had noticed them before but they had made no impression.
Between the cliffs the current was barely perceptible except as
a cool back eddy from the main stream. Once more I tried to
breast the flow but was thrust back as if by a heavy hand.
There was a solidity to the pressure that was unequaled by
any other flow of energy with which I have had experience.
Wind in a violent storm pushes and buffets one about, but
water moving at one-twentieth the speed of a gale of wind
would level everything in its path and tear up the ground
besides.

The sand out in the swath of the tide was moving too. Close
to the bottom the grains were rolling and bumping, creating
small dust storms—a strange phenomenon under water—and
long curving ridges and valleys a foot or more in depth which
formed in endless parallel arcs at right angles to the course
of the water. On a larger scale they were precisely like the
smaller ripples seen on the mud bars when the tide is out.
The whole ocean bottom seemed on the move, as though it
were alive and were creeping towards an unknown destination.

Crouching in the shelter of the outermost boulder, I made
myself comfortable and sat down to contemplate this stupendous event. For it was exactly that. All along the hundreds of

miles of coast all over the world this same action was taking place. Great rivers of liquid were surging past thousands of headlands into bays, creeks, rivers, and lagoons, over shallow bars and in the hollows of deep channels, rolling countless sand grains and bringing oxygen, food, life and death to millions of swarming creatures. I remembered another tide I had watched in the murky green waters of the Chesapeake Bay in Maryland. In comparison to this Inaguan tide, it was a dull slow affair, but before I was through witnessing it from the windows of a steel cylinder hung from a barge anchored in the mouth of the Patuxent River near Solomons Island, I was completely overwhelmed at the mass of life it had brought past my small sphere of vision. The Chesapeake at that time was full of ctenophores, wraith-like comb-jellies belonging to the genus *Mnemiopsis*. The range of vision from the window of the cylinder was limited because of the haze to about six square feet. With a companion I began counting these organisms as they swirled helplessly by on the rising current. For six long hours we tabulated ctenophores and found that an average of 48 went by every minute or over 23,000 for the entire period. Then by computing the width of the river and the square surface of the tidal flow in a line across the river at its narrowest point, we reached the almost astronomical figure of 1,218,-816,000 ctenophores! This did not consider any of the other forms of life which abounded in the water. This was only one small river, so unimportant that it does not even appear on a map of the Eastern United States. When we realize that every inch of this tide-impelled water all over the oceans from the poles to the equator is swarming with similar billions of living things we can only be silent with awe.

The Chesapeake tide, however, had none of the gigantic sweep and force of this Inaguan occurrence. It was a small scale flow, performed in a landlocked bay. This, of Inagua, was a full-fledged deep sea current with the pressure of two immense oceans forcing it on. While I watched, it increased in intensity until even the backwaters of my quiet eddy began to circle and tug at my bare flesh. The algae on the outer rocks were all streamed in one direction, straining at their fastenings as though they would momently tear loose. There was none of the gentle swaying and graceful undulations of the sea fans that I had seen on the reef. The actions of the marine plants and organisms gave the impression that a vast underwater hurricane was brewing and that they would all be shorn away into the blue abyss beyond. Some had been pulled from their anchorages, for large heads of orange-colored algae went swirling past and were lost in the haze. Clinging to one of them was the curved, ringed torso of a spotted seahorse and the saffron colored carapace of a small crab. They were battling bravely to maintain their positions on the rotating fronds, but they were probably going to a certain death. Sooner or later the buoyant tissues would lose their freshness, become limp and watersoaked, the particles of enclosed gas would escape and the seahorse and crab would coast with the plant to the deep sea bottom far off shore away from their accustomed habitat. Somewhere down in the blackness they would be snatched up by a hungry deep sea creature or would slowly deliquesce amid the abyssal ooze and slime.

While the tide was disaster for the tiny cosmos of the orange algae-head, it was the high road for the larger more vigorous fishes which took full advantage of the current to carry them on errands best known to themselves. A few fish attempted to breast the tide but large numbers permitted themselves to be carried on its strenuous course. How like people they were, taking the path of least resistance, going full speed towards an intangible goal, to be returned again when the tide changed. In just this way human action follows the main stream of thought, climbing on the fashionable bandwagons of a particular movement. Large numbers of big hogfish, gaudy fellows splattered with reds and deep oranges went by in a steady stream. Several times vast schools of blue-striped grunts, gleaming with brilliant iridescence, obscured the sand, so closely packed and so numerous were they. These were followed by a scattering of immense amberjacks which may have accounted for the excessive hurry the grunts were in. Some very stouthearted fishes were breasting the current, but they were not making a very good job of it. Most numerous of this rugged group were the common and vividly colored spot snappers. They moved along in a narrow file, or in congregations of thirty or forty, close to the bottom, taking advantage of every depression or place where the rush of water was moderated even slightly. Their fins vibrated at high speed as they crept along, gaining a few feet, holding their own for a space, then inching forward again. What could have been so important to cause all this expenditure of energy I could not guess, though I rather suspect that the fishes themselves did not know. In many respects they are like sheep and blindly follow the leader. It is even questionable if the leader is fully conscious of its activities, for if by some alarm or other interruption the direction of a schooling mass is changed, the leader relinquishes its place and becomes the led, imitating the motions of the nearest member of the school. There is much that is not understood about the phenomenon of schooling in fish; it has been suggested that the occurrence is a form of natural communism organized by a scheming nature as a means of protection. It is a simple task for a marauder to follow and seize a lone individual, but much more difficult to grasp that same individual when it is one of a great mass of darting, scurrying forms. Numbers mean confusion to the enemy, a sort of primitive and defensive "united we stand, divided we fall." It is a curious fact, however, that very few of the big carnivores resort to gregarious living; the greater number of fishes of this type are the preyed upon. However, like all communisms, the individual is sacrificed for the purposes of the mob, and we have the spectacle of spot snappers following their leader in a useless and energy-spending task.

Not all of the upstream creatures, however, were as foolish as the snappers. Some of these wiser ones were exceedingly cunning in their method of attaining their end. These were mostly small fishes, like the red, dark-eyed squirrelfish, and the silvery burnished moonfish and lookdowns. They went well out of their paths to avoid the current, circling in the lee of rocks, catching the back eddies, pushing through narrow holes and crevices, pausing frequently to catch their breaths, as it were. Of all these the lookdowns were the most amazing. They were characterized by the constancy of their numbers. Whereas the other fishes came singly, in vast schools or in isolated groups of six or seven, the lookdowns always appeared in twos. There is magic in numbers. Seven is a favorite numeral in certain folklore, thirteen forebodes evil, and all good things are supposed to come in threes. The number two will always bring to mind the silvery bodies of these fish. When I first saw these peculiar creatures during some diving in Florida, they were swimming in pairs and I have seldom observed them otherwise. Always two by two, side by side, moving as one individual, they are an underwater Damon and Pythias. Their duality is complete. If one dipped downwards, its companion did likewise; when they turned they turned together; moving or quiescent, what one did so did the other. I can think of no logical explanation for this piscine twinning, for these fishes are not known to pair off and build nests in the manner of some fish.

Even in appearance the pairs were identical. They seemed to have a sad expression, and their name was in keeping with their faces. The forehead sloped steeply downwards and they looked as though they were continually searching for some treasure lost on the bottom. From the tips of their backs long lacy filaments went trailing off in graceful arcs. Not the least remarkable characteristic of these fishes was their thinness. When swimming directly toward or away from one, all that was visible was a narrow line extending in a vertical direction. It was fascinating to watch the thin line suddenly form into a broad oval and then as quickly fade as the fishes wheeled and turned. A sort of now-you-see-me and now-you-don't.

Although the tide was whirling a vast horde of larvae fish and transparent spawn towards the outer wastes of the open ocean, it was also bringing a bounty to the many fishermen crouched on the rocks. Not human fishermen these, but an array of fantastic creatures of considerable variety. They were armed with an astonishing assortment of hooks, entangling snares, poisoned arrows and cleverly designed nets. Among the netmen were those most enchanting, highly successful and amazing creatures, the barnacles. Superficially, nothing is more stupid than a barnacle. Yet these doughty animals are clever enough to maintain themselves all over the world, from the frigid Arctic to the equally frozen Antarctic. There is almost no place in the sea where one cannot expect to find them at their interminable net casting. They think nothing of taking a world voyage on the bottom of some dirty tramp, or to go frolicking off on the hide of a whale. Certain species of whale barnacles are so fastidious that they will most often reside on the whale's lips and the front edge of its flippers, while others are said to prefer the throat and belly to the exclusion of the rest of the animal. Still other species are known to take to the air on the persons of flying fish, and not the least unusual are certain forms that attach themselves to the umbrellas of large dead jellyfish.

As seen from underwater barnacles are creations of considerable beauty, not from their color, for they are always drab, but from the exceedingly graceful and lacy form of their fish-nets. These nets, which are really legs which have been transformed by the mechanics of need into living seines, must be seen to be appreciated. A barnacle's legs—even though these appendages resemble feathers more than they do legs—are as important to a barnacle as hands to a person, fins to a fish, or wings to a bird. Although walking is unthought of, their entire existence is dependent on their limbs; their breathing is possible because these organs circulate the water necessary for the separation of oxygen; and the status of the barnacle's stomach is directly in ratio to the functioning of the legs. A barnacle lives because it kicks.

Contrary to popular belief, a barnacle is not a shell fish, although it spends almost its entire life period tightly encased in a shell. Instead it owes allegiance to the great Class *Crustacea,* and in its family tree are the lobsters, the shrimps, and our other friend of the epicures, the edible crab. The name of its subclass is the Cirripedia, which means, literally, the "feathery-footed."

Biologists, not being above error, for a long time considered the barnacles as aberrant relatives of the mollusks, and it was not until some thoughtful soul undertook to study the early stages of this creature that the truth became apparent. It was discovered that, after hatching, the young barnacle was so unlike the adult that it seemed impossible that the two could be parent and progeny. The infant had no shell at all; it swam and it looked like nothing on earth quite so much as an outlandish mosquito. It was studded with hairs and bristles, with spikes and long trailing appendages. But it obviously was a crustacean, for it was segmented and resembled the young of certain other crustaceans. In time the microscopic monstrosity molted, then again and again, altering its shape until oddly enough it grew a small shell on each side of its changed anatomy. At this period of its development it wandered about seeking a place to settle down to begin housekeeping as a full-fledged, calcium-enclosed barnacle. When, by instinct or simple chance, it discovered a proper locality it turned on its back, firmly cemented itself in place, surrounded itself with a house and began kicking—an activity that it continued to the final chapter. And its legs—which in any other crustacean would have become claws, paddles for swimming, or hooks for grasping—spread out, fringe apart and wound up looking like so many feathers.

I worked my way out to the boulder where there was a considerable colony of barnacles and watched them snaring the manna brought on the tide. They looked like so many active volcanoes, with puffs of light brown smoke beginning to issue from the tips of the cones only to be suddenly snatched in again, as though the eruption had gone inexplicably in reverse. Peering closer I could see that the momentary puffs of smoke were really the interlacings of the feet which were extruded and then quickly withdrawn fully expanded and curved inward to prevent the escape of any life that they had snared. The excess water escaped between the interstices of the fibers.

With my fingers I touched one of the delicate cirri, as the feathers are properly termed. With a snap it was retracted and the entrance barred with two plates of solid ivory. These plates fit so closely that they are airtight and watertight, sealing the barnacle in its shell until it once again desires to open. Thus barnacles can survive low tides when they are helplessly removed from their native element. Crashing surf, preying enemies are all the same to the barnacle. I have often thought that barnacles have their advantages. How nice it would be if we could escape undesirable situations, tax collectors and such, by merely closing our doors and going to sleep!

By this time the chill of moving water began to penetrate every fiber of my being. Some of the current seemed to be welling up from the depths for it carried bands of warm and cold. As the tide increased the cold became more pronounced until I was shivering. So I called a recess for a half hour.

When I again dropped below a great change had taken

place. The current had become so violent that I had difficulty in keeping my position, even in the shelter of the boulders. Practically all the fish had disappeared. Those that were still about were swimming close to the rocks or were snuggled down in depressions where they were slowly undulating their tails. Great numbers had retreated into crevices and fissures in the cliff where they hung motionless. No big fish were in sight, except a half dozen large blue parrotfish that were bunched together in the shadow of a crag. The water had become a veritable avalanche and its speed was so great that even the fish did not consider it prudent to fight against it but took refuge in a philosophical retreat.

I did not descend again until just a few minutes before the tide began to change. The water which had flowed so swiftly before was barely moving. It was nearing the full flood. The aqueous dust storms had all subsided and the limit of visibility had extended thirty feet or more. Only the long curving rows of sand ripples remained to remind one of the deluge. I could stand without danger of being swept away.

In ten minutes all motion ceased and a perfect calm settled over everything, except at the surface where the waves still rolled over the rocks. The greatest change, however, was in the fishes. They no longer hung hidden in deep holes or lay quiescent in hollows on the bottom. The grunts were back again from their indefinite errands, though the amberjacks that pursued them did not return. Most of the fish were busily feeding. A number of brilliant triggerfish had mysteriously appeared from nowhere and were gliding from place to place munching on small tidbits which they scraped from the algae-adorned rocks.

Between the triggerfish were swarming large numbers of porkfish, handsome striped creatures, gleaming with iridescent color. Like the triggers they were feeding off the algae, but their method and food was quite different. The triggerfish were scraping low lying mosses; the porkfish confined their activities to the larger, more rounded heads of vegetation where they seemed to search carefully, probing between the fronds, snatching up the small crustaceans, worms and other invertebrates that made the algae their homes.

With a five-pointed spear that I took down with me I tried

to add one of these porkfish to my collection. I missed it completely but on a second try snared one through the top of the
back. Before I could grasp it to place it in the mesh bag I
carried tucked in my belt for the purpose it had twisted loose,
and squirming in pain it floated lopsidedly past the cliff wall.
Before it had drifted very far there was a rush of fins and it
was seized by a rock hind, a large mottled fish covered with
reddish spots which, unnoticed by me, had been lurking in a
wide crevice. The hind returned to its shelter carrying its
victim with it and I went to try for another porkfish. To my
surprise they would not permit me to approach. Previously
they had swum freely about my legs, but now they kept their
distance. Before I had been considered some strange new kind
of fish; I was now regarded as a potential enemy. I have observed similar behavior among the snappers.

Most fish, however, are quite unconcerned about the death
of their neighbors. Tragedy may strike within a few inches
and they will continue feeding or idling or whatever their
activity might be, as though nothing had happened. The next
fish that I tried to spear exhibited a most surprising reaction.
The barbed point scraped along its side, removed several scales
and retained a small speck of flesh on the point. The victim,
which was a yellow grunt with a flaming scarlet mouth, darted
away, then turned, snatched up the floating scales and bit at
the flesh on the point of the spear. Even when I jabbed at it
again it did not flee but glided to one side and nosed the
blades which had become buried in the sand! I marveled at
the contrast between the two species; one perfectly sure of itself and the other timid and untrusting once danger had been
proved.

Spearing fish is not as easy as it might seem. Although most
fishes appear utterly relaxed, they are ever on the alert for
anything that moves with directness. I have jabbed a spear into
a school of fish, so densely packed that to miss seemed impossible, only to find that my barbs did not touch a scale. Yet the
school, itself, moved scarcely at all. Usually there is a localized
flurry which lasts for a brief moment and subsides.

After my failure at snaring the grunt my attention was attracted to a pair of small dull-colored fish which were cavorting
between two sponge covered masses of dead coral. They were

blennies of the same type that I had found at Lantern Head. They were the most unfish-like creatures I have ever seen. They skittered about the rocks assuming the most unusual attitudes. Heads up, then down, vertically or horizontally, they slithered in and out between the algae like restless insects. In a moment they gave a most remarkable performance. They had climbed down—they seemed to walk rather than swim, so closely did they stick to the moss—to the sand at the base of a boulder. Here they faced each other with only an inch or two of space between. For a second they remained motionless, then began a strange little hopping dance, using their pectorals as stilts. Round and round they went in a circle with their mouths as the axis. Occasionally they halted as though attempting to stare each other down.

Their mouths, which up to this point had been tightly closed, began chattering as if in conversation. Once again the hopping and skipping began and continued for some time. When they again stopped, instead of chattering, they protruded their mouths until they touched. It was a perfect kiss! No such amatory caress was intended, however, for, shortly after, the blennies touched lips once more, established a firm contact and began shoving. The kiss was really a trial of strength, and apparently was their method of establishing ownership over a certain territory, for after quite a bit of pushing one of the blennies suddenly turned and fled, leaving the victor triumphantly poised over its tiny kingdom of a square yard of sand and an equal amount of coral encrusted rock. This seemed a very safe and sane way of settling the question of ownership without resort to bloodshed.

The instinct of curiosity, I am certain, is very highly developed in certain fishes. Sharks possess it in a great degree and so do the gurnards and sea-robins. This victorious blenny was the most inquisitive fish I have ever encountered. When I sat down in the sand close to its domain it came over and very carefully inspected each of my fingers outspread in the loose soil, tiptoeing delicately from one fingernail to the other. It nudged each very gently and then proceeded to crawl over my foot where it examined minutely an old scar inflicted by the sharp edge of an oyster shell years before.

Life in this tide-swept land clung almost exclusively to the

rocks. The outer sand with its curving ridges was too completely unstable to house any permanent organisms. It was a
watery no-man's land, a barren sheet of white against a back-
ground of blue. However, in the temporary quiet of the full
flood, a number of fishes were deserting the rocks and making
short excursions into the open. With the exception of the larger
and more able types, few strayed any great distance. The
sergeant-majors, blueheads, and the demoiselles were restricted
to within eight or ten feet. Within this range they seemed very
confident, frequently passing within easy reach of much larger
forms. They knew that with a twist of a fin they could dart
into the safety of a crevice. The only small forms that strayed
with impunity into the open sand were the trunkfish, which no
doubt felt secure behind their solid casings of jointed armor,
and the porcupine fish, which are the nearest things to a living
pincushion except the sedentary sea urchins. These were utterly
without fear, and little wonder, for even to touch one would be
to invite a painful puncture.

The open water was also inhabited by a small group of
swellfish, drab prickly fellows with gullets capable of tremendous extension when they are alarmed. These fish are supposed
to be very stupid, yet in the Chesapeake Bay I have observed
close relatives of the West Indian forms attacking large blue
crabs in mass and biting with their sharp teeth through the
crabs' hard shells, a task that would be exceedingly dangerous
if attempted singly. No creature that is capable of such organized action can be considered stupid.

Most of the fish that patrolled the outer waters were large
carnivores that swept ceaselessly back and forth waiting for
some rock-dweller to venture too far. They were not very
numerous, but most were capable of great speed. Among this
group were a cornet-fish about three feet long, not including the
long filament attached to the end of its tail, an equally long
trumpet fish which chased a tiny butterfly-fish into the shelter
of a crag, and the long slim torso of a barracuda.

For a half hour the water at the base of the submarine cliff
remained quiet and motionless. The fishes glided about, moving
and turning in an easy effortless way. Then faintly, imper-
ceptibly, the tide began to swing. At first I did not notice it,
so gently did it start. But soon I became aware that the algae

no longer drooped listlessly. They began to point their delicate fronds in the direction of the distant and invisible island of Mariguana. I noticed that the sea fans on the rocks were bending too, and that, unlike the sea fans on the great reef, they were all aligned at right angles to the shore instead of parallel to it. Here the tide, not the surf, was the dominating force. Out on the sand the long ripples began to reform, reversing the position of their slopes, gradual on the upstream side, steep on the lee. The parrots, demoiselles, and other rock feeding species began to drift over to the sheltered side of the boulders where they temporarily resumed their interrupted feeding. The easy relaxation of the past half hour began to disappear. The underwater gale was approaching, and in preparation the fishes and even some of the invertebrates, including a half dozen wandering hermit crabs, began to vanish into little holes or fissures where they drifted into that wide-awake yet apparently restful sleep of the creatures without eyelids. The trunkfish and swellfish came out of the sand to settle down on a smooth spot where the swellfish buried themselves until little more than their eyes were showing. I could not help but wonder what sort of perilous life the creatures of this outermost point must lead, forever hedged in by marauding, patrolling enemies, limited above by the boiling surf, and twice daily forced to battle, or sustain, an almost irresistible deluge of flooding water. I was reminded of the people of Flanders, or of Alsace, who are periodically overwhelmed by floods of conquest or counter conquest, who bravely or hopefully continue living there, building new homes to replace those destroyed by shells or gutted by flames, and who after a time see them destroyed once more and are faced with the necessity of doing it all over again. Yet the comparison is not a completely true one, for a sea-tide is a river of life, not of death, a manifestation of nature which is a normal state of affairs for millions of creatures all over the world.

It was fitting that, as I returned to the dry earth again to avoid the rush of water rapidly welling to its climax, the last creatures I saw before my helmet broke the surface were the *Aurelias,* the moon-jellies. They were the first and only moon-jellies that I saw near Inagua. Their appearance at this opportune moment was significant. More than any other living creatures could have done, they expressed in their filmy iridescent tissues the symbolism of a flowing tide. There were six of them slowly drifting with slight pulsations of their hemispherical umbrellas on the bosom of the current towards the open sea. Pale and glowing they resembled the moon after which they are named; in a translucent shining galaxy they floated aimlessly off into watery space. Like the currents of the ocean they were giving themselves completely and passively to the pull of the invisible moon; the responsive tide was their life, their complete world and their means of conveyance.

Shark Close-Ups

JACQUES-YVES COUSTEAU
with FRÉDÉRIC DUMAS

Undersea exploration is not yet one hundred and fifty years old. Henri Milne-Edwards donned a helmet to explore the marine world in 1844 and initiated an age of discovery that shines among man's accomplishments the way sunlight glows on the sea. William Beebe, Auguste Piccard, and then Jacques-Yves Cousteau opened up a world beneath the sea—"the silent world" Cousteau called it—that is our newest frontier. Captain Jacques-Yves Cousteau is the co-inventor of the Aqua-Lung that was man's first true "passport to inner space." Director of the Oceanographic Museum at Monaco, president of the World Underwater Confederation, he is a great oceanographer and a fine writer. Here, with his co-diver Frédéric Dumas, he encounters one of the greatest underwater mysteries— the shark.

*O*n a goggle dive at Djerba Island off Tunisia is 1939 I met sharks underwater for the first time. They were magnificent gun-metal creatures, eight feet long, that swam in pairs behind their servant remoras. I was uneasy with fear, but I calmed somewhat when I saw the reaction of my diving companion, Simone. She was scared. The sharks passed on haughtily.

The Djerba sharks were entered in a shark casebook I kept religiously until we went to the Red Sea in 1951, where sharks appeared in such numbers that my census lost value. From the data, covering over a hundred shark encounters with many varieties, I can offer two conclusions: The better acquainted we become with sharks, the less we know them, and one can never tell what a shark is going to do.

Man is separated from the shark by an abyss of time. The fish still lives in the late Mesozoic, when the rocks were made: it has changed but little in perhaps three hundred million years. Across the gulf of ages, which evolved other marine creatures, the relentless, indestructible shark has come without need of evolution, the oldest killer, armed for the fray of existence in the beginning.

One sunny day in the open sea between the islands of Boavista and Maio, in the Cape Verde group, a long Atlantic swell beat on an exposed reef and sent walls of flume high into the air. Such a sight is the dread of hydrographers, who mark it off sternly to warn the mariner. But the *Élie Monnier* was attracted to such spots. We anchored by the dangerous reef to dive from the steeply rolling deck into the wild sea, where there is abundant life.

Small sharks came when we dropped anchor. The crew broke out tuna hooks and took ten of them in as many minutes. When we went overside for a camera dive, there were only two sharks left in the water. Under the racing swell we watched them strike the hooks and thrash their way through the surface. Down in the reef we found the savage population of the open ocean, including some extremely large nurse sharks, a class that is not supposed to be harmful to man. We saw three sharks sleeping in rocky caverns. The camera demanded lively sharks. Dumas and Tailliez swam into the caves and pulled their tails to wake them. The sharks came out and vanished into the blue, playing their bit parts competently.

We saw a fifteen-foot nurse shark. I summoned Didi and conveyed to him in sign language that he would be permitted to relax our neutrality toward sharks and take a crack at this one with his super-harpoon gun. It had a six-foot spear with an explosive head and three hundred pounds of traction in its elastic bands. Dumas fired straight down at a distance of twelve feet. The four-pound harpoon tip exploded. We were severely shaken. There was some pain involved.

The shark continued to swim away, imperturbably, with the spear sticking from its head like a flagstaff. After a few strokes the harpoon shaft fell to the bottom and the shark moved on. We swam after it as fast as we could to see what would happen. The shark showed every sign of normal movement, accelerated gradually and vanished. The only conclusion we

could draw was that the harpoon went clear through the head
and exploded externally, because no internal organ could survive a blast that nearly incapacitated us six harpoon lengths
away. Even so, taking such a burst a few inches from the
head demonstrated the extraordinary vitality of sharks.

One day we were finishing a movie sequence on triggerfish
when Dumas and I were galvanized with ice-cold terror. It is a
reaction unpleasant enough on land, and very lonely in the
water. What we saw made us feel that naked men really do not
belong under the sea.

At a distance of forty feet there appeared from the gray
haze the lead-white bulk of a twenty-five-foot *Carcharodon
carcharias,* the only shark species that all specialists agree is a
confirmed man-eater. Dumas, my bodyguard, closed in beside
me. The brute was swimming lazily. In that moment I thought
that at least he would have a bellyache on our three-cylinder
lungs.

Then, the shark saw us. His reaction was the last conceivable
one. In pure fright, the monster voided a cloud of excrement
and departed at an incredible speed.

Dumas and I looked at each other and burst into nervous
laughter. The self-confidence we gained that day led us to a
foolish negligence. We abandoned the bodyguard system and
all measures of safety. Further meetings with sharp-nosed
sharks, tiger sharks, mackerel sharks, and ground sharks, inflated our sense of shark mastery. They all ran from us. After
several weeks in the Cape Verdes, we were ready to state flatly
that all sharks were cowards. They were so pusillanimous they
wouldn't hold still to be filmed.

One day I was on the bridge, watching the little spark jiggle
up and down on the echo-sound tape, sketching the profile of
the sea floor nine thousand feet below the open Atlantic off
Africa. There was the usual faint signal of the deep scattering
layer twelve hundred feet down. The deep scattering layer is
an astounding new problem of oceanography, a mystifying
physical mezzanine hovering above the bedrock of the sea. It is
recorded at two to three hundred fathoms in the daytime and
it ascends toward the surface at night.

The phenomenon rises and falls with the cycle of sun and
dark, leading some scientists to believe it is a dense blanket
of living organisms, so vast as to tilt the imagination. As I

watched the enigmatic scrawls, the stylus began to enter three distinct spurs on the tape, three separate scattering layers, one above the other. I was lost in whirling ideas, watching the spark etch the lowest and heaviest layer, when I heard shouts from the deck, "Whales!" A herd of sluggish bottlenosed whales surrounded the *Élie Monnier*.

In the clear water we studied the big dark forms. Their heads were round and glossy with bulbous foreheads, the "bottle" which gives them their name. When a whale broke the surface, it spouted and the rest of the body followed softly, stretching in relaxation. The whale's lips were curved in a fixed smile with tiny eyes close to the tucks of the lips, a roguish visage for such a formidable creature. Dumas skinned down to the harpoon platform under the bow while I stuck a film in the underwater camera. The whales were back from a dive. One emerged twelve feet from Dumas. He threw the harpoon with all his might. The shaft struck near the pectoral fin and blood started. The animal sounded in an easy rhythm and we paid out a hundred yards of harpoon line, tied to a heavy gray buoy. The buoy was swept away in the water—the whale was well hooked. The other whales lay unperturbed around the *Élie Monnier*.

We saw Dumas's harpoon sticking out of the water; then it, the whale and buoy disappeared. Dumas climbed the mast with binoculars. I kept the ship among the whales, thinking they would not abandon a wounded comrade. Time passed.

Libera, the keen-eyed radioman, spotted the buoy and there was the whale, seemingly unhurt, with the harpoon protruding like a toothpick. Dumas hit the whale twice with dum-dum bullets. Red water washed on the backs of the faithful herd, as it gathered around the stricken one. We struggled for an hour to pick up the buoy and tie the harpoon line to the *Élie Monnier*.

A relatively small bottlenosed whale, heavily wounded, was tethered to the ship. We were out of sight of land, with fifteen hundred fathoms of water under the keel, and the whale herd diving and spouting around the ship. Tailliez and I entered the water to follow the harpoon line to the agonized animal.

The water was an exceptionally clear turquoise blue. We followed the line a few feet under the surface, and came upon the whale. Thin streams of blood jetted horizontally from the bullet holes. I swam toward three other bottlenoses. As I neared them, they turned up their flukes and sounded. It was the first time I had been underwater to actually see them diving and I understood the old whaler's word, "sound." They did not dive obliquely as porpoises often do. They sped straight down, perfectly vertical. I followed them down a hundred feet. A fifteen-foot shark passed way below me, probably attracted by the whale's blood. Beyond sight was the deep scattering layer; down there a herd of leviathans grazed; more sharks roamed. Above in the sun's silvery light were Tailliez and a big whale dying. Reluctantly I returned to the ship.

Back on deck I changed into another lung and strapped a tablet of cupric acetate on an ankle and one on my belt. When this chemical dissolves in water it is supposed to repulse sharks. Dumas was to pass a noose over the whale's tail, while I filmed. Just after we went under he saw a big shark, but it was gone before I answered his shout. We swam under the keel of the ship and located the harpoon line.

A few lengths down the line in a depth of fifteen feet we sighted an eight-foot shark of a species we had never before seen. He was impressively neat, light gray, sleek, a real collector's item. A ten-inch fish with vertical black-and-white stripes accompanied him a few inches above his back, one of the famous pilot fish. We boldly swam toward the shark, confident that he would run as all the others had. He did not retreat. We drew within ten feet of him, and saw all around the shark an escort of tiny striped pilots three or four inches long.

They were not following him; they seemed part of him. A thumbnail of a pilot fish wriggled just ahead of the shark's snout, miraculously staying in place as the beast advanced. He probably found there a compressibility wave that held him. If he tumbled out of it, he would be hopelessly left behind. It was some time before we realized that the shark and his courtiers were not scared of us.

Sea legends hold that the shark has poor eyesight and pilot fish guide him to the prey, in order to take crumbs from his table. Scientists today tend to pooh-pooh the attribution of the pilot as a seeing-eye dog, although dissection has confirmed the low vision of sharks. Our experiences lead us to believe they probably see as well as we do.

The handsome gray was not apprehensive. I was happy to have such an opportunity to film a shark, although, as the first wonder passed, a sense of danger came to our hearts. Shark and company slowly circled us. I became the film director, making signs to Dumas, who was co-starred with the shark. Dumas obligingly swam in front of the beast and along behind it. He lingered at the tail and reached out his hand. He grasped the tip of the caudal fin, undecided about giving it a good pull. That would break the dreamy rhythm and make a good shot, but it might also bring the teeth snapping back at him. Dumas released the tail and pursued the shark round and round. I was whirling in the center of the game, busy framing Dumas. He was swimming as hard as he could to keep up with the almost motionless animal. The shark made no hostile move nor did he flee, but his hard little eyes were on us.

I tried to identify the species. The tail was quite asymmetrical with an unusually long top, or heterocercal caudal fin. He had huge pectorals, and the large dorsal fin was rounded with a big white patch on it. In outline and marking he resembled no shark we had seen or studied.

The shark had gradually led us down to sixty feet. Dumas pointed down. From the visibility limit of the abyss, two more sharks climbed toward us. They were fifteen-footers, slender, steel-blue animals with a more savage appearance. They leveled off below us. They carried no pilot fish.

Our old friend, the gray shark, was getting closer to us, tightening his slowly revolving cordon. But he still seemed manageable. He turned reliably in his clockwise prowl and the pilots held their stations. The blue pair from the abyss hung back, leaving the affair to the first comer. We revolved inside the ring, watching the gray, and tried to keep the blues located at the same time. We never found them in the same place twice.

Below the blue sharks there appeared great tunas with long fins. Perhaps they had been there since the beginning, but it was the first time we noticed them. Above us flying fish gamboled, adding a discordant touch of gaiety to what was becoming a tragedy for us. Dumas and I ransacked our memories for advice on how to frighten off sharks. *"Gesticulate wildly,"* *said a lifeguard.* We flailed our arms. The gray did not falter. *"Give 'em a flood of bubbles," said a helmet diver.* Dumas waited until the shark had reached his nearest point and released a heavy exhalation. The shark did not react. *"Shout as loud as you can," said Hans Hass.* We hooted until our voices cracked. The shark appeared deaf. *"Cupric acetate tablets fastened to leg and belt will keep sharks away if you go into the drink," said an Air Force briefing officer.* Our friend swam through the copper-stained water without a wink. His cold, tranquil eye appraised us. He seemed to know what he wanted, and he was in no hurry.

A small dreadful thing occurred. The tiny pilot fish on the shark's snout tumbled off his station and wriggled to Dumas. It was a long journey for the little fellow, quite long enough for us to speculate on his purpose. The mite butterflied in front of Dumas's mask. Dumas shook his head as if to dodge a mosquito. The little pilot fluttered happily, moving with the mask, inside which Dumas focused in cross-eyed agony.

Instinctively I felt my comrade move close to me, and I saw his hand clutching his belt knife. Beyond the camera and the knife, the gray shark retreated some distance, turned and glided at us head on.

We did not believe in knifing sharks, but the final moment had come, when knife and camera were all we had. I had my hand on the camera button and it was running, without my knowledge that I was filming the oncoming beast. The flat snout grew larger and there was only the head. I was flooded with anger. With all my strength I thrust the camera and banged his muzzle. I felt the wash of a heavy body flashing past and the shark was twelve feet away, circling us as slowly as before, unharmed and expressionless, I thought, *Why in hell doesn't he go to the whale? The nice juicy whale. What did we ever do to him?*

The blue sharks now climbed up and joined us. Dumas and I decided to take a chance on the surface. We swam up and thrust our masks out of the water. The *Élie Monnier* was three hundreds yards away, under the wind. We waved wildly and saw no reply from the ship. We believed that floating on the surface with one's head out of the water is the classic method of being eaten away. Hanging there, one's legs could be plucked like bananas. I looked down. The three sharks were rising toward us in a concerted attack.

We dived and faced them. The sharks resumed the circling maneuver. As long as we were a fathom or two down, they hesitated to approach. It would have been an excellent idea for us to navigate toward the ship. However, without landmarks, or a wrist compass, we could not follow course.

Dumas and I took a position with each man's head watching the other man's flippers, in the theory that the sharks preferred to strike at feet. Dumas made quick spurts to the surface to wave his arms for a few seconds. We evolved a system of taking turns for brief appeals on the surface, while the low man pulled his knees up against his chest and watched the sharks. A blue closed in on Dumas's feet while he was above. I yelled. Dumas turned over and resolutely faced the shark. The beast broke off and went back to the circle. When we went up to look we were dizzy and disoriented from spinning around underwater, and had to revolve our heads like a lighthouse beacon to find the *Élie Monnier*. We saw no evidence that our shipmates had spied us.

We were nearing exhaustion, and cold was claiming the outer layers of our bodies. I reckoned we had been down over a half-hour. Any moment we expected the constriction of air in our mouthpieces, a sign that the air supply nears exhaustion. When it came, we would reach behind our backs and turn the emergency supply valve. There was five minutes' worth of air in the emergency ration. When that was gone, we could abandon our mouthpieces and make mask dives, holding our breath. That would quicken the pace, redouble the drain on our strength, and leave us facing tireless, indestructible creatures that never needed breath. The movement of the sharks grew agitated. They ran around us, working all their strong propulsive fins, turned down and disappeared. We could not believe it. Dumas and I stared at each other. A shadow fell across us. We looked up and saw the hull of the *Élie Monnier*'s launch. Our mates had seen our signals and had located our bubbles. The sharks ran when they saw the launch.

We flopped into the boat, weak and shaken. The crew were as distraught as we were. The ship had lost sight of our bubbles and drifted away. We could not believe what they told us; we had been in the water only twenty minutes. The camera was jammed by contact with the shark's nose.

On board the *Élie Monnier,* Dumas grabbed a rifle and jumped into the small boat to visit the whale. He found it faintly alive. We saw a brown body separate from the whale and speed away, a shark. Dumas rowed around to the whale's head and gave the *coup de grâce,* point-blank with a dumdum bullet. The head sank with the mouth open, streaming bubbles from the blowhole. Sharks twisted in the red water, striking furiously at the whale. Dumas plunged his hands in the red froth and fastened a noose to the tail, which is what he had started out to do when we were diverted by our friend.

We hoisted the whale aboard and were impressed by the moon-shaped shark bites. The inch-thick leather of the whale had been scooped out cleanly, without rips, ten or fifteen pounds of blubber at a bite. The sharks had waited until we were cheated away from them before they struck the easy prey.

The whale became Surgeon Longet's biggest dissection. He swept his scalpel down the belly. Out on deck burst a slimy avalanche of undigested three-pound squids, many of them intact, almost alive. In the recesses of the stomach were thousands of black squid beaks. My mind leaped back to the fathogram of the deep scattering layer. The coincidence of the whale's lunch and the lines drawn on the fathogram may have been entirely fortuitous. It was not strict proof. But I could not dispel an unscientific picture of that dark gloaming of the scattering layer twelve hundred feet down, and whales crashing into a meadow writhing with a million arms of squids.

Standing for Dakar we met a porpoise herd. Dumas harpooned one in the back. It swam like a dog on tether, surrounded by the pack. The mammals demonstrated a decided sense of solidarity. Save that the whale was now a porpoise, Dumas and Tailliez dived into a re-enactment of the previous drama. This time the dinghy carefully followed their air bubbles.

I watched the porpoise swimming on its leash like a bait goat a lion hunter has tied to a stake. The sharks went for the porpoise. It was cruelty to an animal but we were involved with a serious study of sharks, and had to carry it out.

The sharks circled the porpoise as they had circled us. We stood on deck remarking on the cowardice of sharks, beasts as powerful as anything on earth, indifferent to pain, and splendidly equipped as killers. Yet the brutes timidly waited to attack. Attack was too good a word for them. The porpoise had no weapons and he was dying in a circle of bullies.

At nightfall Dumas sent a *coup de grâce* into the porpoise. When it was dead, a shark passed closely by the mammal, and left entrails in the water. The other sharks passed across the porpoise, muddying the sea with blood. There was no striking and biting. The sharks spooned away the solid flesh like warm butter, without interrupting their speed.

Sharks have never attacked us with resolution, unless the overtures of our friend and the two blues may be called pressing an attack. Without being at all certain, we suppose that sharks more boldly strike objects floating on the surface. It is there that the beast finds its usual meals, sick or injured fish and garbage thrown from ships. The sharks we have met took a long time surveying submerged men. A diver is an animal they may sense to be dangerous. Aqua-Lung bubbles may also be a deterrent.

After seeing sharks swim on unshaken with harpoons through the head, deep spear gashes on the body and even after sharp explosions near their brains, we place no reliance in knives as defensive arms. We believe better protection is our "shark billy," a stout wooden staff four feet long, studded with nail tips at the business end. It is employed, somewhat in the manner of the lion tamer's chair, by thrusting the studs into the hide of an approaching shark. The nails keep the billy from sliding off the slippery leather, but do not penetrate far enough to irritate the animal. The diver may thus hold a shark at his proper distance. We carried shark billies on wrist thongs during hundreds of dives in the Red Sea, where sharks were commonplace. We have never had occasion to apply the billy, and it may prove to be merely another theoretical defense against the creature which has eluded man's understanding.

The Palaus
and the Best Spearfisherman

EUGENIE CLARK

The seas are rich in food—food so full of protein that it could feed all mankind if the proper technology were pursued. One of the earliest fishing "technologies" was the spear, and even today the fishermen of the Pacific islands are unusually proficient in its use.

Eugenie Clark, who is in charge of the Cape Haze Marine Biological Laboratory in Florida, discovered the skill of the Palaus of the Pacific.

I *was permitted* to look through the wide front windshield, over the pilot's shoulder, as our "tramp steamer of the airways" approached the Palauan Islands. An intricate mass of hundreds of green pieces of land lay scattered ahead. I couldn't figure out which was Koror.

Our seaplane docked at what they said was Arakabesan, an island next to Koror. I could see a group of people watching us from shore. A blonde head stood out among them, reflecting the sun almost like a mirror. As we disembarked I found it belonged to an attractive and charming young lady who thrust a bouquet of gardenias into my hands. "Welcome to the Palaus!" she greeted me warmly. With her was a tall, lanky fellow with glasses and sharp features. These were the Hills, newlyweds from Michigan, who were in charge of the Pacific War Memorial Station on Koror where I was supposed to make my headquarters for the rest of my stay in the Pacific.

"I warned you in my letters not to expect anything fancy," Peter Hill emphasized as we drove up to a two-story building in a bomb-blasted area. "This used to be a Japanese weather station. The Navy still uses the upstairs as such—you'll notice a balloon going up every night. We live in one half of the ground floor, the other half is being made into a lab. Actually, we're far from ready to accommodate visiting scientists."

In the next few weeks several other SIM scientists passed through the Palaus: a zoology professor from Swarthmore who was studying the types and distribution of Pacific rats; a young orchid specialist and an elderly sponge expert from the University of Hawaii; a malacologist from the Bishop Museum who was studying a control measure for the fiercely spreading African land snail that the Japanese had introduced. Each came to the Station expecting nothing fancy but just some little haven where he could sort his collection and camp and chat with fellow field collectors. We were all prepared to "rough it" —in fact that is part of the fun of field work. As it turned out, the sponge expert and I shared a half-built but comfortable Quonset hut belonging to the Memorial Station and the rest lived at the Navy BOQ.

I was permitted to eat at the BOQ, but as it was some five miles away and I had no regular means of transportation I took to eating at a little native restaurant, less than two miles away, that served Palauan and Japanese food. The proprietress always joined me when she saw I was eating alone. She spoke no English but she made an effort to understand my attempts at Japanese and would try to teach me some Palauan. The latter was very hard for me to grasp. As most Palauans speak Japanese, I thought it best to struggle with that language during my few months' stay here.

Most of the Navy personnel on Koror were not exactly fond of visiting scientists. They didn't like to be disturbed by a group of eccentrics out collecting fish, rats, snails, orchids, and sponges. Fortunately most of my dealings were with the always kind and helpful natives and the few members of the Navy who were more tolerant. Lt. Harry Stille, who handled native affairs, and Harry Uyehara, a Japanese-Hawaiian who worked mainly as an interpreter, were a great help to me from the beginning. They took me to a native "Congress" meeting, explaining to the Congress that I was making a study of poisonous fishes. I was introduced to the magistrates and chieftains of most of the native districts in the Palaus. While

Harry interpreted, the native leaders told me about the types of poisonous fishes in the local waters, where I might find them, and which fishermen I might rely on for more help. And so I started making contacts with the natives.

The Palauan people have an odd mixture of native and adopted names. The first two fishermen who took me trap fishing were Ngiraibuuch and Milimara. There was a native called Stanislaus who helped me poison pools with my rotenone preparation. He also tried to poison himself by eating the ripe eggs of a blowfish when his wife left him. And there was Bismark who showed me how to use the fresh roots of the local Derris plant to poison fish in open reef waters. But the name Siakong recalls the most wonderful underwater adventures I experienced in the South Seas.

Siakong was a betel-chewing, wife-beating drunkard. But he was the best spearfisherman in the Palaus—or maybe in the whole world, I sometimes think now. I'm not just biased because he taught me spearfishing and one hundred other things about the underwater world. His stupendous skill was an undisputed fact among all the Palauans.

Siakong was just over fifty when I knew him. What he was like in his youth will be a legend of the Palaus. The stories about him are unbelievable—probably exaggerated by the tellers, including Siakong himself. But I will tell you what facts I know about him—my firsthand experiences with him in the waters around the Palaus.

Siakong worked for the Hills. He was their most valuable general handy man for he could do the work that required the physical strength of three average Palauans. Although Siakong had been recommended to me as the best fisherman I could find, and I had but a few precious weeks to spend in those islands, Peter Hill would not allow me to borrow Siakong during working hours. Fortunately the work day ended at 3 P.M. and so I could hire him to come with me on late afternoon trips and all day Sunday.

Siakong knew a native, Niraibui, who owned a one-cylinder inboard motorboat that could hold up to six people. So besides the three of us we sometimes took other fishermen and on Sundays we'd invite Harry Uyehara and one or two of the

SIM scientists who happened to be there that week. The professor from Swarthmore was as impressed by Siakong's magnificent build and strength as the rest of us and promptly nicknamed him King Kong.

A small red loincloth and homemade goggles formed Siakong's diving outfit. The rest of the time he wore an old pair of khaki shorts over his loincloth, a dirty handkerchief tied around his head and a decrepit straw hat over the handkerchief. When he took these off to go into the water he was suddenly metamorphosed from a bum into a Greek God.

Siakong knew the best places to get the plectognaths I was after and these seemed to be where there were the most beautiful coral reefs. These reefs were a long way out from the town of Koror. We usually went there via Malakal Harbor where we could look deep down into the clear water and see sunken battleships from the war days. Niraibui's motor conked out every so often and sometimes we found ourselves paddling back so late that the water was inky black, except where our paddles made a trail of phosphorescence given off by the microorganisms we disturbed.

Siakong had an exceptionally nice lightweight throw net which he had made himself out of nylon. Even I learned to use this net a little. I had no luck at all with the heavy, bulky cotton throw nets of other fishermen. Siakong's spears, however, were his main equipment. They had metal heads and bamboo handles and were deftly balanced so that you could maneuver them underwater with ease, regardless of their length. Some of them were over twelve feet. And they were just light enough for the bamboo end to float so you could recover them easily. He also had several shorter-handled, four-pronged spears for catching small fish. The prongs on these were small and fine and Siakong could get me a tiny filefish without perceptibly damaging it.

It was great fun to watch Siakong spear fish from above the water. He would stand on the bow of Niraibui's boat as we putt-putted to the outer reefs, a long spear in each hand. I would sometimes stand up searching the water too but I could never spot a fish before Siakong did. A spear was flying through the air as I opened my mouth to call out, "There's a fish!" If the first spear missed, the second one was on its way in a flash and Siakong seemed to predict the direction in which the fish would dodge the first spear. Whether he got the fish or not this was a noisy affair once the spears were thrown, for Siakong would be either cheering or cursing himself at the top of his lungs.

Underwater it was different. He never made a sound but I could see him grinning broadly and his eyes sparkled through his water goggles. Here, there was no suspense about whether or not Siakong would get the fish he was after. It was only a question of how long it would take him and by what trick he would get it.

The first fish I speared was a triggerfish. But it never made a specimen for a museum. It was a beauty about nine inches long of pastel orange and yellow and with a large, black spot in the middle of its body. I'd never seen this species before although I had read about it. I chased it with no more finesse than a child reaching for an ice-cream cone. When I managed to get above it and made ready to lunge with my spear, it turned on its side to give me a last good look and then slipped into a small hole in the reef. But its tail end was still half out. What a cinch, I thought to myself. It was like spearing a stationary object. The first thrust of the spear didn't penetrate the tough skin but the second did. "Got you!" I muttered triumphantly to myself.

Then I tried to pull the fish up by the spear but it was stuck tight in the hole. I pulled and pulled but only succeeded in pulling out my spear and leaving a big gash in my specimen. I speared it again and pulled with the same result. I stuck the spearhead into the hole and then into the front end of the triggerfish. Still no luck. By this time I had done a fine job of tearing my specimen to shreds, but its head was still tightly fixed in the hole. I gave up and joined Siakong, who was spearing fish some distance away.

A large brown triggerfish swam within sight of us. I pointed to it but Siakong was already slowly swimming after it, circling around it to head it off from going into deep water. Finally it went into a hole—but again the rear end was sticking out.

Then Siakong did something I thought was odd. He let his

spear float to the surface and he dove after the fish empty-handed. Siakong went right to the hole and, gripping a piece of heavy coral with his left hand, he slipped his right hand into the hole with the fish. He looked up at me with a triumphant grin as he withdrew the fish with his hand.

Then it dawned on me what he had done. Triggerfish are so named because of an ingenious mechanism in their first dorsal fin. This fin has three spines, the first of which is large and tough. When swimming around, triggerfish usually keep this fin folded flat on their backs. When frightened, however, a triggerfish will often slip into a small opening and then erect its large spine, thus locking itself in its hiding place. No amount of pushing or pulling can lower this spine and it is very hard to break.

But the third spine on that same fin, although sometimes so small it shows as nothing more than a tiny button, is actually the *releaser* for the first spine. A slight pressure on it and the whole fin collapses. Siakong of course knew this trick and had simply pushed the right button to back the fish out of its hole!

It wasn't always quite so simple, however. Sometimes a triggerfish would go deep into a crevice in the coral until it was out of sight and a hand could not reach the release spine on the fin. For this situation Siakong had a chisel and with the help of a stone, he'd break away the coral around the hiding fish. It wasn't easy for a fish to escape Siakong.

Once I pointed out a fish to him it was as good as mine. He was a keen observer and his years of underwater experience made him an expert fish psychologist. He knew the ways of every one of the hundreds of varieties of reef fishes. He didn't always go directly after a fish but would watch it a few seconds, calculate its next move, and then head it off into a place where it could easily be caught.

One of Siakong's methods of spearing fish underwater was literally breath taking, as well as remarkably simple. He would find a reef well populated with fish and then dive calmly to about ten or twenty feet, sometimes weighting himself with a rock so he could sink without swimming. He'd get a firm grip on the reef with his legs or his free arm, poise his spear in readiness and then *wait* for the fish to come to him!

The first time I watched him do this it alarmed me. He

dived and lay motionless on the reef, like an animal about to spring on its prey. His brown body and red loincloth blended in with the kaleidoscope of colors on the surrounding reef. The fish began to regard him as part of the corals and came very close.

I was watching from above. Not used to Siakong's extraordinary lung capacity, I began to worry after a long time passed and he didn't move. So I swam down to him and tapped him on the head to make sure he was all right. He turned and looked up at me with his usual underwater grin as I reached for a piece of coral to hold myself down. I tried to make a gesture with my face to ask him what he was doing but he was looking at my hand and the grin had dropped from his face. He reached for my arm as I felt the "coral" under my hand suddenly move.

I was holding onto the side of a giant "man-eating" clam. The clam had just snapped shut and my fingers were only a fraction of an inch from the opening between the two halves of the shell. These close with a viselike grip that can hold a diver's arm or leg until he drowns.

As we swam up to the surface, Siakong pointed to the wall of coral along which I had carelessly descended. Partly imbedded in the corals were dozens of these clams, all with their shells gaping open. The shells looked like gray dead corals. Inside, the soft flesh had the beautiful colors of the surrounding living corals and the plants and animals that encrust them. Some were iridescent green, others blue, purple, and shades of brown mingled with irregular darker patches. They were well camouflaged but from then on I learned to distinguish them from anything else.

Siakong taught me, however, that even the largest of these clams can be handled safely and that they are among the most delicious of raw sea foods. He would dive down to an open clam and wave his hand over it. Often this was enough to stimulate the light-sensitive flesh inside and the clam would close. If not, he tapped the side of the shell. Then he pried the clam loose and brought it up with him. With a rock or his chisel he chipped open a part of the curved meeting edges of the shell—just enough to slip in the blade of his knife. Then a little cut in just the right place and the shell would fall right open and we could reach in and pull out all the "meat."

Almost every part of the giant clam can be eaten raw though actually I think the soft reproductive organs and tough colored parts are better cooked. But the adductor muscle—the large white muscle that connects the two halves of the shell and closes the clam with such force—is truly a gourmet's delight. I have never tasted anything more delicious. It need only be washed off in sea water and it is ready for eating. It has a texture that is like biting into a crisp cucumber. It has a sweet, clean, indescribably pleasant flavor. From the first time I tried it, the raw adductor muscle of the giant clam has been my favorite sea food. It became a regular part of our reef picnics along with raw fish, a tasty pinkish seaweed that grew in spaghettilike strands, and tiny limpets.

Limpets are distant relatives of snails but with low conical shells that resemble the hats of Chinese coolies. The species we ate clung to the rocks near the water line by the thousands in some places. A twist of a small knife would free the flesh (sometimes no more than the size of a pea) from the shell. The first time we came across them, Niraibui and I sat in the boat eating them by the dozens as fast as a grinning Siakong could pick them off the rocks. We never had to bring any lunches with us, for we were always swimming among more good sea food than we could ever eat. Sometimes, if the day was exceptionally cool or rainy, we might head for the nearest island, make a fire, and cook some of our sea food.

Ordinarily rain didn't stop us from spearfishing. The reef water was so clear that it took more than average rain clouds to make vision bad. The first time we started spearfishing in the rain, however, I thought it would prove a waste of time. When I got into the water and looked around it was full of wavy lines and everything was blurred as if I weren't wearing my face mask. But Siakong and Niraibui were diving without concern. Then I took a dive too and when my face reached about four feet below the surface, the water became its usual clear self. Then I realized that the blurring near the surface was the result of the fresh rain water mixing with salt water, something that always happens when two liquids of unequal densities are first put together. I've never come across an

English word for it but German chemistry books refer to the phenomenon as *Schlieren*. So for spearfishing in the rain, one merely has to dive below the *Schlieren* layer and reach the homogeneous sea water to see clearly.

It was on such a day that we came across the largest giant clam I ever saw alive. Siakong and I were swimming across some open water toward the reef where the boat was anchored. Niraibui was sitting in it chewing betel nut and keeping his head dry under Siakong's straw hat. We swam along, diving now and then below the *Schlieren* layer for a look around.

Whenever I swim in deep open water, I keep glancing around through my face mask with a mingled feeling of fear and hope. I don't want to miss seeing it if a large shark should be cruising nearby. But on each of these dives I saw only empty water in all directions. Not the smallest fish was in sight. From above I could see Niraibui was still over one hundred yards away and I looked forward to reaching him and seeing the comforting walls of reef and the mass of familiar fish that would be swimming there. It is a strange feeling to swim underwater away from any signs of rock, coral, the bottom, or sea life. It's like swimming in the middle of the ocean. It was nice to be able to find Siakong in the water nearby.

I was getting a little ahead of Siakong, as he was stopping for deeper dives, when I heard him call me back.

"Nechan, come see here."

I swam over to him, dove under the *Schlieren*, and looked where he was pointing down below. I couldn't make out much until I was down a few more feet. Then I could see a sandy bottom and sitting in the sand was a clam. It looked like an average-size giant clam. However, there was nothing around to compare it with and I couldn't estimate the depth.

We swam to the surface and treaded water easily and forced a long series of deep breaths. We had been swimming for quite a while and I wasn't prepared for a deep dive. When I felt a little rested and saturated with fresh air, I nodded to Siakong. He started to dive toward the clam and I followed, swallowing to adjust my ears to the increasing pressure.

I've never measured how deep I can dive, but I know that at more than twenty feet under, my face mask cuts into my head and my ears and nose feel uncomfortable. Usually I don't go much deeper for I have always found enough activity in the top twenty-five feet to keep me occupied and satisfied. But this time I followed Siakong until I felt I was well below my usual limit and I knew my breath wouldn't last descending any deeper. Perhaps if I had dived with a weight and not spent so much energy swimming downward, I might have been able to stand another ten feet—but I still wouldn't have been anywhere near bottom. From the depth I did manage to reach, I could see Siakong far below me getting smaller and smaller until he reached the clam.

Then I saw it was truly a giant.

Siakong looked like a midget beside the clam which seemed nearly four feet across. I saw him give it a kick to close the huge jaws which could have held all of Siakong with ease. And then I had to shoot for the surface. I was still panting heavily when Siakong finally came up with no sign of strain.

We got Niraibui to come over with the boat. The anchor wouldn't reach bottom. It hung loose, far above the clam. We couldn't improvise anything long enough to reach bottom and help us haul up the clam. Then the three of us dived toward the clam again but I stopped at a comfortable depth and clung to the dangling anchor while Niraibui continued on with Siakong. I doubted that even the two of them together could lift it an inch.

The clam's jaws were open again. Siakong reached it and kicked it shut. Niraibui hovered about Siakong's head for a second and then headed back for the surface, where we met, both well out of breath.

"O kina ne!" (It's a big one isn't it?) Niraibui exclaimed to me. His eyes were bloodshot and I figured he must have been drinking as well as chewing betel nut for his wind was usually much longer than mine.

Siakong still had not come up. Niraibui and I dived under again. As we descended I made out a sight that sickened me with horror. Siakong was caught in the clam.

The jaws of the gigantic mollusc were clamped tight and Siakong's arm was in it up to the elbow. Siakong wasn't moving. I expected Niraibui to dive all the way and at least attempt a rescue but the bleary-eyed fellow swam back to the surface. In the excitement my breath was shorter than ever. I came up gasping and started hollering at Niraibui in panic. My flimsy Japanese came out all mixed up and he looked at me surprised and then blankly. I felt helpless and desperate. Siakong was trapped and would be dead in a few seconds if we couldn't find some way to help him. How could Niraibui tread water there so calmly even if he was drunk!

Short of breath and good for nothing, I nevertheless adjusted my mask to dive again. But just then Siakong popped up beside us—panting but grinning! He lifted his arm out of the water, the one I had seen in the jaws of the clam, and held up the biggest adductor muscle I had ever laid eyes on.

I was doing a mixture of laughing and crying as the three of us climbed back into the boat. Niraibui of course had understood all along that the clam—which must have weighed at least a quarter of a ton—was impossible to lift off the bottom and that Siakong had broken the lip of the huge shell enough to reach into the clam and cut loose the adductor muscle with his knife. The two men got a big kick out of my fright.

"She was ready to kill me because I didn't try to save you!" Niraibui told Siakong, who howled with delight. I started to feel a little ridiculous, but when they went on to kid me unmercifully, I got angry. Finally they stopped and the rain which was still falling cooled me back to normal. Soon we all sat contentedly in the boat, munching on a delicious adductor muscle the size of a man's thigh. Niraibui and Siakong stuffed their mouths to keep from laughing any more.

I never saw Siakong spear a shark underwater, although several times he showed up with six- and seven-foot specimens neatly speared through the gills. He explained that the gills were the best place to spear a shark because the skin was too tough and if you missed getting the spear in, the shark might not give you the opportunity for a second try.

The same is true for moray eels. They stay mostly in their holes in the reefs, usually with only their ferocious-looking heads sticking out. You can get fairly close to one without endangering yourself if you don't wave an arm or leg carelessly in front of its lair. And it's safe to spear one through the head —if you're sure you won't miss.

The first time I saw a large moray I was full of confidence. Luckily I speared it neatly but then had to get Niraibui's help to get the four feet of writhing body off the spear. However, the more I continued to see of large morays, the less I toyed with them. I decided not to invite trouble without a good reason.

All of Siakong's spears were of the primitive hand type. He had none of the fancy arbaletes or CO_2 cartridged spearguns that shoot sixty feet through the water—the equipment of the hundreds of modern skin divers in Europe and the United States these days. When Siakong speared a fish his powerful arms were the only propelling force behind the spear. And the fish, though it be a shark, was then caught on one end of the spear while Siakong held on to the other.

I'm glad I first learned to use a hand spear. It made speargun fishing seem easy later on. And a simple hand spear needs no fancy repairs. It doesn't run out of "shells" and you don't lose twenty to one hundred dollars if you spear a big fish and lose your grip on the whole works. But of course a hand spear has its limitations—especially when you're not a diver like Siakong.

There was a time, however, when Siakong missed getting a rare specimen for me. The day started off wrong to begin with. It was a Sunday and we had invited Harry Uyehara to come along with us. We were to meet at Niraibui's boat at 7 A.M. but at 7:30 Siakong had not yet shown up. He was unreliable when it came to many things but not a spearfishing trip. He was always sober on such mornings no matter how wild had been his night before.

We finally went to his house.

"Siakong not here!" his wife said as she slammed the door in our faces. A little boy standing outside whispered to us, "He's in the calaboose."

"What's he in for?" we asked the jailkeeper when we reached Siakong's other quarters. We learned that the night before he had beaten up several men, including a policeman, and then had gone home and thrown his wife off the back porch into the taro patch. We also learned that this wasn't unusual for Siakong.

We were allowed to visit the jail. Through the bars we saw a big room with a number of drunks strewn about but Siakong was pacing the floor like a wild alert beast. When he saw us he came over and hung his head. "*Gomenasai, Nechan.*" (Forgive me, big sister.)

Harry, one of the most diplomatic and well-liked persons in the Palaus, somehow talked the jailer into letting Siakong out in our custody and off we went to the reefs.

We went to a reef I hadn't seen before. The corals grew on a wide ledge about fifteen feet underwater. The ledge dropped off suddenly at its outer edge into what seemed to be deep ocean. Harry and Niraibui climbed back in the anchored boat when they had their fill of spearfishing while Siakong and I continued our favorite sport. There were a number of balloon fish and other easy-to-spear plectognaths around and we worked our way after them toward the edge of the reef.

I was struggling to get a triggerfish to fold up so I could pull him out of a crevice, when Siakong tapped me on the shoulder. He was pointing off the reef. As I watched I saw an incredible sight coming from the deep water.

At first I couldn't make out much except a light haze in the otherwise richly blue water. The haze was moving toward us. As it came closer it resolved into huge forms. It was like a flotilla of submarine dirigibles. There were so many I couldn't count them. Each was like a huge fat pig and had no color except a uniform gray-white.

They were fish undoubtedly, but a kind I had never seen before. They looked uncanny. Their heads were grotesque as if swollen and distorted. If I had seen only one I would have thought it was an anomaly. But here was a whole school of the weird beasts facing us. I had seen a head somewhat resembling theirs on only one other fish—the freakish-looking, artificially inbred lion-headed goldfish. But I knew these fish were not even distant monster relatives of any goldfish.

As they came closer we came up for air. "Are they dangerous? Can you spear one?" I asked Siakong and then quickly ducked under again to see how close they had gotten without waiting for his answer. Siakong gave me his usual reassuring look and then started swimming after them. In one movement the whole school made an about-face and headed back for deep water. They looked less formidable going in this direction and their tail ends were more fishlike than their monstrous heads. They had a fluffy look as they once again blended into just a light haze and disappeared—a herd of phantoms that Saikong could not catch up with.

Later Siakong told me had seen these fish several times before and once they were fighting among themselves, butting with their heads. He had never succeeded in spearing one but he believed they were very powerful fish.

It was only recently that I decided these must have been a species of large wrasse, related to the group known as "sheepsheads," the adults of which grow fatty humps on their heads. While at the Red Sea, I saw a fisherman's photograph of a rare fish he had caught on a line. No one I consulted in Egypt could identify the fish but it resembled the school I had seen in the Palaus. From my notes and descriptions, Dr. L. P. Schultz of the Smithsonian Institute believes the species to be *Cheilinus undulatus*. He once saw a school of these in the Phoenix Islands. Each appeared to be three to four feet long and the school reminded him of a flock of sheep. The ones I saw were easily this size. At the time, I estimated between four and five feet long, although I may have been overimpressionable then as many of us tend to be with "the fish that got away." Siakong didn't get close enough for me to compare and accurately estimate their size. However, I have since examined many pictures of sheepsheads and have never seen any with head swellings that approach those of the fish I saw with Siakong. I think they must have been exceptionally large adults to have developed such heads, if indeed they were any known species of sheepshead.

That same day when Siakong missed getting me a specimen of what was such a mystery fish for me, he and Niraibui put on an underwater turtle rodeo. They were in a clowning mood. Siakong caught hold of Niraibui's foot and tickled the bottom of it until Niraibui had to laugh out all his breath and almost drowned before Siakong let him go to the surface for air. They were having great fun. Then Niraibui spotted a large sea turtle resting quietly on the bottom and he sat on its back. Siakong latched onto Niraibui's back and they began taking turns knocking each other off the turtle and riding the bewildered animal around underwater. They could steer it any way they liked by holding the shell just behind the poor turtle's neck, pulling back to make it swim upward, pressing down to make it dive, and leaning sideways to make it bank and turn. All the while the turtle flapped its finlike legs desperately and strained its long neck forward trying helplessly to get rid of the mischievous tormentors.

Finally they brought the turtle on the boat. Niraibui was pleased when I took his picture with it and I promised to give him a print. I didn't know then, that that was our last trip with him.

A few days later I asked Siakong if we could get together with Niraibui for another fishing trip. "I don't think so," he answered with a strange expression.

"What's the matter?"

"I think because he's dead," Siakong said sadly.

The whole story came out later. Niraibui had spied some metal drums marked "alcohol" on a Navy truck. That was the one word he could read in English. The fact that the complete label read "methyl alcohol" didn't concern him. He punctured a hole in one of the drums and drank to his heart's content and end.

His widow sold his boat immediately. There was no other motor boat available to me and thereafter Siakong and I had to go to the reefs in outriggers. It took very long so we went only on Sundays.

As my weeks in the Palaus came to an end, Siakong asked when I would be back again. "Perhaps many years later," I said because I hated to tell him, "Probably never." "That's O.K., Nechan, I'll still be a good spearfisherman when I'm eighty." And he might have been, too. But a few years later I learned that Siakong, after being released from a long stretch in jail, went on a fishing trip, took a deep dive after a turtle, and never came up again. The area was combed by other divers but they couldn't find a sign of him nor a clue to his disappearance. Perhaps with his great skill in the water, Siakong found a way to stay alive underwater indefinitely and just decided not to bother coming back to a world that was constantly throwing him in the calaboose. He may still be happily swimming around those reefs that he loved so much, playing with the turtles and fish. Who knows what the story of his mysterious disappearance will be when the Palauan children of today tell it to their grandchildren?

Boy Beneath the Sea

ARTHUR C. CLARKE
with MIKE WILSON

Stories of sunken treasure are part of the folklore of every sea. But sometimes these stories are true, as two boys discovered off the Great Reef of Ceylon.

*M*ark and Bobby were practically amphibious; they spent all their spare time in the water. We would often meet them cycling down to the sea, with their spearfishing gear tied to their bicycles—and see them coming back with fish draped across their handlebars. They were a complete contrast; Mark was very small built and blond, looking much younger than his thirteen years, while Bobby was big and husky. And whereas Mark had just one sister, Bobby was one of a large and handsome family that never stayed still long enough to be counted.

However, both were remarkably mature for their years, and were extremely anxious to use the aqualung. On their very first lesson in the local swimming pool, they were able to throw all their equipment—masks, fins, weightbelt and aqualung—into the water, dive down, and put it all on again before coming to the surface.

They talked very little, but when they did say something, it was always constructive. This does not mean that they were solemn and serious—indeed, they were full of high spirits—but they realized that diving requires care and concentration. After a very few lessons, Mike was confident that they could tackle all ordinary underwater jobs quite safely, and wouldn't lose their heads in an emergency.

The three explorers set off from Colombo in our Volkswagen

Microbus loaded with diving gear, and that was the last we heard of them for almost two weeks, except for a brief "All well" message flashed one night by Morse from the lighthouse. There was no telephone from Colombo to Kirinda, so we did not expect any real news of the expedition until it returned.

It was a great relief to everybody when, late one afternoon, Mike and the boys arrived back safely and started unloading the bus. When I asked them eagerly, "Well, how did it go?" they avoided a straight answer, but mumbled something like "Oh, not so badly," as they staggered into my office carrying a battered tin trunk.

On the outward trip, that trunk had contained our cameras; it seemed much heavier now, but I thought nothing of it until Mike locked the office door and said mysteriously: "Look at this."

He threw open the lid—and there were two beautiful little brass cannon, badly worn but gleaming brilliantly where the sea had polished them, and obviously very old. I cried out in excitement. "You've found an old wreck!" Like all divers, we'd been dreaming of this for years, but had never taken the idea very seriously.

Then, without saying a word, Mike lifted the guns and showed me what lay underneath them. At first, I thought I was looking at dirty lumps of coral, about the size of coconuts. Then I realized just what those lumps were; and I was too astonished to say anything.

It was one of the unforgettable moments of a lifetime, for I knew then that I was staring at something that very few men have ever seen—genuine, honest-to-goodness treasure. These unimpressive looking lumps were masses of coins—hundreds of them, cemented together. When I bent down to pick one up, I could hardly lift it. It was not—alas!—heavy enough for gold, but it could only be the next best thing—silver.

Besides these big lumps, there were hundreds of loose coins. Many were badly corroded, but most of them seemed to be in remarkably good condition. They were covered with Persian lettering, and the total weight of silver came to about one hundred and fifteen pounds. "But," said Mike, "there's a lot more where we found this."

In addition to the coins and the little cannon, the expedition had recovered some small copper bars and about twenty lead musketballs. Altogether, the salvaged material weighed about two hundredweight, and it was a major feat to have recovered it from the seabed, got it safely to the lighthouse, then to the relief boat and across ten miles of sea, and finally unloaded it on land—all without anyone seeing it.

That evening, we asked the boys' parents round to our house; at our request, Mark and Bobby, had not breathed a word about the discovery, though this must have been something of a strain. Then we had the pleasure of watching the Smiths and the Kriegels do a double take, exactly as I had done, when they looked into the treasure box and realized just what it held. During the next few days, we were to grow accustomed to watching perplexity, wonder, disbelief, and finally excitement spread across the faces of the few trusted friends we introduced to the finds, which now rested safely in a massive wooden chest with a big brass padlock.

That chest had been designed to carry explosives, at a time when Mike fancied he could build up a business as an underwater demolition expert. (He couldn't, and we are still the embarrassed owners of a quarter of a ton of submarine blasting gelignite.) I could not help thinking that the chest's new contents were almost as explosive as the old; what it now held would undoubtedly change our lives, in ways that it was impossible to predict.

For two years that chest has stood in the corner of my office, where I can see it when I raise my eyes from the typewriter; it is in front of me now. At first there was an aura of unreality about it; I could not quite believe that all this had actually occurred. I am not an unimaginative person, but I would never have imagined that anything so improbable could have happened to us.

From time to time, to reassure myself, I will open the lid, and look at the evidence with my own eyes. But even with my eyes shut, a reminder is always there. Out of the chest wells a curious metallic tang as of iodine and seaweed—not at all unpleasant. It is now one of the most evocative smells I know; for the rest of my life it will bring back vivid memories of the sea, and of spray-drenched rocks glistening beneath the equatorial sun.

It is the scent of treasure.

The other day, I came across Mark Smith's diary of the expedition; it's so brief, and so tantalizing, that I would like to quote it in full. The first entry says simply: "*March 12, 1961.* Arrived."

That one word covers the 175-mile drive down the beautiful, palm-fringed coast of Ceylon—surely one of the loveliest in the world—past dozens of fishing villages with their picturesque outrigger boats drawn up on the beaches. The journey goes through the ancient port of Galle which, say some historians, may be the Tarshish of the Bible—and beyond that into a lonely landscape of still lagoons and patches of jungle. You may meet wild elephants here, but they seldom bother motorists.

At Kirinda, the jumping-off point for the reef, Mike and the boys unloaded all their gear, and by next day had recovered somewhat. "*March 13.* Surfed all day—in late afternoon repacked gear."

They went to bed early that night, because the *Pharos* would leave at 4 A.M., when the sea was at its calmest. The ten-mile journey to the lighthouse, the giddy trip up the swaying rope, and the transfer of tons of equipment from pitching boat to the spray-drenched rocks at the base of the great tower, Mark sums up as follows: "*March 14.* Left for G.B. Stowed gear, etc."

Having been through all this myself, I am not in the least surprised that he had no energy to write any more. But by the next morning operations were in full swing, and Mark becomes positively garrulous. I will give the rest of his diary without a break:

March 15. Sea bad, strong current, big chop. No SCUBA diving, snorkeled. Met Sindbad and Ali Baba, regained friendship.

March 16. Took first SCUBA dive. Saw and filmed groupers, Mike saw barracuda, big shark.

March 17. Sea good, took two dives. 1st. Filmed Sindbad and Ali Baba. 2nd. Saw dozen tunas, from 75 to 200 pounds.

Had big giant grouper (300 pounds) chase us. Took stills of
caves, batfish and groupers. Bobby saw same (?) big shark as
seen yesterday (10 ft.).

This was not a bad beginning for any underwater expedition; after that, however, things got too hectic for Mark
to continue his literary activities. Fortunately, we have a full
account of what happened next, for as soon as they returned
to the mainland, I interviewed both boys with a tape recorder,
while their impressions were still sharp and clear. So in what
follows, I am able to give their actual words, spoken while
they were still gripped by the excitement of the discovery.

For the next four days, they continued diving and filming.
They would jump off the rugged, barnacle-encrusted edge of
the reef and swim out to the groupers' home, about a hundred
yards away, towing a large inflated inner tube from which the
aqualungs and cameras were hung. If the currents were
against them, this could be very hard work; it sometimes took
half an hour to cover this short distance.

After anchoring the float, they would put on their lungs
and dive down to the bottom, where the groupers would at
once greet them with open mouths. Sometimes, if they were not
fed immediately, they would become impatient, and on one
occasion a greedy Sindbad swallowed Mark's arm up to the
elbow. As the grouper was more than twice his size, there was
nothing that Mark could do but wait until he got his arm
back. Fortunately, groupers have very small teeth, and the
incident left only a few scars which Mark displayed proudly
until they healed. Perhaps it was lucky that nothing like this
happened with the *really* big grouper seen on March 17—an
unfriendly character who was left strictly alone.

Then, on March 22—but let Bobby Kriegel tell you the
story in his own words, as taken down on the tape recorder:

Well, the sea was unusually calm; in fact, it was so calm
that there was no current to take away the sand in the water.
So it wasn't very clear and we couldn't get any pictures. That
day, some porpoises came unusually close, about fifty feet away
from the lighthouse, and Mike, Mark and I set off to see how
close we could get to them. We saw them and when they
disappeared, we went away. Since there was no tide and we
couldn't take any pictures, we decided to go down and explore

one of the reefs which had never been seen underwater. So we went down there and on the way Mike told us later that he thought he saw a cannonball. Then we saw a small cannon, about two and one-half feet long. Mike dived down—no, Mike didn't dive down to it. He showed it to me and pointed. I dived down and tried to pull it up. I couldn't do it. So then Mike dived down and lifted it free, then put it back down. Mike said that the wreck might have hit on one side of the reef and some more might be on the other side; so we swam round the edge of it.

After we got to the other side the first thing we saw was a shiny cannon, about two and one-half feet long, sitting on the edge of a big canyon; and it was worn smooth by the water, and shining as though someone had put it there the other day.

These two little cannon (their correct name is "swivel guns") had been polished by the waves and the sand until their brass gleamed like gold. From a distance, indeed, they looked brand new. They were the unmistakable signposts without which the wreck might never have been discovered. We now think that they must have been well up on the tall stern of the ship, and fell on the higher part of the reef when she went aground. They had been lying there for centuries, rolling back and forth in the swell which surges almost continually across the reef in bad weather and in good, waiting for Mike to spot them.

It is nearly always the cannon that betray an old wreck. When the hull decays and collapses—which takes only a few years—they remain intact. Even when they become completely covered with coral, their straight lines are an immediate give-away, for nothing natural in the sea is perfectly straight.

But back to Mike and the boys—

They were a long way from the lighthouse—more than a thousand feet, which was a tremendous distance, even for a good swimmer, against the powerful currents that sweep along the reef. And they had no aqualungs, no underwater cameras— for, after all, they had merely been on a sightseeing trip. So they decided that the best thing to do was to go back to the lighthouse, have lunch, and return properly equipped in the afternoon.

After a hasty meal, they were back on the site with their aqualungs and the big inner tube. Now they were able to make a more thorough investigation, and slowly the pattern of the wreck began to emerge. The hull had been smashed to pieces, and no trace of it was left. In fact, ninety-nine skin-divers out of a hundred would have swum right over the site without seeing a thing—except for one cannon, about five feet long, which lay on the seabed like the fallen column from some Greek temple. Not far from it were shapeless mounds which, on more careful inspection, turned out to be two huge anchors tangled together. And near what must have been the middle of the ship was a pile of about a dozen large iron cannon, jumbled together like matchsticks spilt from a box.

It was that afternoon, on their second dive, that they made the big discovery that turned this from another old wreck to something even more exciting. Listen to Mark Smith's rather breathless account, which I think conveys the drama of that moment very well:

> We took out the big inner tube and were going to take out the filming equipment, but Bob drifted down the current so fast that Mike put the film equipment away and we went out with aqualungs. Then, when we got near the spot, we turned on our aqualungs and went down and Mike was hitting everything he saw with his knife. Then Mike came over to us and showed us the cannon, and Bob pointed out something shining right near it. Mike examined it and said it was silver, underwater with his mouthpiece on!

Both boys were much impressed by this last feat. It is virtually impossible to talk underwater when you are gripping an aqualung mouthpiece between your teeth; but Mike yelled "Silver!" so loudly that they both heard him.

Then the hunt was on; listen to Mark again:

> Then we all three started to uncover the sand. We pushed it away and then we saw all the coins stuck to the rock. So we started working on the coins and that day we got a small bag full of loose coins and a few little pieces of coral with coins in it. Then we took it back to the lighthouse at the time that the lighthouse keepers were taking a nap . . .

Already the little expedition was up against the problem that would give us one of our biggest headaches in the future— security. They could not guess the importance of this find, but it was obviously wise to keep it secret for the present. There were four lighthouse men with them on the rock, and if the news got back to land there was always a possibility that some-one else might come out and clean up the wreck. We were not the only divers in Ceylon.

While the lighthouse staff was still having its afternoon siesta, continues Mark:

> We spread all the treasure out and the two cannon that we'd got, and Mike photographed them. We put the silver inside a kit bag, but we didn't show the lighthouse keepers the treasure, though we showed them the two cannon that we'd got. The next day, early morning, the water was still not clear around the lighthouse, so we went out to the wreck—this time with all the equipment—knives, crowbars, chisels, and the big inner tube. This time we also took the still cameras. We went off to the place and this time we got a lot of bags full of loose coins and some chunks of silver coins. Then we went back to the lighthouse and that afternoon we spent our time chipping out the coins and washing them. The next morning, we went out and got the big hunks of silver coins—four big lumps and some loose ones. And that was the last time we went out to the wreck; we paddled back to the lighthouse and squared everything away.

The underwater photographs that Mike took on these two trips are, as far as I know, the only ones ever made showing treasure at the actual moment of recovery from the seabed. We have kept them secret for over two years, but we do not mind publishing them now; for this section of the reef looks quite different today, thanks to the hard work done by our latest expedition.

Altogether, Mike and the boys spent only two days diving on the wreck, without proper equipment, and with no boat. Yet they brought back some two hundred pounds of material—including the two little swivel guns, which weigh about thirty pounds each. As the swim to the lighthouse often took more than an hour, this was a really astonishing performance. Now that I have visited the site myself, I am still more amazed at what they accomplished.

Batfish

CAPTAIN EDWARD L. BEACH, U.S.N.

Captain Edward L. Beach knows the underwater world with rare intimacy. His ship the USS Triton *was the first submarine to circle the globe underwater. He knows all phases of the "submarine world"—a world of high adventure where survival depends upon skill and patience; the world of the* Batfish, *for example.*

*U*SS *Batfish* got under way from Pearl Harbor on December 30, 1944, on what was to be her sixth war patrol. It was also to be one of the epoch-making patrols of the war, one whose influence may be discerned even at this late date. Her skipper was Commander J. K. Fyfe, a Naval Academy graduate of the class of 1936, who had already built up an outstanding record of successful submarine action. From the time when the PC boat escorting her out of Pearl Harbor was dismissed until she arrived at Guam, Jake Fyfe kept his ship at flank speed. He, in common with most submariners, saw no reason for delay in getting into the war zone, except the necessity of conserving fuel. The capture of Guam removed that necessity, insofar as the first leg of the trip was concerned. After leaving Guam or Saipan it usually paid to be a bit conservative, in case you ran into a long chase, or were given a prolonged special mission.

On January 9, 1945, *Batfish* arrived at Guam, and on the next day she departed en route to an area north of the Philippines. On January 12 she sighted what was probably her first enemy contact on this particular patrol, presaging the turn which the whole patrol would subsequently take. A periscope suddenly popped out of the water some distance ahead.

Since you don't stick around to argue with an enemy submarine which has the drop on you, and since, besides, Jake
was in a hurry to get to his area where he was scheduled
for immediate lifeguard services, he simply bent on everything
she would take and got out of there. Sightings of Japanese
periscopes by our boats were fairly numerous during the war.
The Japs never learned how *doubly* cautious you must be
when stalking one of your own kind; we never learned a lesson
better.

Between January 13 and February 9 *Batfish* had rather a
dull time. She wasted two days of looking for several aviators
who were reported ditched near her track; investigated twenty-
eight junks to see what kind of cargo they were carrying;
dived at occasional aircraft alarms. Then, on February 9, while
she was patrolling in Babuyan Channel, south of Gamiguin
Island, the radar operator sounds a warning.

Something in his radar arouses his attention—he looks closely
—there it is again—and again. It is not a pip which he sees; if it
were, he would not wait to sing out "Radar contact" and
thereby immediately mobilize the ship for action. This is something more difficult to evaluate. A faint shimmering of the
scopes—a momentary unsteadiness in the green and amber
cathode ray tubes—which comes and goes. Almost unconsciously
he times them, and notices the bearing upon which the radar
head is trained each time the faint wobble in the normal
"grass" presentation is noticed. A few moments of this, and—
"Captain to the conn!" No time to wait on ceremony. This
particular lad wants his skipper, and he wants him badly.

A split second later the word reaches Jake Fyfe in his cabin,
where he had lain down fully clothed for a few minutes of
shut-eye. In a moment the skipper is in the conning tower.

The radar operator points to his scope. "There it is, sir!
There it is again! I just noticed it a minute ago!" The operator
is doing himself an injustice; from the time he first noticed
there was something out of the ordinary to the moment Fyfe
himself was beside him could not have been more than thirty
seconds.

The captain stares at the instrument, weighing the significance of what he sees. This is something new, something
portentous—there is a small stirring in the back of his mind—
there seems to be a half-remembered idea there, if he can

only dig it up—then, like a flash, he has it! If he is right, it means they are in grave danger, with a chance to come out of it and maybe add another scalp to their belts; if he is wrong, what he is about to do may make a bad situation infinitely worse. But Jake knows what he is doing. He is not playing some farfetched hunch.

"Secure the radar!" he orders. The operator reaches to the cutoff switch and flips it, looking questioningly at his skipper.

"What do you think it is?" Fyfe asks the lad.

"It looked like another radar to me, Captain." The reply is given without hesitation.

"What else?"

The boy is at a loss for an answer, and Jake Fyfe answers his own question:

"Japanese submarine!"

Submarine *vs.* submarine! The hunter hunted! The biggest fear of our submarine sailors during World War II was that an enemy submarine might get the drop on them while they were making a passage on the surface. It would be quite simple, really. All you have to do is detect the other fellow first, either by sight or by radar, submerge on his track, and let go the fish as he passes. *All you have to do is to detect him first!*

Our submarines ran around the coast of Japan as though they were in their own back yards. They usually condescended to patrol submerged only when within sight of the enemy shore line in order not to be spotted by shore watchers or aircraft patrols, for you can't sink ships which stay in port because they know you are waiting outside. But when out of sight of land, and with no planes about, United States submarines usually remained on the surface. Thus they increased their search radius and the speed with which they could move to new positions. And it should not be forgotten that the fifty-odd boats doing lifeguard duty at the end of the war were required to stay on the surface whether in sight of land or not! Small wonder that our submarine lookouts were the best in the Navy.

United States submariners were, as a class, far too well acquainted with the devastating surprise which can be dealt with a pair of well-aimed torpedoes to take any preventable risk of being on the receiving end themselves. Submarines are rugged ships, but they have so little reserve buoyancy that a torpedo hit is certain to permit enough water to flood in to overbalance what remaining buoyancy there is. Even though the submarine might be otherwise intact, she would instantly sink to the bottom of the sea with most of her crew trapped inside. *Tang* was a prime example. Ordinarily there are no survivors from sunken submarines, with the exception of the Germans, who had a habit of surfacing and abandoning ship when under attack.

The submarine, which hunts by stealth, is therefore itself peculiarly susceptible to attack by stealth. But don't make the mistake of underestimating the enemy submarine crew. The fact that they are operating a submarine at all indicates that they are picked men, who know as much about the game, in all probability, as you do. The odds are definitely even, and it is a question of dog eat dog. The only advantage lies in superior ability and equipment.

Not counting midgets, the first Japanese submarine sunk by our forces was the *I-173*, which fell victim to the *Gudgeon* on January 27, 1942. The last such was sunk by the *Spikefish* on August 13, 1945. Between these dates twenty-three additional Japanese subs were destroyed by our own undersea warriors. And we regret to chronicle that some five of our own subs, it is thought, went down under the periscope sights of Japanese submarines. Unfortunately the Jap records are so poor that the precise manner in which all of our lost submarine vessels met their doom will never be discovered. The fact remains that our submarines were convinced that the Japs were sending the two-man midgets out at night, looking for them. And almost every patrol report turned in by our people toward the end of the war records that one or more torpedoes had been fired at them.

The most outstanding record of enemy subs sunk was the one hung up by *Batfish*, beginning that fateful February 9.

"Secure the radar!" Jake Fyfe turned to a shocked conning tower crew, and ordered crisply, "Battle stations torpedo!"

The helmsman instinctively had already extended his hand in the direction of the general alarm. Now he grasped it, pulled it out, and then down. The low-pitched chime of the alarm resounded through the ship, penetrating every corner, waking men who had turned in dead tired, vowing to sleep for a year— meaning only until their next watch—bringing them upright, fully alert, instinctively racing to their battle stations, all in the space of an instant.

What is it? What is it?

Don't know. Something on the radar.

Skipper says a Jap sub out there.

How does he know that?

The process of deduction by which Fyfe arrived at the conclusion that the source of the radar peculiarities was an enemy submarine was not at all illogical. The wavering of his radar scope was probably due to the presence of another radar. It was known that the Japs had radar, though of an inferior type to ours. If this radar came from a vessel as large as a destroyer, he should have been detected on *Batfish's* radar before the emanations from his low-powered radar had been noticed. This, of course, was the usual case. Since the radar waves had been the first to be picked up, it followed that the ship producing them must be small and low on the water. Yet it must be a valuable ship, sufficiently important to rate one of the relatively few radar sets the Nips possessed. *Hence, a submarine.*

The reason why Fyfe ordered his own radar temporarily secured was simply to deny the Jap the same information which he himself had just received, while he and his Executive Officer, Lieutenant C. K. Sprinkle, USNR, broke out the charts and did some very rapid figuring.

The enemy radar emanations have been from 220, approximately southwest. Babuyan Channel runs more or less north and south. Therefore the target must be on a northerly course, approaching from the south.

To check this deduction *Batfish's* radar is cautiously turned on for only a moment. Sure enough, the bearing of the other radar has changed slightly. It is now 225.

"All ahead full! Right full rudder!" *Batfish* leaps ahead and steadies on a course calculated to get to the north of the approaching enemy vessel. She runs for a short time, every now and then checking the situation with her radar. All clear—no other ships around. Just the Jap, and his signals are becoming stronger, while his bearing is now drawing to the southward. This is as it should be.

But Fyfe does not, of course, propose to make his approach and attack on bearings alone. He wants to close the range, but on his own terms, with his bow on the enemy, his torpedoes ready—in short, with the drop on him.

Finally, Jake Fyfe and Sprinkle figure their position is about right. *Batfish* turns toward the enemy and ghosts in, keeping the darkest section of the midnight horizon behind her, and sweeping frequently, but at odd intervals, with her radar.

"Radar contact!" The word from Radar this time startles nobody—they have all been expecting it for several minutes. The tracking party now goes to work in earnest, with some concrete information instead of the rather sporadic and unprecise dope they have had up to now.

Target is on course 310, speed 12. The dials whirl on the TDC in the conning tower, where Sprinkle is in charge.

The range continues to decrease, the radar operator and the TDC operator tirelessly feeding in the essential information on the fire-control instruments. The plotting party also has its part in this, for all solutions must check before torpedoes may be fired.

On the bridge, the captain strains his eyes, and so do the lookouts up there with him. Suppose the Jap has somehow learned of the presence of the American submarine! It is possible. In this case, if he deduces what is going on, he might very logically turn the situation to his own advantage by firing his torpedoes first. After all, when you make an approach on another ship, there is a period during which you are in a much better position for him to shoot torpedoes at you than you at him—at a somewhat longer range, of course. Or, more probably, he might simply dive, thus spoiling the shot *Batfish* has worked for so long, not to mention making it immediately imperative for her to get the hell out of there!

Closer and closer comes the unsuspecting enemy sub. It is so dark that as yet he cannot be seen by the tense bridge party. As the situation develops, it is apparent that he will pass through the firing position at just under 2000 yards' range. This is a little long for optimum torpedo fire, but Fyfe wants to take no chances of being detected. On he comes—only a little more now—then from the conning tower, "On the firing bearing, Captain!" This from the exec.

"Let them go when ready, Sprink. Shoot on radar bearings. I still can't see him from up here." From the skipper.

Silently, four torpedoes are loosed into the water. Four new wakeless electric fish start their run toward the target. They have 1800 yards to go; it will take awhile. The watch hands crawl slowly and maddeningly around their faces. The wait grows longer, more anxious. *Something should have happened by now! Those fish should surely have arrived! We could not have been so far off that our spread missed also!*

But miss they do, all four torpedoes. Finally there is no escaping that conclusion. The whole careful and well-executed approach—wasted! All hands are bitterly disappointed. What can have gone wrong?

The question is answered by Plot, dramatically. "Target has speeded up! Speed now fourteen knots!" Too bad this was not detected a minute or two earlier. At least it explains the trouble, and allays the suspicious doubts which had already inevitably crept into the minds of both skipper and exec.

But the target continues serenely on his way, giving no sign of being aware of having been fired upon. Maybe *Batfish* will be able to try again.

No sooner thought than tried. The four murmuring diesels of the hunter lift their voices, and the submarine slips away through the water, seeking another position from which to launch her deadly missiles. But by this time, of course, the target has passed beyond *Batfish*, and in order to regain firing position it will be necessary to execute an end around.

Jake Fyfe has elected to remain on the surface for the whole attack, crediting to his superior radar the fact that he had been alerted before the Jap; and trusting to his belief that he could keep the enemy from detecting him. His plan is to get up ahead of the other submarine, and to head in toward him while the unsuspecting Nip is pounding along in nearly the opposite direction. Thus the range would close rapidly, and the amount of warning the other submarine could expect before torpedo junction would be very little. It was surprising that the Jap sub gave no indication of being aware he had been shot at. Whereas Fyfe had expected only one chance at him, he now finds another. "Obviously the fellow isn't as good as I gave him credit for!" And concurrent with this came the resolution to get in closer the next time, play his luck a little harder. If he could only sight the enemy, and fire on optical bearings instead of radar bearings, he would have a much neater solution to his fire-control problem—and thus greater certainty of hitting.

And besides, although Jake was morally certain the ship he was stalking was another submarine—and therefore Japanese, for he knew positively there were no friendly submarines in that area—he naturally wanted very badly to see him, just by way of confirming things. He had thought that visibility was good enough to see 2000 yards—a mile—and therefore had settled on about eighteen hundred yards for firing range. Events had proved him too optimistic, and he had not been able to see him at that range. This time he *would* get a look!

All the while, *Batfish* is racing through the black night at full speed. She has pulled off abeam of her quarry, just within maximum radar range in order to be outside range of the less-efficient radar carried by the enemy, and she is rapidly over-hauling him. Jake is still very careful with his own radar, searching all around and getting a radar range and bearing on the enemy as frequently as he dares, but he is not going to take a chance on being detected. All this time, of course, the radar emanations from the Jap have been coming in regularly, and their unchanged characteristics add proof that he is still sound asleep.

The skipper stands on the bridge of his ship during the whole of the new approach, for the situation could change so radically and so quickly that he must remain where he can take immediate action. So he must trust the coordination of everything below decks to Sprinkle.

Batfish has worked up somewhat ahead of the enemy's beam. Fyfe is trying to visualize the chart of the channel, for if he remembers rightly, some kind of a change is going to have to be made at the rate they are covering ground. The sea is fairly smooth, as it so often is in these southern waters, and hardly any solid water comes over *Batfish's* main deck, although considerable spray is whipped across it by the wind of her passing. It is an absolutely pitch-black night. No distinction can be seen between sky and water—the horizon simply doesn't exist. All about is warm, dank, murky grayness, broken only by the white water boiling along your side. It is as though *Batfish* were standing still, dipping and rising slightly, and occasionally shaking herself free from the angry sea which froths and splashes beneath her.

In a moment Clark Sprinkle's voice is heard on the interior communication system: "Plot says target is changing course. They'll let us know for sure in a minute."

The skipper presses a large heavy button on the bulkhead beside him and leans forward to speak into the bridge speaker: "Fine! As soon as you're sure, we'll change too."

About a minute later a speaker mounted to the overhead of the conning tower squawks: "This is Plot. Target has changed course to the right. New course, zero one five."

"I've got the same, Sprink," says the TDC operator. "New course about zero two zero, though."

Sprinkle pulls a portable microphone toward him, presses the button. "Bridge, Plot and TDC have the target on new course between zero one five and zero two zero. Suggest we come to zero two zero."

"Right full rudder! Come right to new course zero two zero!" The order to the helm is sufficient acknowledgment.

"Rudder is right full, sir! Coming to zero two zero!" the helmsman shouts up the hatch.

Batfish heels to port as she whips around. Her white wake astern shows nearly a sharp right-angle turn as her stern slides across the seas.

Several more minutes pass. Fyfe is on the point of asking for more information, when again the bridge speaker blares its muffled version of Sprinkle's voice: "Captain, we've got him on zero two zero, making fourteen knots. Range is seven oh double oh, and distance to the track is two five double oh. This looks pretty good to me. Recommend we come left and let him have it!"

"Okay, Sprink. Give me a course to come to." The captain's voice has assumed a grim finality, a flat quality of emotionless decision. This is always a big hurdle; until now you really have the option of fighting or not fighting—of risking your neck or not—that is, if you can remain undetected. But when you start in, you are committed. You go in with the bow of your ship pointed directly at the enemy; you get well inside his visibility range, and radar range, too, for that matter; and you depend upon the quickness with which the attack develops to give the opportunity to get it off. Keeping your bow on him gives him less to look at, a very important factor in the night surface attack; but if you change your mind and try to pull out of there you've got to change course, give him your broadside—and set yourself up for a beautiful counterattack on his part. Destroyers are supposed to be able to get a half-salvo in the air within seconds after having been alerted; submarines always carry one or two torpedoes at the ready, which can be fired instantly from the bridge. Small wonder that starting in is a crucial decision!

"Left full rudder!" Fyfe's command whips down the conning tower hatch to the helmsman.

"Rudder is left full, sir!"

"All ahead two thirds!" Fyfe has waited a moment before slowing, in order to make the turn faster.

"Answered all ahead two thirds!" Maneuvering room has matched annunciators with the conning tower, thus indicating that they have the word.

Sprinkle has been following things closely from the conning tower—checking bearings, ranges, courses, and speeds. He performs a rapid mathematical computation, drawing arrows this way and that, and measuring angles. Then he speaks into his little mike: "Captain, if we steady up on two four oh we'll have him ten degrees on our port bow, going across. His angle on the bow is now starboard forty."

"Steady on new course two four oh!" The ship has about thirty degrees more to swing, and the helmsman eases the rudder upon receipt of the command from the bridge.

"Steady on two four oh, sir!"

The exec speaks again. "Captain, he is on course zero two oh, making fourteen knots. Angle on the bow is starboard forty-five, and he now bears five degrees on our port bow. The distance to the track is two three double oh. Range, five oh double oh."

No answer from the bridge, but that doesn't bother Sprinkle. He knows he will hear quickly if the skipper isn't satisfied with the way things are going or the reports he is getting.

A few more tense moments pass. Again the speaker near the skipper's left elbow reproduces Sprinkle's familiar voice. "He's crossing our bow now. Range, four oh double oh."

"Come right to two five oh." Fyfe, who is working the same problem in his head that Sprinkle is solving mechanically in the conning tower, has the situation firmly fixed in his mind. He wants to keep coming around to head for the enemy, and has anticipated by seconds only the latter's recommendation.

"What is the distance to the track?"

"Two oh double oh, Captain."

"All ahead one third." *Batfish* is closing the target's projected track too quickly, and the firing range will be too short, or the target might detect her before firing. Fyfe's brain is now in high gear, and he can feel every part of the problem falling into place. In fact, it is almost as if he could reach out and control the movements of the Japanese skipper also, and his mind wills the enemy to keep on coming, to keep on the course and speed as set up; to come unerringly and steadily on to his doom.

And on and on he comes, totally unaware of the trap set for him, totally unaware that he is springing the trap on himself, that any change whatsoever which he might make would be to his advantage, that the most serious mistake you can make, when it's submarine against submarine, is to relax— *ever.* Of course, to give him his due, the Jap doesn't know he is being shadowed. But he knows very well that he is proceeding through a submarine-infested area—and in this little game no excuses are accepted.

At 1500 yards the keen eyes on *Batfish's* bridge distinguish a blur in the gray murk, and at 1000 yards the sinister outline of a Japanese I class submarine is made out—the first time during the whole evening that the enemy has actually been sighted. He wallows heavily in the slight chop of the sea—low, dark, and ungainly.

At 1000 yards the Jap is broadside to *Batfish:* Fyfe's plan has borne fruit, for his own bow is exactly toward the enemy, and he has all the advantage of sighting. Furthermore, the darkest portion of the overcast is behind him.

Sprinkle is beside himself with eagerness. For about thirty seconds he has been imploring his skipper to shoot. He has a perfect solution and doesn't want to let it get away from him. "We've got them cold! Ready to shoot any time, Captain!" He repeats the same formula over and over, a veteran of too many patrols to say what he really means, which would be more on the order of, *"Let's go, Captain! What are we waiting for?"*

But Fyfe refuses to be hurried. He's worked too long for this moment, and he has already missed once, possibly because of a little haste in firing. Carefully he takes a bridge bearing and has it matched into the TDC, swings the TBT and takes another, to make sure there is no transmission lag which might cause an error. Then, for the first time using the word, he says, in a curious flat voice, "Fire torpedoes!"

"Fire one!" Sprinkle's voice is a split second behind that of his skipper's.

Almost immediately the telephone talker standing under the conning tower hatch shouts loudly, so that his message is heard in the conning tower as well as on the bridge:

"Number one did not eject! Running hot in the tube!"

Something has gone wrong. The torpedo should have been pushed out of the torpedo tube by the high-pressure air ejection system. Instead, it has stuck in the tube, and the torpedomen forward can hear it running in the tube. This is critical, for it will be armed within a matter of seconds, and then almost anything could set it off. Besides, the motor is overspeeding in the tube, and it could conceivably break up under the strain and vibration—which might itself produce sufficient shock to cause an explosion.

But there isn't time to think much about possibilities. The skipper's reaction is instant. "Tubes forward, try again, by hand. Use full ejection pressure!" Full pressure is used only when firing at deep submergence, but this is an emergency.

The next command is for Clark Sprinkle in the conning tower. "Check fire!" Fyfe is not going to let the Jap get away while he waits for the casualty to be straightened out, but neither does he want the faulty torpedo to be ejected at the same time as a good one, and possibly interfere with it. If it does not eject on the second try, he will shoot the remaining tubes, and then return to the balky one.

"Number one tube fired by hand. Tube is clear!" The very

welcome report is received after a few anxious seconds with a profound sense of relief. Only half-a-dozen seconds have been lost, altogether, and the situation is still good for the remaining fish.

"Resume fire, Clark!" But the exec has not needed that command. Number two torpedo is already on its way, followed a few seconds later by number three. Torpedoes number four, five, and six are held in reserve in case the first salvo misses.

Because these are wakeless electric torpedoes, Jake Fyfe, on the bridge, does not have the pencil-like wakes of steam and air to mark where they have gone. There is a slight disturbance of the surface of the water to show the direction they took, but that is all. Seven pairs of binoculars are glued to the Jap's low, lumbering silhouette and his odd-shaped bridge.

Down in the conning tower, the radar operator and the exec are staring at their screen, where the blip which is the target is showing up strongly and steadily, showing radar emanations still at the same uninterrupted interval. Suddenly, however, the radar waves become steady, as though the enemy operator had steadied his radar on a just-noticed blip, possibly to investigate it.

"I think he's detected us, sir!" whispers Radar. "See—it's steadied on us!"

Sprinkle has also seen. Eyes fixed on the cathode tube face he reaches for the portable mike to tell the skipper about this new development, when he drops it again. Before his eyes the blip has suddenly, astoundingly, grown much larger. It is now nearly twice the size it had been an instant before. Small flashes of light can be seen on the screen, going away from the outsized pip and disappearing. Then, swiftly, the pip reduces in size and disappears entirely. Nothing is left on the scope whatsoever.

At this moment a jubilant shout from the bridge can be heard. "We got him! We got him! He blew up and sank!" Sprinkle mops his brow.

The watchers on *Batfish*'s bridge had hardly expected anything quite so dramatic as what they saw. One torpedo had evidently reached the target, and must have hit into a magazine or possibly into a tank carrying gasoline. The Nip sub had simply exploded, with a brilliant red-and-yellow flame which shot high into the night sky, furiously outlined against the somber, sober grayness. And as quickly as the flame reached its zenith, it disappeared, as 2500 tons of broken twisted Japanese steel plunged like a rock to the bottom of the ocean.

There was nothing left for torpedo number three—following a few seconds behind number two—to hit, and it passed over the spot where the enemy ship had been.

Batfish immediately proceeded to the spot where the sub had sunk, hoping to pick up a survivor or two, but the effort was needless. Undoubtly all hands had been either killed instantly by the terrific explosion, or had been carried down in the ship. There had been absolutely no chance for anyone not already topside to get out. All Jake Fyfe could find was a large oil slick extending more than two miles in all directions from the spot where the enemy had last been seen.

Strangely—delighted and happy through he was over his success in destroying the enemy sub—the American skipper felt a few twinges of a peculiar emotion. This was very much like shooting your own kind, despite the proven viciousness and brutality exhibited by some of the enemy—and but for the superiority of his crew and equipment, the victim might have been *Batfish* instead of HIJMS *I-41*.

The final attack on the Jap sub had been made at exactly two minutes after midnight on the morning of February 10. Then, an hour or so after sunset on the 11th, at 1915—

"Captain to the conn!" The skipper is up there in an instant.

The radar operator points to his radar scope. "There's another Jap sub, Captain!"

Sure enough, there, if you watch closely, is the same tiny disturbance which alerted *Batfish* two nights ago. This time there is less doubt as to what action to take. The same tactics which were heralded with such signal success on the first occasion are immediately placed into effect. The crew is called to battle stations, the tracking parties manned, and all is made ready for a warm reception. The radar party is cautioned—unnecessary precaution—to keep that piece of gear turned off except when a range and bearing are actually required.

If anything, it is even darker than it was the first night. Having found how ineffective the Jap radar really is—or was it simply that the Jap watch standers were asleep?—Fyfe determines to make the same kind of attack as before.

The situation develops exactly as it did before, except that this submarine is heading southeast instead of northeast. At 1800 yards he is sighted from the bridge of the American submarine. He is making only 7 knots, somewhat slower than the other, and it takes him a little longer to reach the firing bearing. Finally everything is just about set. Sprinkle has made the "ready to shoot" report, and Fyfe will let them go in a moment, as soon as the track improves a bit and the range decreases to the optimum. About one minute to go—it won't be long now, chappy.

"Hello, he's dived! He dived right on the fire bearing!" Where there had been an enemy submarine, there is now only the rolling undulation of the sea. Nothing to do now but get out of there. *Batfish* must have waited too long and been detected. The Jap was keeping a slightly better watch than Fyfe had given him credit for, and now *Batfish* is being hunted. Just as quickly as that the whole situation has changed. With an enemy submarine known to be submerged within half a mile of you, there is only one of two things to do. Dive yourself, or beat it.

If you dive, you more or less give up the problem, and concentrate on hiding, which many skippers probably would have done. If you run away on the surface, however, there is a slight chance that he'll come back up, and you'll have another shot at him. Jake Fyfe is a stubborn man, and he doesn't give up easily: he discards the idea of diving. "Left full rudder!" he orders instead. His first object is to get away; and his second is to stay in action. Maybe the Jap will assume that he has continued running—which is precisely what Jake hopes he will do.

"All ahead flank!"

The Jap was on a southeasterly course before he dived. Knowing that his periscope must be up and watching his every move, Fyfe orders a northerly course, and *Batfish* roars away from the spot, steadying on a course slightly west of north. Three miles Fyfe lets her run, until he is reasonably sure to be beyond sonar as well as visual range. Then he alters course to the left, and within a short time arrives at a position *southwest* of the position at which the Jap sub dived.

In the conning tower, at the plotting station, and on the bridge there is some rapid and careful figuring going on. "Give the son of a gun four knots," mutters Sprinkle to himself. "That puts him on this circle. Give him six knots, and he's here. Give him eight knots—oh, t'hell with 8 knots!" Clark Sprinkle's exasperation is almost comical as he grips his pencil in sweaty stubby fingers and tries to decide what he'd do if he were a Jap.

The point is that *Batfish* wants to arrive at some point where she will be assured of getting a moderately long-range radar contact the instant the Nip surfaces, in a position to be able to do something about it. *But don't let her spot us through the periscope, or wind up near enough for her to torpedo us while still submerged.* This is where the stuff you learned in school really pays off, brother.

Naturally, *Batfish* cannot afford to remain overly long in the vicinity. Every extra minute she spends there increases by that much the diameter of the circle upon which the enemy may be; and even at that very moment he may be making a periscope approach—while she hangs around and makes it easy for him. But Fyfe has no intentions of making it any easier than he can help. Once he has put his ship in what he has calculated to be a logical spot to await developments, he slows down to one third speed—about 4 knots. Then he orders the sound heads rigged out. With his stern toward the direction from which the enemy submarine would have to come, were he making an attack, and making 4 knots away from there, *Batfish* is forcing the Jap to make high submerged speed in order to catch her; she is banking on detecting him by sound before he can get close enough to shoot, or on detecting the torpedo itself if a long-range shot is fired.

Twenty minutes pass. Fyfe cannot guess how long the Nip sub will stay down, but his game is to outwit him. If his initial gambit of running away to the northward has fooled him, he'll probably show within an hour after diving. The soundmen listen with silent intensity, their headphones glued to their heads. The radar operator scrutinizes his scope with equal urgency. It would not do to miss any indication.

Suddenly, both sound operators look up at the same time. The senior one speaks for both. "Mr. Sprinkle! There's a noise, bearing zero one five!"

Clark is there in an instant. "What's it like?" He flips on the loud-speaker switch.

Clearly, a rushing sound can be heard, a sort of powerful swishing sound. It changes somewhat in intensity and tone, then suddenly stops. Like a flash the exec grabs the portable mike. "Captain," he bellows to the bridge. "He's blown his tanks, bearing zero one five. He'll be up directly!"

The blast from the bridge speaker nearly blows everyone off the bridge, for Sprinkle has a powerful voice. All binoculars are immediately turned to the bearing given. But the black night conceals its secrets well. Nothing can be seen.

The bridge speaker blares again. "Radar contact, zero one eight. That's him all right!"

Apparently convinced that all is clear, the Japanese submarine has surfaced, and is evidently going to continue on his way. *Batfish* is to get another chance. Whether the target saw them, or thought he saw them; heard them or thought he did; detected them on radar, or simply made a routine night dive, will never be known. One thing Jake is definite on, however: he will get no chance to detect *Batfish* this time.

Once again *Batfish* goes through all the intricate details of the night surface approach—with one big difference. The skipper is not going to go in on the surface. The Jap detected him the last time. He's got more strings to his bow than that.

The Jap has speeded up and changed course slightly. *Batfish* again seeks a position in front of him, and when the range and distance to the track are to Fyfe's liking, *Batfish* dives— but not entirely. Since the radar antennae are normally on top of the highest fixed structure of the ship, it follows that they are the last things to go under when a submarine dives. All Fyfe had done was dive his ship so that these vital antennae were still out of water, although nearly all the rest of the submarine is beneath the surface. This is a good trick; that *Batfish* had been able to do it so neatly is a tribute to the state of training and competence of her crew. With her radar antennae dry and out of water, they still function as well as when she was fully surfaced, and the dope continues to feed into the fire-control gear, even though not a thing can be seen through the periscope.

And of course the Jap, probably alerted and nervous—maybe he has heard of the failure of one of his brother subs to get through this same area two nights ago—has no target to see or detect by radar, unless you consider a few little odd-shaped pieces of pipe a target.

So on he comes, making 12 knots now, fairly confident that he has managed to avoid the sub which had stalked him a couple of hours ago. He doesn't even notice or pay any attention to the curious structure in the water a few hundred yards off his starboard beam—for Jake Fyfe has resolved to get as close as possible—and four deadly fish streak his way out of the dark night.

Mercifully, most of the Nip crew probably never knew what hit them. The first torpedo detonated amidships with a thunderous explosion, virtually blowing the ill-fated ship apart. As the two halves each upended and commenced to sink swiftly amid horrible gurgles of water and foaming of released air and fuel oil, the second and third torpedoes also struck home. Their explosions were slightly muffled, however, as though they might have struck some stray piece of metal and gone off mostly in water; but they served to increase the probability that none of the enemy crew had survived the initial attack.

Three minutes later Fyfe logged two more blasts from deep beneath his ship, evidently some kind of internal explosions in the broken hulk of the sinking submarine. Eight minutes later one terrifically loud explosion rocked *Batfish*. First thought to be an aircraft bomb, the explosion was finally put down to part of the swan song of the Nipponese sub. All during this period, and for some time later, Sound heard the usual noises of a sinking submarine—mainly small internal explosions and escaping air.

This time Jake Fyfe was prevented from trying to rescue any of the possible survivors of the catastrophe by the presence of a plane, which was detected just as *Batfish* was getting ready to surface. It is highly doubtful, however, that there could have been any survivors, in view of the triple-barreled blow the submarine had received.

Shortly after midnight, some twenty-four hours later, one of the more irrepressible members of *Batfish*'s crew was heard to mutter, "What, again? Ho hum; here we lose another night's sleep playing tag with these slant-eyed submarines!"—as Captain Jake Fyfe rushed past en route to the conning tower.

For the third time in four days the radar operator has called his skipper—unfortunately the patrol reports of our submarines do not usually list the names of the crew, nor their stations—it would be interesting to know whether the same man spotted the enemy each time. From the times of the three contacts, however, 2210, 1915, and 0155, it would appear that one contact was made by each of the three watch sections, and that therefore the three men standing the radar watches each can lay claim to one Nip sub.

Naturally, the particular peculiarity in the appearance of the radar scope which had first served to alert *Batfish*, had been carefully explained to all radar watchers, and they all knew what to look for. In this case, as in the last, the operator simply pointed to his scope and stated flatly, "There's another one of those Jap subs, Captain!"

One look at the screen, and Jake Fyfe raps out the command to sound the general alarm.

This time Fyfe himself gets on the ship's interior announcing system. "It looks like another Nip submarine, boys," he says. "We ought to be written right into their operation orders by this time. Let's see if we can't help him along the same road as the other two!"

Fyfe and his tracking party are pretty fine hands by this time, and it only takes a short while before the Jap is picked up for sure on the radar; and his course and speed are known. The United States submariners are fairly certain he will either be on the northerly course of the first sub, or the southeasterly one of the second. It proves to be the latter— course one two zero, speed 7. *Batfish* heads to intercept, playing it cagily, as always, but a little more self-confident this time. Somehow these Japs don't seem to have as good equipment as our own—we can thank the home front for that—and they surely are not using what they have to the best advantage—for which we can thank *them*. And we will— in our own unique fashion.

But with the range still quite long, and before *Batfish* is able to get into attack position, the Japanese sub dives. Just why he does, no one knows. Possibly he detected an aircraft, or thought he did—although *Batfish* sees no planes on her radar—or perhaps he got a momentary contact on *Batfish* through some unexplained vagary of his radar equipment. The most probable explanation is that he has heard of the failure of two other boats to get through this particular stretch, and is attempting to make pursuit more difficult by diving occasionally.

But Jake Fyfe has the answer for this one cold. Last night qualified him in its implementation. He heads, despite this new development, to the spot originally selected for attack position. Then, instead of diving, he proceeds down the track at 4 knots, sound gear rigged out, radar sweeping steadily and deliberately, lookouts alerted and tensely watching.

Half an hour after the Jap dived, *Batfish*'s radar once again picks up the faint, shimmering emanations of the Nip radar. He's back up again, though this time no blowing of tanks has been heard. Fyfe, Sprinkle, and the tracking party start the same old approach game.

The first thing to do is to get actual radar contact; this wobble in the scope is no good for tracking, even though it does give a vague indication of the enemy's bearing. So *Batfish* heads for the source of what her radar operators now term the "wobbly," expecting to get contact momentarily. Several thousand yards are covered in this manner, with no result, except that the wobbly is getting stronger. Fyfe and his exec become worried over this development. They know the Jap is surfaced—or can he have thought of the same dodge they themselves used only last night? Suppose the Jap is even then in the process of making the same type of approach on *Batfish*! An unpleasant thought to entertain. The lookouts redouble their vigilance, especially directing their search at the water surface within half a mile around them. At the skipper's order everything else in the ship is subordinated to the sound watch. Fans and blowers are secured. Unnecessary gear throughout the ship is turned off. Most important, the diesel engines are secured and propulsion shifted to the battery. Silently, eerily, *Batfish* glides through the water, peering and listening for the telltale swoosh of a torpedo coming at her. If the Jap is very smart indeed, he will silence also, and will get so close before shooting that *Batfish* will not have a chance of avoiding the torpedoes, even though she might actually hear them on the way.

The lapping of the water alongside is excruciatingly loud in the unnatural stillness. The very air seems stifling and oppressive on the bridge, as it most certainly is down below, with all blowers turned off. Your breath seems to stop, and your heart beats with a muffled thump. The tiny blower motor in the radar gear whines insistently in the conning tower; impossible to shut it down because it keeps the radar tubes from overheating. Sprinkle makes a mental note to have it pulled out and overhauled at the first opportunity.

Down below everyone talks in whispers, not that whispering could do any good, but in tacit recognition of the deadly desperateness of the situation. The Jap sub, submerged, possibly making an approach, and *themselves still on the surface!*

The basic problem, of course, is to compute how far the Jap sub can travel toward them, assuming his most probable course and speed for the time since he dived, and then to stay at least that distance, plus a little to be on the safe side, away from the spot where he submerged. Fyfe, straining for that elusive radar contact which his reasoned deductions say should come soon, allows *Batfish* to go as far as he dares before reversing course again. Just as he gives the order, someone in one of the engine rooms drops a wrench on the steel deck. The sharp noise is carried up the silent main induction pipe and hits the tensely waiting and watching bridge with a shock. All hands are visibly startled, and one lookout almost drops his binoculars. The skipper half opens his mouth, then shuts it again. It wouldn't do to show exasperation at this point.

And then, finally, with *Batfish* still swinging to her hard-over rudder, it comes at last. "Radar contact, bearing three three six!" Fyfe's judgment and nerve have been vindicated again. The Jap was probably just being cagey himself, and had no knowledge of the presence of the United States submarine.

It happens that there are only two torpedoes left forward

in *Batfish*, which really does not matter much since she is due shortly to depart station en route to Pearl Harbor. But it must be admitted that no one expected to run into three nearly identical situations like this—and until the third submarine was detected Fyfe had held no qualms whatever at being nearly dry forward. Now, however, a problem presents itself.

It is necessary to maneuver *Batfish* so that the Jap goes across her stern instead of her bow. Not too easy to do, since you have to be going away instead of toward the target. Fyfe plays his target slowly and carefully, somewhat like an expert fisherman campaigning against a crafty big one. The cast has been made, the fly has landed, the big fellow is nosing toward it, ready to head back for the deep water at the slightest suspicious sign.

This particular submarine has shown considerably more wariness than either of the other two. His peculiar actions on surfacing have proved him to be astute and careful, and Jake Fyfe is not the man to underrate his opponent. His recent scare is rather fresh in mind, and the ice is still mighty thin, measured as it is only in the superiority of United States equipment and alertness.

So *Batfish* tracks the target, gets his course and speed entirely by radar without ever having seen him, and finally submerges dead ahead of him, several miles away. Once again Fyfe uses the stunt of leaving his radar antennae out of water, so that the all-important information on the target's movements will continue to be available to his fire control party and the intricate instruments they operate. Only this time he keeps his stern toward the target and moves slowly away from him, turning as he does so, with the result that the doomed Jap passes directly across his stern at the desired range, and three torpedoes are on their way to meet him. This is really a deliberate shot.

It also is slightly longer in range than the two previous attacks, and there is a longer wait in *Batfish*'s conning tower after the fish are finally sent on their way.

The skipper is watching through the periscope. He can now clearly see the long, low shape of the enemy, his odd-shaped bridge, and his peculiar undulating deckline. He is not a bad-looking ship, Fyfe must admit to himself, and most of these big Jap boats are pretty fast—at least as fast as our own. Not much is known about how they handle under water, however, and, like all United States submariners, Fyfe will reserve his judgment on that score. Our experience with big boats is that you pay for size with submerged maneuverability, and that the well-established theory about efficiency varying with the size of the vessel does not apply to submarines. The Nip is painted black, which makes him just a little easier to see against the gray night, and on the side of his bridge can quite plainly be seen a white rectangle with a dark disk in the center.

On he comes, ominous and a bit pathetic, entirely unaware of the three messengers of doom speeding his way. Fyfe, in the meantime, is a bit anxious. Without taking his eyes from the periscope, he calls out, "How long since the first one?"

Clark Sprinkle answers obliquely, "About fifteen seconds to go, Captain."

"Fifteen seconds! Damn!"

But the torpedoes run true and as intended, and Fyfe's impatience finally is brought to an end. "A hit!" he shouts, "a beautiful hit!" And so it is: a single hit which produces a brilliant orange explosion right in the center of the stricken ship.

Simultaneously, a wide diffusion of pips is noted on the radar screen, indicating that the target has blown apart. Then all the pips die away. The whole catastrophe has been silent; no sound whatsoever has reached the eager listeners in *Batfish*. A moment later, however, the noise of the explosion with its terrifying aftermath crackles over the sound gear into the headsets of the operators, and, indeed, comes right through the pressure hull, so that no man in the crew need have it described to him.

The loud WHAM of the warhead going off is followed instantly, and almost as though it were a single explosion, but a much louder and more prolonged WHRROOOM. This undoubtedly must be the enemy's magazines going up—and there exists a strong probability that he is carrying an extra heavy load, possibly intended for the beleaguered Japs in the Philippines.

One of the three stop watches is stopped with the first

hit and there is no doubt that this was the first torpedo running
the calculated range at exactly the calculated speed. But there
are no further hits, despite the care with which the other fish
had been launched on their way. This occasions no disappoint-
ment, however, since there is simply nothing left for the last
two fish to hit.

As for *Batfish*, Jake Fyfe had her fully on the surface
again within three minutes after the torpedo hit. Though he
strongly doubted that there could possibly be any survivors
of the terrific explosion he had witnessed, he was determined,
as before, to give them a chance for their lives. It was nearly
dawn, and no good came from use of the searchlight, which
Fyfe had ordered turned on and played upon the water, so
the decision was made to wait until daylight, in hopes that
Jap planes patrolling the area would somehow not be immediately in evidence.

Parenthetically, one cannot help comparing *Batfish*'s re-
peated magnanimous attempts to succor the victims of her
attacks with the treatment meted out in similar circumstances
by the Japanese. There is one instance on record in which
most of the crew of an American submarine were picked up
by a Japanese destroyer; one man was injured, and was
promptly thrown overboard. Another had swallowed so much
salt water that he was retching heavily, and would also have
gone overboard had he not fought clear of his saviors and
joined the remainder of the group of survivors. In the case of
Tang, the pitifully small number of survivors were mercilessly
beaten and clubbed about the head and body. By contrast,
Batfish deliberately exposed herself by turning on a searchlight
to assist in locating survivors of her night's handiwork, and
then voluntarily remained on the surface in these enemy waters
until long after daybreak, in hopes of possibly finding one or
two. Since her position was well within enemy aircraft patrols,
the unofficial rules by which most United States submarines
guided their actions required that she be submerged during
daylight.

Several of our submarines were enabled to rescue enemy
survivors in some manner or other, after either they or someone else had torpedoed them. In more than one instance
American sailors or officers had to go overboard after sur-

vivors and force them to accept their hospitality. In no case was such a prisoner badly treated after rescue; most of them gained weight during their sojourn on board, and were so well treated that instructions had finally to be issued to treat them with greater severity in order not to "spoil" them.

With the dawn *Batfish* sighted much oil, bits of wood and paper, debris of various kinds, all newly in the water and quite evidently from the sunken submarine. No Japanese were seen, however—dead or alive. It appeared that once again there was to be nothing tangible to reward Jake Fyfe for his brilliant achievement, but finally a small wooden box recovered from the water was found to contain the Jap navigator's workbook and navigational instruments. Evidently he had just brought it topside, perhaps preparatory to taking a sight or two despite the not-too-favorable weather, but had not yet opened it.

Because the Japanese use Arabic numerals for navigational purposes, there was no difficulty in reading the workbook. Apparently the Jap departed Nagoya for Formosa, and had left there for Luzon—where he never arrived.

Batfish left her area for Guam three days later, and on February 21 she moored alongside the submarine tender *Apollo* in Apra Harbor, Guam.

To say that Jake Fyfe was received with open arms by the submarine brethren is putting it mildly. Though no public announcement of his magnificent feat could be made, owing to the well-laid policy of cloaking our submarine activities in anonymity, it instantly became known and broadcast throughout the submarine force. Here was another patrol nearly on a par with Sam Dealey's famous five-destroyers cruise. Here was additional proof that the spirit of the submarine force, so beautifully exemplified by Dealey and O'Kane and Morton, was still going strong, and that those who came after had not lost the touch of their predecessors.

Ships and Sailors

Mutiny!

WILLIAM LAY *and* C. HUSSEY

The date January 25, 1824 has gone down in history for on that day there took place what was perhaps the most terrible of all mutinies on the high seas, the one that occurred on the whaleship Globe, *out of Nantucket. Whaling was a job for young men—the oldest man on the* Globe *was under thirty, the youngest was fourteen. The following story is by the two survivors of the mutiny and it is an important original document.*

*T*he ship *Globe*, on board of which vessel occurred the horrid transactions we are about to relate, belonged to the Island of Nantucket; she was owned by Messrs. C. Mitchell & Co. and other merchants of that place; and commanded on this voyage by Thomas Worth, of Edgartown, Martha's Vineyard. William Beetle, mate, John Lumbert, 2nd mate, Nathaniel Fisher, 3rd mate, Gilbert Smith, boat-steerer, Samuel B. Comstock, do., Stephen Kidder, seaman, Peter C. Kidder, do., Columbus Worth, do., Rowland Jones, do., John Cleveland, do., Constant Lewis, do., Holden Henman, do., Jeremiah Ingham, do., Joseph Ignasius Prass, do., Cyrus M. Hussey, cooper, Rowland Coffin, do., George Comstock, seaman, and William Lay, do.

On the 15th day of December, we sailed from Edgartown, on a whaling voyage, to the Pacific Ocean, but in working out, having carried away the crossjack-yard, we returned to port, and after having refitted and sent aloft another, we sailed again on the 19th and on the same day anchored in Holmes Hole. On the following day a favorable opportunity offering to proceed to sea, we got under way, and after having cleared the land, discharged the pilot, made sail, and performed the necessary duties of stowing the anchors, unbending and coiling away the cables, etc. On the 1st of January 1823, we experienced a heavy gale from N.W. which was but the first in the catalogue of difficulties we were fated to encounter. As this was our first trial of a seaman's life, the scene presented to our view, "mid the howling storm," was one of terrific grandeur, as well as of real danger. But as the ship scudded well, and the wind was fair, she was kept before it, under a close reefed main-topsail and foresail, although during the gale, which lasted forty-eight hours, the sea frequently threatened to board us, which was prevented by the skillful management of the helm. On the 9th of January we made the Cape Verde Islands, bearing S.W. twenty-five miles distant, and on the 17th, crossed the Equator. On the 29th of the same month we saw sperm whales, lowered our boats, and succeeded in taking one; the blubber of which, when boiled out, yielded us seventy-five barrels of oil. Pursuing our voyage, on the twenty-third of February we passed the Falkland Islands, and about the 5th of March, doubled the great promontory of South America, Cape Horn, and stood to the northward.

We saw whales once only before we reached the Sandwich Islands, which we made on the first of May early in the morning. When drawing in with the Island of Hawaii about four in the afternoon, the man at the mast head gave notice that he saw a shoal of black fish on the lee bow; which we soon found to be canoes on their way to meet us. It falling calm at this time prevented their getting along side until night fall, which they did, at a distance of more than three leagues from the land. We received from them a very welcome supply of potatoes, sugar cane, yams, coconuts, bananas, fish, etc., for which we gave them in return pieces of iron hoop, nails, and similar articles. We stood off and on during the next day, and after obtaining a sufficient supply of vegetables and fruit, we shaped our course for Oahu, at which place we arrived on the following day, and, after lying there twenty hours, sailed for the coast of Japan, in company with the whaling ship *Palladium* of Boston, and *Pocahontas* of Falmouth; from which ships we parted company when two days out. After cruising in the Japan seas several months, and obtaining five hundred and fifty barrels of oil, we again shaped our course for the Sandwich Islands, to obtain a supply of vegetables, etc.

While lying at Oahu, six of the men deserted in the night; two of them having been retaken were put in irons, but one of them having found means to divest himself of his irons set the other at liberty, and both escaped.

To supply their places, we shipped the following persons, viz: Silas Payne, John Oliver, Anthony Hanson, a native of Oahu, Wm. Humphries, a black man, and steward, and Thomas Lilliston. Having accommodated ourselves with as many vegetables and much fruit as could be preserved, we again put to sea, fondly anticipating a successful cruise, and a speedy and happy meeting with our friends. After leaving Oahu we ran to the south of the equator, and after cruising a short time for whales without much success, we steered for Fanning Island, which lies in lat. 3°49′ N. and long. 158°29′ W. While cruising off this Island an event occurred which, whether we consider the want of motives, or the cold blooded and obstinate cruelty with which it was perpetrated, has not often been equaled. We speak of the want of motives because, although some occurrences which we shall mention had given the crew some ground for dissatisfaction, there had been no abuse or severity which could in the least degree excuse or palliate so barbarous a mode of redress and revenge. During our cruise to Japan the season before, many complaints were uttered by the crew among themselves with respect to the manner and quantity in which they received their *meat,* the quantity sometimes being more than sufficient for the number of men, and at others not enough to supply the ship's company; and it is fair to presume that the most dissatisfied deserted the ship at Oahu.

But the reader will no doubt consider it superfluous for us to attempt an unrequired vindication of the conduct of the officers of the *Globe* whose aim was to maintain a correct discipline, which should result in the furtherance of the voyage and be a benefit to all concerned, more especially when he is informed that part of the men shipped at Oahu, in the room of the deserters, were abandoned wretches, who frequently were the cause of severe reprimands from the officers, and in one instance one of them received a severe flogging. The reader will also please to bear in mind that Samuel B. Comstock, the ringleader of the mutiny, was an officer (being a boat-steerer) and as is customary, ate in the cabin. The conduct and deportment of the Captain towards this individual was always decorous and gentlemanly, a proof of intentions long premeditated to destroy the ship. Some of the crew were determined to leave the ship provided she touched at Fanning Island, and we believe had concerted a plan of escape, but of which the perpetration of a deed chilling to humanity precluded the necessity. We were at this time in company with the ship *Lyra,* of New Bedford, the Captain of which had been on board the *Globe* during the most of the day, but had returned in the evening to his own ship. An agreement had been made by him with the Captain of the *Globe* to set a light at midnight as a signal for tacking. It may not be amiss to acquaint the reader of the manner in which whalemen keep watch during the night. They generally carry three boats, though some carry four, five, and sometimes six; the *Globe,* however, being of the class carrying three. The Captain, mate, and second mate stand no watch except there is *blubber* to be boiled; the boat-steerers taking charge of the watch and managing the ship with their respective boat's crews, and in this instance dividing the night into three parts, each taking a third. It so happened that Smith, after keeping the first watch, was relieved by Comstock (whom we shall call by his surname in contradistinction to his brother George) and the *waist boat's crew,* and the former watch retired below to their berths and hammocks. George Comstock took the helm, during his *trick,* received orders from his brother to "keep the ship a good full," swearing that the ship was too nigh the wind. When his time at the helm had expired he took the *rattle* (an instrument used by whalemen to announce the expiration of the hour, the watch, etc.) and began to shake it, when Comstock came to him, and, in the most peremptory manner, ordered him to desist, saying, "If you make the least damn bit of noise, I'll send you to hell!" He then lighted a lamp and went into the steerage. George, becoming alarmed at this conduct of his unnatural brother, again took the *rattle* for the purpose of alarming some one; Comstock arrived in time to prevent him, and, with threatenings dark and diabolical,

Eugenie Clark spearfishing in the Red Sea.

This is the gear used by treasure hunters.

The heroic submarine, USS *Batfish*.

A contemporary print depicting the mutiny on the whaleship *Globe*. Here Comstock runs Lumbert through the body.

The execution of Humphries—a contemporary print.

The whaleship *Globe,* of Nantucket, as she appeared off the Mulgrave Islands on February 11, 1824—a contemporary print.

The death of Samuel Comstock—a contemporary print.

A famous nineteenth-century painting of Blackbeard boarding a sloop.

The *Cachalot* in which
Frank Bullen sailed.

Moonlight on a frozen Antarctic sea.

Sir Ernest Shackleton, the Antarctic explorer.

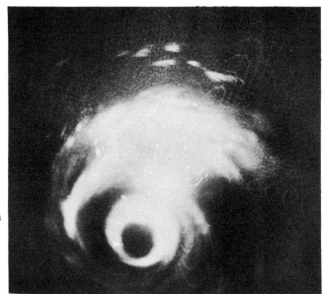

The eye of the 1944 typhoon
as it appeared on radar.

The bow of the USS *New Jersey* is nearly buried in heavy seas during the typhoon of December 1944.

An August day's sail off the coast of Maine.

so congealed the blood of his trembling brother, that even had he possessed the power of alarming the unconscious and fated victims below, his life would have been the forfeit of his temerity!

Comstock now laid something heavy upon a small work bench near the cabin gangway, which was afterwards found to be a boarding knife. It is an instrument used by whalers to cut the *blubber* when hoisting it in, is about four feet in length, two or three inches wide, and necessarily kept very sharp, and, for greater convenience when in use, is two edged.

In giving a detail of this chilling transaction, we shall be guided by the description given of it by the younger Comstock, who, as has been observed, was upon deck at the time, and afterwards learned several particulars from his brother, to whom alone they could have been known. Comstock went down into the cabin, accompanied by Silas Payne or Paine, of Sag Harbour, John Oliver, of Shields, Eng., William Humphries, the steward of Philadelphia, and Thomas Lilliston; the latter, however, went no farther than the cabin gangway, and then ran forward and *turned in*. According to his own story he did not think they would attempt to put their designs in execution, until he saw them actually descending into the cabin, having gone so far, to use his own expression, to show himself as brave as any of them. But we believe he had not the smallest idea of assisting the villains. Comstock entered the cabin so silently as not to be perceived by the man at the helm, who was first apprised of his having begun the work of death by the sound of a heavy blow with an axe, which he distinctly heard.

The Captain was asleep in a hammock, suspended in the cabin, his state room being uncomfortably warm; Comstock approaching him with the axe, struck him a blow upon the head, which was nearly severed in two by the first stroke! After repeating the blow, he ran to Payne, who it seems was stationed with the before mentioned boarding knife, to attack the mate, as soon as the Captain was killed. At this instant, Payne making a thrust at the mate, he awoke, and terrified, exclaimed. "What! what! what!" "Is this— Oh! Payne! Oh! Comstock!" "Don't kill me, don't." "Have I not always—." Here Comstock interrupted him saying, "Yes! you have always been a d—d rascal; you tell lies of me out of the ship will you?

It's a d—d good time to beg now, but you're too late." Here the mate sprang, and grasped him by the throat. In the scuffle, the light which Comstock held in his hand was knocked out and the axe fell from his hand; but the grasp of Mr. Beetle upon his throat did not prevent him from making Payne understand that his weapon was lost, who felt about until he found it, and, having given it to Comstock, he managed to strike him a blow upon the head, which fractured his skull; when he fell into the pantry where he lay groaning until dispatched by Comstock! The steward held a light at this time, while Oliver put in a blow as often as possible!

The second and third mates, fastened in their state rooms, lay in their berths listening, fearing to speak, and being ignorant of the numerical strength of the mutineers, and un-armed, thought it best to wait the dreadful issue, hoping that their lives might yet be spared.

Comstock, leaving a watch at the second mate's door, went up on deck to light another lamp at the binnacle, it having been again accidentally extinguished. He was there asked by his terrified brother, whose agony of mind we will not attempt to portray, if he intended to hurt Smith, the other boat-steerer. He replied that he did; and inquired where he was. George, fearing that Smith would be *immediately* pursued, said he had not seen him. Comstock then perceiving his brother to be shedding tears asked sternly, "What are you crying about?" "I am afraid," replied George, "that they will hurt me!" "I *will* hurt you," said he, "if you talk in that manner!"

But the work of death was not yet finished. Comstock took his light into the cabin, and made preparations for attacking the second and third mates, Mr. Lumbert, and Mr. Fisher. After loading two muskets, he fired one through the door, in the direction as near as he could judge of the officers, and then inquired if either was shot! Fisher replied, "Yes, I am shot in the mouth!" Previous to his shooting Fisher, Lumbert asked if he was going to kill him? To which he answered with ap-parent unconcern, "Oh no, I guess not."

They now opened the door, and Comstock, making a pass at Mr. Lumbert, missed him, and fell into the state room. Mr. Lumbert collared him, but he escaped from his hands. Mr. Fisher had got the gun, and actually presented the bayonet to the monster's heart! But Comstock assuring him that his life should be spared if he gave it up, he did so; when Comstock immediately ran Mr. Lumbert through the body several times!!

He then turned to Mr. Fisher, and told him there was no hope for *him!!* "You have got to die," said he, "remember the scrape you got me into, when in company with the *Enterprise* of Nantucket." The "scrape" alluded to was as follows. Comstock came up to Mr. Fisher to wrestle with him. Fisher being the most athletic of the two, handled him with so much ease, that Comstock in a fit of passion *struck* him. At this Fisher seized him, and laid him upon deck several times in a pretty rough manner.

Comstock then made some violent threats, which Fisher paid no attention to, but which now fell upon his soul with all the horrors of reality. Finding his cruel enemy deaf to his remonstrances, and entreaties, he said, "If there is no hope, I will at least die like a man!" and having, by order of Comstock, turned back too, said in a firm voice, *"I am ready!!"*

Comstock then put the muzzle of the gun to his head, and fired, which instantly put an end to his existence! Mr. Lumbert, during this time, was begging for life, although no doubt mortally wounded. Comstock, turned to him and said, "I am a bloody man! I have a bloody hand and *will* be avenged!" and *again* run him through the body with a bayonet! He then begged for a little water; "I'll give you water," said he, and once more plunging the weapon in his body, left him for dead!

Thus it appears that this more than demon, murdered with his own hand, the whole! Gladly would we wash from "memory's waste" all remembrance of that bloody night. The compassionate reader, however, whose heart sickens within him at the perusal, as does ours at the recital, of this tale of woe, will not, we hope, disapprove our publishing these melancholy facts to the world. As, through the boundless mercy of Providence we have been restored to the bosom of our families and homes, we deemed it a duty we owe to the world to record our "unvarnished tale."

Smith, the other boat-steerer, who had been marked as one of the victims, on hearing the noise in the cabin, went aft, apprehending an altercation between the Captain and some of the other officers, little dreaming that innocent blood was flowing in torrents. But what was his astonishment when he beheld Comstock brandishing the boarding knife, and heard him exclaim, "I am the bloody man, and will have revenge!" Horror struck, he hurried forward, and asked the crew in the forecastle what he should do. Some urged him to secrete himself in the hold, others to go aloft until Comstock's rage should be abated; but alas! the reflection that the ship afforded no secure hiding place determined him to confront the ring-leader, and if he could not save his life by fair means, to sell it dearly! He was soon called for by Comstock, who upon meeting him threw his bloody arms around his neck, and embracing him, said, "You are going to be with us, are you not?" The reader will discover the good policy of Smith when he unhesitatingly answered, "Oh yes, I will do any thing you require."

All hands were now called to make sail, and a light at the same time was set as a signal for the *Lyra* to tack;—while the *Globe* was kept upon the same tack, which very soon caused a separation of the two ships. All the reefs were turned out, top-gallantsails set, and all sail made on the ship, the wind being quite light.

The mutineers then threw the body of the Captain over-board, after wantonly piercing his bowels with a boarding knife, which was *driven with an axe,* until the point protruded from his throat!! In Mr. Beetle, the mate, the lamp of life had not entirely gone out, but he was committed to the deep.

Orders were next given to have the bodies of Mr. Fisher and Mr. Lumbert brought up. A rope was fastened to Fisher's neck, by which he was hauled upon deck. A rope was made fast to Mr. Lumbert's feet, and in this way was he got upon deck, but when in the act of being thrown from the ship, he caught the plank-shear; and appealed to Comstock, reminding him of his promise to save him, but in vain; for the monster forced him from his hold, and he fell into the sea! As he appeared to be yet capable of swimming, a boat was ordered to be lowered, to pursue and finish him, fearing he might be picked up by the *Lyra;* which order was as soon countermanded as given, fearing, no doubt, desertion of his murderous companions.

We will now present the reader, with a journal of our passage to the Mulgrave Islands, for which group we shaped our course.

1824, Jan. 26th. At 2 A.M. from being nearly calm a light breeze sprung up, which increased to a fresh breeze by 4 A.M. This day cleaned out the cabin, which was a scene of blood and destruction of which the recollection at this day chills the blood in our veins. Every thing bearing marks of the murder was brought on deck and washed.

Lat. 5°50′ N., long. 159°13′ W.

Jan. 27th. These twenty-four hours commenced with moderate breezes from the eastward. Middle and latter part calm. Employed in cleaning the small arms which were fifteen in number, and making cartridge boxes.

Lat. 3°45′ N., long. 160°45′ W.

Jan. 28th. This day experienced fine weather, and light breezes from N. by W. The black steward was hung for the following crime.

George Comstock who was appointed steward after the mutiny, and business calling him into the cabin, he saw the former steward, now called the purser, engaged in loading a pistol. He asked him what he was doing that for. His reply was, "I have heard something very strange, and I'm going to be ready for it." This information was immediately carried to Comstock, who called to Payne, now mate, and bid him follow him.

On entering the cabin they saw Humphries, still standing with the pistol in his hand. On being demanded what he was going to do with it, he said he had heard something which made him afraid of his life!

Comstock told him if he had heard any thing, that he ought to have come to him, and let him know, before he began loading pistols. He then demanded to know what he had heard. Humphries answered at first in a very suspicious and ambiguous manner, but at length said that Gilbert Smith, the boat-steerer who was saved, and Peter Kidder were going to retake the ship. This appeared highly improbable, but they were summoned to attend a council at which Comstock presided, and asked if they had entertained any such intentions. They positively denied ever having had conversation upon the subject. All this took place in the evening. The next morning the parties were summoned, and a jury of two men called. Humphries under a guard of six men, armed with muskets, was arraigned, and Smith and Kidder seated upon a chest near him. The prisoner was asked a few questions touching his intentions, which he answered but low and indistinctly. The trial, if it may be so called, had progressed thus far, when Comstock made a speech in the following words. "It appears that William Humphries *has been accused guilty*, of a *treacherous and base act*, in loading a pistol for the purpose of shooting Mr. Payne and myself. Having been tried the jury will now give in their verdict, whether Guilty or not Guilty. If guilty he shall be hanged to a studdingsail boom, rigged out eight feet upon the foreyard, but if found not guilty, Smith and Kidder shall be hung upon the aforementioned gallows!" But the doom of Humphries had been sealed the night before, and kept secret *except from the jury*, who returned a verdict of Guilty. Preparations were immediately made for his execution! His watch was taken from him, and he was then taken forward and seated upon the rail, with a cap drawn over his face, and then the rope placed round his neck.

Every man was ordered to take hold of the execution rope, to be ready to run him up when Comstock should give the signal, by ringing the ship's bell!

He was now asked if he had any thing to say, as he had but fourteen seconds to live! He began by saying, "Little did I think I was born to come to this—"; the bell struck! and he was immediately swung to the yard-arm! He died without a struggle; and after he had hung a few minutes, the rope was cut, to let him fall overboard, but getting entangled aloft, the body was towed some distance along side, when a *runner hook**
was attached to it, to sink it, when the rope was again cut and the body disappeared. His chest was now overhauled, and sixteen dollars in specie found, which he had taken from the Captain's trunk. Thus ended the life of one of the mutineers, while the blood of innocent victims was scarcely washed from his hands, much less the guilty stain from his soul.

* [A large hook used when hoisting in the blubber.]

Feb. 7th. These twenty-four hours commenced with thick squally weather. Middle part clear and fine weather. Hove to at 2 A.M., and 6 made sail, and steered W. by S. At ½ past 8 made an Island ahead, one of the Kingsmill group. Stood in with the land and received a number of canoes along side, the natives in them however having nothing to sell us but a few beads of their own manufacture. We saw some coconut, and other trees upon the shore, and discovered many of the natives upon the beach, and some dogs. The principal food of these Islanders is a kind of bread fruit, which they pound very fine and mix it with fish.

Feb. 8th. Commences squally with fresh breezes from the northward. Took a departure from Kingsmill Island; one of the group of that name, in lat. 1°27′ N. and long. 175°14′ E. In the morning passed through the channel between Marshall and Gilbert Islands; luffed to and dispatched a boat to Marshall Island, but did not land, as the natives appeared hostile, and those who swam off to the boat endeavored to steal from her. When about to leave, a volley of musketry was discharged at them, which probably killed or wounded some of them. The boat then gave chase to a canoe, paddled by two of the natives, which were fired upon when within gunshot, when they immediately ceased paddling; and on the boat approaching them, discovered that one of the natives was wounded. In the most supplicating manner they held up a jacket, manufactured from a kind of flag, and some beads, being all they possessed, giving their inhuman pursuers to understand that all should be theirs if they would spare their lives! The wounded native laid down in the bottom of the boat, and from his convulsed frame and trembling lip, no doubt remained but that the wound was mortal. The boat then returned on board and we made sail for the Mulgrave Islands. Here was another sacrifice; an innocent child of nature shot down, merely to gratify the most wanton and unprovoked cruelty, which could possibly possess the heart of man. The unpolished savage, a stranger to the more tender sympathies of the human heart, which are cultivated and enjoyed by civilized nations, nurtures in his bosom a flame of revenge, which only the blood of those who have injured him can damp; and when years have rolled away, this act of cruelty will be remembered by these Islanders, and made the pretext to slaughter every white man who may fall into their hands.

Feb. 11th. Commenced with strong breezes from the Northward. At ½ past meridian made the land bearing E.N.E. four leagues distant. Stood in and received a number of canoes along side. Sent a boat on shore, and brought off a number of women, a large quantity of coconuts, and some fish. Stood off shore most of the night, and

Feb. 12th, in the morning stood in shore again and landed the women. We then stood along shore looking out for an anchorage, and reconnoitering the country, in the hope of finding some spot suitable for cultivation; but in this we were disappointed, or more properly speaking, they, the mutineers; for we had no will of our own, while our bosoms were torn with the most conflicting passions, in which Hope and Despair alternately gained the ascendancy.

Feb. 13th. After having stood off all night, we in the morning stood in, and after coasting the shores of several small Islands, we came to one, low and narrow, where it was determined the ship should be anchored. When nearly ready to let go, a man was sent into the chains to sound, who pronounced twelve fathoms; but at the next cast, could not get bottom. We continued to stand in, until we got regular sounding, and anchored within five rods of the shore, on a coral rock bottom, in seven fathoms water. The ship was then moored with a kedge astern, sails furled, and all hands retired to rest, except an *anchor watch.*

Feb. 14th, was spent in looking for a landing place. In the morning a boat was sent to the Eastward, but returned with the information that no good landing place could be found, the shore being very rocky. At 2 P.M. she was sent in an opposite direction, but returned at night without having met with better success; when it was determined to land at the place where we lay; notwithstanding it was very rocky. Nothing of consequence was done, until

Sunday, 15th Feb. 1824, when all hands were set to work to construct a raft out of the spars, upon which to convey the provisions, etc., on shore.

The laws by which we were now governed had been made by Comstock, soon after the mutiny, and read as follows:

"That if any one saw a sail and did not report it immediately, he should be put to death! If any one refused to fight a ship he should be put to death; and the manner of their death, this— They shall be bound hand and foot and boiled in the *try pots*, of boiling oil!" Every man was made to seal and sign this instrument, the seals of the mutineers being *black*, and the remainder, *blue* and *white*. The raft or stage being completed, it was anchored, so that one end rested upon the rocks, the other being kept seaward by the anchor. During the first day many articles were brought from the ship in boats, to the raft, and from thence conveyed on shore. Another raft, however, was made, by laying spars upon two boats, and boards again upon them, which at high water would float well up on the shore. The following, as near as can be recollected, were the articles landed from the ship: (and the intention was when all should have been got on shore, to haul the ship on shore, or as near it as possible and burn her) One mainsail, one foresail, one mizen-topsail, one spanker, one driver, one maintop gallantsail, two lower studdingsails, two royals, two topmast-studdingsails, two top-gallant-studdingsails, one mizenstaysail, two mizen-top-gallantsails, one fly-gib (thrown overboard, being a little torn), three boat's sails (new), three or four casks of bread, eight or ten barrels of flour, forty barrels of beef and pork, three or more 6o gal. casks of molasses, one and a half barrels of sugar, one barrel dried apples, one cask vinegar, two casks of rum, one or two barrels domestic coffee, one keg W. I. coffee, one and a half chests of tea, one barrel of pickles, one do. cranberries, one box chocolate, one cask of towlines, three or more coils of cordage, one coil rattling, one do. lance warp, ten or fifteen balls spunyarn, one do. worming, one stream cable, one larboard bower anchor, all the spare spars, every chest of clothing, most of the ship's tools, etc. The ship by this time was considerably unrigged.

On the following day, Monday 16th February, Payne, the second in the mutiny, who was on board the ship attending to the discharge of articles from her, sent word to Comstock, who with Gilbert Smith and a number of the crew were on shore attending to the landing of the raft: "That if he did not act differently with regard to the plunder, such as making presents to the natives of the officers' fine clothing, etc., he would do no more, but quit the ship and come on shore." Comstock had been very liberal to the natives in this way, and his object was, no doubt, to attach them as much as possible to his person, as it must have been suggested to his guilty mind that however he himself might have become misanthrope, yet there were those around him whose souls shuddered at the idea of being forever exiled from their country and friends, whose hands were yet unstained by blood, but who might yet imbrue them for the purpose of escape from lonely exile, and cruel tyranny.

When the foregoing message was received from Payne, Comstock commanded his presence immediately on shore, and interrogated him, as to what he meant by sending such a message. After considerable altercation, which took place in the tent, Comstock was heard to say, "I helped to take the ship, and have navigated her to this place. I have also done all I could to get the sails and rigging on shore, and now you may do what you please with her; but if any man wants any thing of *me*, I'll take a musket with him!"

"That is what I want," replied Payne, "and am ready!" This was a check upon the murderer, who had now the offer of becoming a duelist; and he only answered by saying, "I will go on board once more, and then you may do as you please."

He then went on board, and after destroying the paper upon which were recorded the "Laws," returned, went into the tent with Payne, and putting a sword into a scabbard, exclaimed, "*This* shall stand by me as long as I live."

We ought not to omit to mention that during the time he was on board the ship, he challenged the persons there to fight him, and as he was leaving, exclaimed, "I am going to leave you; *look out for yourselves!*"

After obtaining from Payne permission to carry with him a cutlass, a knife, and some hooks and lines, he took his departure, and as was afterwards ascertained, immediately joined a gang of natives, and endeavored to excite them to slay Payne and his companions! At dusk of this day he passed the tent, accompanied by about 50 of the natives, in a direction of their village, upwards of a league distant. Payne came on board, and after expressing apprehensions that Comstock would persuade the natives to kill us all, picked out a number of the crew to go on shore for the night, and stationed sentinels around the tent, with orders to shoot any one, who should attempt to approach without giving the countersign. The night, however, passed without any one's appearing; but early on the morning of the

17th Feb.; Comstock was discovered at some distance coming towards the tent. It had been before proposed to Smith by Payne, to shoot him; but poor Smith, like ourselves, dare do no other than remain upon the side of neutrality.

Oliver, whom the reader will recollect as one of the wretches concerned in the mutiny, hurried on shore, and with Payne and others, made preparations to put him to death. After loading a number of muskets they stationed themselves in front of the tent, and waited his approach—a bushy spot of ground intervening, he did not make his appearance until a short distance of the tent, which as soon as he saw, drew his sword and walked quick towards it, in a menacing manner; but as soon as he saw a number of the muskets leveled at him, he waved his hands and cried out, "Don't shoot me, don't shoot me! I will not hurt you!" At this moment they fired, and he fell! Payne fearing he might *pretend* to be shot, ran to him with an axe, and nearly severed his head from his body! There were four muskets fired at him, but only two balls took effect, one entered his right breast, and passed out near the backbone, the other through his head.

Thus ended the life of perhaps as cruel, bloodthirsty, and vindictive a being as ever bore the form of humanity.

All hands were now called to attend his burial, which was conducted in the same inconsistent manner which had marked the proceedings of the actors in this tragedy. While some were engaged in sewing the body in a piece of canvas, others were employed in digging a grave in the sand, adjacent to the place of his decease, which, by order of Payne, was made five feet deep. Every article attached to him, including his cutlass, was buried with him, except his watch; and the ceremonies consisted in *reading a chapter from the Bible over him, and firing a musket!*

Only twenty-two days had elapsed after the perpetration of the massacre on board the ship, when, with all his sins upon his head, he was hurried into eternity.

No duty was done during the remainder of the day, except the selection by Payne of six men to go on board the ship and take charge of her, under the command of Smith; who had communicated his intentions to a number of running away with the ship. We think we cannot do better than to give an account of their escape in the words of Smith himself. It may be well to remark that Payne had ordered the two binnacle compasses to be brought on shore, they being the only ones remaining on board, except a hanging compass suspended in the cabin. Secreting one of the binnacle compasses, he took the hanging compass on shore and the exchange was not discovered.

"At 7 P.M. we began to make preparations for our escape with the ship. I went below to prepare some weapons for our defense should we be attacked by Payne, while the others, as silently as possible, were employed in clearing the running rigging, for everything was in the utmost confusion. Having found one musket, three bayonets, and some whale lances, they were laid handy, to prevent the ship from being boarded. A handsaw well greased was laid upon the windlass to saw off the cable, and the only remaining hatchet on board was placed by the mizen mast, to cut the stern moorings when the ship should have sufficiently swung off. Taking one man with me, we went upon the foretop-sailyard, loosed the sail and turned out the reefs, while two others were loosing the main-topsail and mainsail. I will not insult the reader's good sense, by assuring him, that this was a duty, upon the success of which seemed to hang our very existence. By this time the moon was rising, which rendered it dangerous to delay for those who had formed a resolution to swim on board and accompany us. The *bunts* of the sails being yet confined aloft, by their respective gaskets, I sent a man on the foreyard and another upon the foretop-sailyard, with orders to *let fall*, when I should give the word; one man being at the helm, and two others at the fore tack.

"It was now half past nine o'clock, when I took the handsaw, and in less than two minutes the cable was off! The ship *payed off* very quick, and when her head was off the land, there being a breeze from that quarter, the hawser was cut and all the sail we could make upon the ship immediately set, a fine fair wind blowing. A raft of iron hoops, which was towing along side, was cut adrift, and we congratulated each other upon our fortunate escape; for even with a vast extent of ocean to traverse, hope excited in our bosoms a belief that we should again embrace our friends, and our joy was heightened by the reflection that we might be the means of rescuing the innocents left behind, and having the guilty punished."

After a long and boisterous passage the ship arrived at Valparaiso, when she was taken possession of by the American Consul, Michael Hogan, Esq., and the persons on board were put in irons on board a French frigate, there being no American man-of-war in port. Their names were Gilbert Smith, George Comstock, Stephen Kidder, Joseph Thomas, Peter C. Kidder, and Anthony Hanson.

Enter Blackbeard the Pirate

FRANK R. STOCKTON

"Go tell your King, he is King of the Land; But I am King of the Sea!" said the pirate Barbarossa to a messenger from Charles V.

King of the Sea! Every pirate and buccaneer thought himself that, and stories of piracy are part of the story of the oceans. None, however, was more fierce than Blackbeard, who harried our Atlantic Coast.

So long as the people of the Carolinas were prosperous and able to capture and execute pirates who interfered with their trade the Atlantic sea robbers kept away from their ports, but this prosperity did not last. Indian wars broke out, and in the course of time the colonies became very much weakened and impoverished, and then it was that the harbor of Charles Town began to be again interesting to the pirates.

About this time one of the most famous of sea robbers was harassing the Atlantic coast of North America, and from New England to the West Indies he was known as the great pirate Blackbeard. This man, whose real name was Thatch, was a most terrible fellow in appearance as well as action. He wore a long, heavy, black beard, which it was his fancy to separate into tails, each one tied with a colored ribbon, and often tucked behind his ears. Some of the writers of that day declared that the sight of this beard would create more terror in any port of the American seaboard than would the sudden appearance of a fiery comet. Across his brawny breast he carried a sort of a sling in which hung not less than three pairs of pistols in leathern holsters, and these, in addition to his cutlass and a knife or two in his belt, made him a most formidable-looking fellow.

Some of the fanciful recreations of Blackbeard show him to have been a person of consistent purpose. Even in his hours of rest when he was not fighting or robbing, his savage soul demanded some interesting excitement. Once he was seated at table with his mate and two or three sailors, and when the meal was over he took up a pair of pistols, and cocking them put them under the table. This peculiar action caused one of the sailors to remember very suddenly that he had something to do on deck, and he immediately disappeared. But the others looked at their captain in astonishment, wondering what he would do next. They soon found out; for crossing the pistols, still under the table, he fired them. One ball hit the mate in the leg, but the other struck no one. When asked what he meant by this strange action, he replied that if he did not shoot one of his men now and then they would forget what sort of a person he was.

At another time he invented a game; he gathered his officers and crew together and told them that they were going to play that they were living in the lower regions. Thereupon the whole party followed him down into the hold. The hatches and all the other openings were closed, and then Blackbeard began to illuminate the scene with fire and brimstone. The sulphur burned, the fumes rose, a ghastly light spread over the countenances of the desperados, and very soon some of them began to gasp and cough and implore the captain to let in some fresh air, but Blackbeard was bound to have a good game, and he proceeded to burn more brimstone. He laughed at the gasping fellows about him and declared that he would be just as willing to breathe the fumes of sulphur as common air. When at last he threw open the hatches, some of the men were almost dead, but their stalwart captain had not even sneezed.

In the early part of the eighteenth century Blackbeard made his headquarters in one of the inlets on the North Carolina coast, and there he ruled as absolute king, for the settlers in the vicinity seemed to be as anxious to oblige him as the captains of the merchantmen sailing along the coast were anxious to keep out of his way. On one of his voyages Blackbeard went down the coast as far as Honduras, where he took a good many prizes, and as some of the crews of the captured vessels enlisted under him, he sailed north with a stronger force than ever before, having a large ship of forty guns, three smaller vessels, and four hundred men. With this little fleet Blackbeard made for the coast of South Carolina, and anchored outside the harbor of Charles Town. He well understood the present condition of the place and was not in the least afraid that the citizens would hang him up on the shores of the bay.

Blackbeard began work without delay. Several well-laden ships—the Carolinians having no idea that pirates were waiting for them—came sailing out to sea and were immediately captured. One of these was a very important vessel, for it not only carried a valuable cargo, but a number of passengers, many of them people of note, who were on their way to England. One of these was a Mr. Wragg, who was a member of the Council of the Province. It might have been supposed that when Blackbeard took possession of this ship, he would have been satisfied with the cargo and the money which he found on board, and having no use for prominent citizens, would have let them go their way; but he was a trader as well as a plunderer, and he therefore determined that the best thing to do in this case was to put an assorted lot of highly respectable passengers upon the market and see what he could get for them. He was not at the time in need of money or provisions, but his men were very much in want of medicines, so he decided to trade off his prisoners for pills, potions, plasters, and all sorts of apothecaries' supplies.

He put three of his pirates in a boat, and with them one of the passengers, a Mr. Marks, who was commissioned as Blackbeard's special agent, with orders to inform the governor that if he did not immediately send the medicines required amounting in value to about three hundred pounds, and if he did not allow the pirate crew of the boat to return in safety, every one of the prisoners would be hanged from the yardarm of his ship.

The boat rowed away to the distant town, and Blackbeard waited two days for its return, and then he grew very angry, for he believed that his messengers had been taken into custody, and he came very near hanging Mr. Wragg and all his companions. But before he began to satisfy his vengeance, news came from the boat. It had been upset in the bay, and had had great trouble in getting to Charles Town, but it had arrived there at last. Blackbeard now waited a day or two longer; but as no news came from Mr. Marks, he vowed he would not be trifled with by the impudent people of Charles Town, and swore that every man, woman, and child among the prisoners should immediately prepare to be hanged.

Of course the unfortunate prisoners in the pirate ship were in a terrible state of mind during the absence of Mr. Marks. They knew very well that they could expect no mercy from Blackbeard if the errand should be unsuccessful, and they also knew that the Charles Town people would not be likely to submit to such an outrageous demand upon them; so they trembled and quaked by day and by night, and when at last they were told to get ready to be hanged, every particle of courage left them, and they proposed to Blackbeard that if he would spare their lives, and that if it should turn out that their fellow citizens had decided to sacrifice them for the sake of a few paltry drugs, they would take up the cause of the pirates; they would show Blackbeard the best way to sail into the harbor, and they would join with him and his men in attacking the city and punishing the inhabitants for their hard-hearted treatment of their unfortunate fellow citizens.

This proposition pleased Blackbeard immensely; it would have been like a new game to take Mr. Wragg to the town and make him fight his fellow members of the Council of the Province, and so he rescinded his order for a general execution, and bade his prisoners prepare to join with his pirates when he should give the word for an assault upon their city.

In the meantime there was a terrible stir in Charles Town. When the governor and citizens received the insolent and brutal message of Blackbeard they were filled with rage as well as consternation, and if there had been any way of going out to sea to rescue their unhappy fellow citizens, every able-bodied man in the town would have enlisted in the expedition. But they had no vessels of war, and they were not even in a position to arm any of the merchantmen in the harbor. It seemed to the governor and his council that there was nothing for them to do but to submit to the demands of Blackbeard, for they very well knew that he was a scoundrel who would keep his word, and also that whatever they did must be done quickly, for there were the three swaggering pirates in the town, strutting about the streets as if they owned the place. If this continued much longer, it would be impossible to keep the infuriated citizens from falling upon these blustering rascals and bringing their impertinence to a summary end. If this should happen, it would be a terrible thing, for not only would Mr. Wragg and his companions be put to death, but the pirates would undoubtedly attack the town, which was in a very poor position for defence.

Consequently the drugs were collected with all possible haste, and Mr. Marks and the pirates were sent with them to Blackbeard. We do not know whether or not that bedizened cutthroat was satisfied with the way things turned out; for having had the idea of going to Charles Town and obliging the prisoners to help him confiscate the drugs and chemicals, he may have preferred this unusual proceeding to a more commonplace transaction; but as the medicine had arrived he accepted it, and having secured all possible booty and money from the ships he had captured, and had stripped his prisoners of the greater part of their clothing, he set them on shore to walk to Charles Town as well as they could. They had a miserably difficult time, making their way through the woods and marshes, for there were women and children among them who were scarcely equal to the journey. One of the children was a little boy, the son of Mr. Wragg, who afterward became a very prominent man in the colonies. He rose to such a high position, not only among his countrymen, but in the opinion of the English government, that when he died, about the beginning of the Revolution, a tablet to his memory was placed in Westminster Abbey, which is, perhaps, the first instance of such an honor being paid to an American.

Having now provided himself with medicines enough to keep his wild crew in good physical condition, no matter how much they might feast and frolic on the booty they had obtained from Charles Town, Blackbeard sailed back to his North Carolina haunts and took a long vacation, during which time he managed to put himself on very good terms with the governor and officials of the country. He had plenty of money and was willing to spend it, and so he was allowed to do pretty much as he pleased, provided he kept his purse open and did not steal from his neighbors.

But Blackbeard became tired of playing the part of a make-believe respectable citizen, and, having spent the greater part of his money, he wanted to make some more. Consequently he fitted out a small vessel, and declaring that he was going on a legitimate commercial cruise, he took out regular papers for a port in the West Indies and sailed away, as if he had been a mild-mannered New England mariner going to catch codfish. The officials of the town of Bath, from which he sailed, came down to the ship and shook hands with him and hoped he would have good success.

After a moderate absence he returned to Bath, bringing with him a large French merchant vessel, with no people on board, but loaded with a valuable cargo of sugar and other goods. This vessel he declared he had found deserted at sea, and he therefore claimed it as a legitimate prize. Knowing the character of this bloody pirate, and knowing how very improbable it was that the captain and all the crew of a valuable merchant vessel, with nothing whatever the matter with her, would go out into their boats and row away, leaving their ship to become the property of anyone who might happen along, it may seem surprising that the officials of Bath appeared to have no doubt of the truth of Blackbeard's story, and allowed him freely to land the cargo on the French ship and store it away as his own property.

But people who consort with pirates cannot be expected to have very lively consciences, and although there must have been persons in the town with intelligence enough to understand the story of pitiless murder told by that empty vessel, whose very decks and masts must have been regarded as silent witnesses that her captain and crew did not leave her of their own free will, no one in the town interfered with the thrifty Blackbeard or caused any public suspicion to fall upon the propriety of his actions.

Feeling now quite sure that he could do what he pleased on shore as well as at sea, Blackbeard swore more, swaggered more, and, whenever he felt like it, sailed up and down the coast and took a prize or two to keep the pot boiling for himself and his men.

On one of these expeditions he went to Philadelphia, and, having landed, he walked about to see what sort of a place it was, but the governor of the state, hearing of his arrival, quickly arranged to let him know that the Quaker city allowed no black-hearted pirate, with a ribbon-bedecked beard, to promenade on Chestnut and Market streets, and promptly issued a warrant for the sea robber's arrest. But Blackbeard was too sharp and too old a criminal to be caught in that way, and he left the city with great despatch.

The people along the coast of North Carolina became very tired of Blackbeard and his men. All sorts of depredations were committed on vessels, large and small, and whenever a ship was boarded and robbed or whenever a fishing vessel was laid under contribution, Blackbeard was known to be at the bottom of the business, whether he personally appeared or not. To have this busy pirate for a neighbor was extremely unpleasant, and the North Carolina settlers greatly longed to get rid of him. It was of no use for them to ask their own state government to suppress this outrageous scoundrel, and although their good neighbor, South Carolina, might have been willing to help them, she was too poor at that time and had enough to do to take care of herself.

Not knowing, or not caring for, the strong feeling of the settlers against him, Blackbeard continued in his wicked ways, and among other crimes he captured a small vessel and treated the crew in such a cruel and atrocious manner that the better class of North Carolinians vowed they would stand him no longer, and they therefore applied to Governor Spotswood, of Virginia, and asked his aid in putting down the pirates. The Virginians were very willing to do what they could for their unfortunate neighbors. The legislature offered a reward for the capture of Blackbeard or any of his men; but the governor, feeling that this was not enough, determined to do something on his own responsibility, for he knew very well that the time might come when the pirate vessels would begin to haunt Virginia waters.

There happened to be at that time two small British men-of-war in Hampton Roads, and although the governor had no authority to send these after the pirates, he fitted out two sloops at his own expense and manned them with the best fighting men from the war vessels. One of the sloops he put under Captain Brand, and the other under Captain Maynard, both brave and experienced naval officers. All preparations were made with the greatest secrecy—for if Blackbeard had heard of what was going on, he would probably have decamped—and then the two sloops went out to sea with a commission from the governor to capture Blackbeard, dead or alive. This was a pretty heavy contract, but Brand and Maynard were courageous men and did not hesitate to take it.

The Virginians had been informed that the pirate captain and his men were on a vessel in Ocracoke Inlet, and when they arrived they found, to their delight, that Blackbeard was there. When the pirates saw the two armed vessels sailing into the inlet, they knew very well that they were about to be attacked, and it did not take them long to get ready for a fight, nor did they wait to see what their enemy was about to do. As soon as the sloops were near enough, Blackbeard, without waiting for any preliminary exercises, such as a demand for surrender or any nonsense of that sort, let drive at the intruders with eight heavily loaded cannon.

Now the curtain had been rung up, and the play began, and a very lively play it was. The guns of the Virginians blazed away at the pirate ship, and they would have sent out boats to board her had not Blackbeard forestalled them. Boarding was always a favorite method of fighting with the pirates. They did not often carry heavy cannon, and even when they did, they had but little fancy for battles at long distances. What they liked was to meet foes face to face and cut them down on their own decks. In such combats they felt at home, and were almost always successful, for there were few mariners or sailors, even in the British navy, who could stand against these brawny, glaring-eyed dare-devils, who sprang over the sides of a vessel like panthers, and fought like bulldogs. Blackbeard had had enough cannonading, and he did not wait to be boarded. Springing into a boat with about twenty of his men, he rowed to the vessel commanded by Maynard, and in a few minutes he and his pirates surged on board her.

Now there followed on the decks of that sloop one of the most fearful hand-to-hand combats known to naval history. Pirates had often attacked vessels where they met with strong resistance, but never had a gang of sea robbers fallen in with such bold and skilled antagonists as those who now confronted Blackbeard and his crew. At it they went—cut, fire, slash, bang, howl, and shout. Steel clashed, pistols blazed, smoke went up, and blood ran down, and it was hard in the confusion for a man to tell friend from foe. Blackbeard was everywhere, bounding from side to side, as he swung his cutlass high and low, and though many a shot was fired at him, and many a rush made in his direction, every now and then a sailor went down beneath his whirling blade.

But the great pirate had not boarded that ship to fight with common men. He was looking for Maynard, the commander. Soon he met him, and for the first time in his life he found his match. Maynard was a practised swordsman, and no matter how hard and how swiftly came down the cutlass of the pirate, his strokes were always evaded, and the sword of the Virginian played more dangerously near him. At last Blackbeard, finding that he could not cut down his enemy, suddenly drew a pistol, and was about to empty its barrels into the very face of his opponent, when Maynard sent his sword blade into the throat of the furious pirate; the great Blackbeard went down upon his back on the deck, and in the next moment Maynard put an end to his nefarious career. Their leader dead, the few pirates who were left alive gave up the fight, and sprang overboard, hoping to be able to swim ashore, and the victory of the Virginians was complete.

The strength, toughness, and extraordinary vitality of these feline human beings who were known as pirates have often occasioned astonishment in ordinary people. Their sun-tanned and hairy bodies seemed to be made of something like wire, leather, and India rubber, upon which the most tremendous exertions, and even the infliction of severe wounds, made but little impression. Before Blackbeard fell, he received from Maynard and others no less than twenty-five wounds, and yet he fought fearlessly to the last, and when the panting officer sheathed his sword, he felt that he had performed a most signal deed of valor.

When they had broken up the pirate nest in Ocracoke Inlet, the two sloops sailed to Bath, where they compelled some of the unscrupulous town officials to surrender the cargo which had been stolen from the French vessel and stored in the town by Blackbeard; then they sailed proudly back to Hampton Roads, with the head of the dreaded Blackbeard dangling from the end of the bowsprit of the vessel he had boarded, and on whose deck he had discovered the fact, before unknown to him, that a well-trained, honest man can fight as well as the most reckless cutthroat who ever decked his beard with ribbons, and swore enmity to all things good.

Our First Whale

FRANK T. BULLEN

*"It is immense," wrote Rudyard Kipling. "There is no other word.
I have never read anything that equals it in its deep sea wonder
and mystery. Nor do I think that any book before has so completely covered the whole business of whale fishing and at the
same time given such real and new sea pictures. It is a new world
that you've opened the door to."*

*So wrote Rudyard Kipling to Frank Bullen when he published
his book entitled* The Cruise of the Cachalot, *about his experiences
on a whaling ship when he was eighteen years old. Bullen wrote
it, he said, for a coming generation, and that generation is now
here—one with a great affection for the sea and one which will
explore it more than any other generation has done before.*

*S*imultaneous ideas occurring to several people, or thought
transference, whatever one likes to call the phenomenon, is too
frequent an occurrence in most of our experience to occasion
much surprise. Yet on the occasion to which I am about to
refer, the matter was so very marked that few of us who took
part in the day's proceedings are ever likely to forget it.

We were all gathered about the fo'c'sle scuttle one evening,
and the question of whale-fishing came up for discussion. Until
that time, strange as it may seem, no word of this, the
central idea of all our minds, had been mooted. Every man
seemed to shun the subject, although we were in daily ex-
pectation of being called upon to take an active part in
whale-fighting. Once the ice was broken, nearly all had something to say about it, and very nearly as many addle-headed
opinions were ventilated as at a Colney Hatch debating society.

For we none of us *knew* anything about it. I was appealed to
continually to support this or that theory, but as far as whaling
went I could only, like the rest of them, draw upon my
imagination for details. How did a whale act, what were the
first steps taken, what chance was there of being saved if your
boat got smashed, and so on unto infinity. At last, getting very
tired of this "Portuguee Parliament" of all talkers and no
listeners, I went aft to get a drink of water before turning in.
The harpooners and other petty officers were grouped in the
waist, earnestly discussing the pros and cons of attack upon
whales. As I passed I heard the mate's harpooner say, "Feels
like whale about. I bet a plug (of tobacco) we raise sperm
whale tomorrow." Nobody took his bet, for it appeared that
they were mostly of the same mind, and while I was drinking
I heard the officers in dignified conclave talking over the same
thing. It was Saturday evening, and while at home people
were looking forward to a day's respite from work and care, I
felt that the coming day, though never taken much notice of
on board, was big with the probabilities of strife such as I at
least had at present no idea of. So firmly was I possessed by the
prevailing feeling.

The night was very quiet. A gentle breeze was blowing, and
the sky was of the usual "Trade" character, that is, a dome of
dark blue fringed at the horizon with peaceful cumulus clouds,
almost motionless. I turned in at four a.m. from the middle
watch and, as usual, slept like a babe. Suddenly I started
wide awake, a long mournful sound sending a thrill to my very
heart. As I listened breathlessly other sounds of the same
character but in different tones joined in, human voices monot-
onously intoning in long drawn-out expirations the single word
"bl-o-o-o-o-w." Then came a hurricane of noise overhead, and
adjurations in no gentle language to the sleepers to "tumble
up lively there, no skulking, sperm whales." At last, then,
fulfilling all the presentiments of yesterday, the long dreaded
moment had arrived. Happily there was no time for hesitation,
in less than two minutes we were all on deck, and hurrying
to our respective boats. There was no flurry or confusion, and
except that orders were given more quietly than usual, with a
manifest air of suppressed excitement, there was nothing to
show that we were not going for an ordinary course of boat

drill. The skipper was in the main crow's-nest with his binoculars. Presently he shouted, "Naow then, Mr. Count, lower
away soon's y'like. Small pod o'cows, an' one 'r two bulls
layin' off to west'ard of 'em." Down went the boats into the
water quietly enough, we all scrambled in and shoved off. A
stroke or two of the oars were given to get clear of the ship,
and one another, then oars were shipped and up went the
sails. As I took my allotted place at the main-sheet, and the
beautiful craft started off like some big bird, Mr. Count leant
forward, saying impressively to me, "Y'r a smart youngster, an'
I've kinder took t'yer; but don't ye look ahead an' get gallied,
'r I'll knock ye stiff wi' th' tiller; y'hear me? N' don't ye dare
to make thet sheet fast, 'r ye'll die so sudden y' won't know
whar y'r hurted." I said as cheerfully as I could, "All right,
sir," trying to look unconcerned, telling myself not to be a
coward, and all sorts of things; but the cold truth is that I
was scared almost to death because I didn't know what was
coming. However, I did the best thing under the circumstances,
obeyed orders and looked steadily astern, or up into the
bronzed impassive face of my chief, who towered above me,
scanning with eagle eyes the sea ahead. The other boats were
coming flying along behind us, spreading wider apart as they
came, while in the bows of each stood the harpooner with his
right hand on his first iron, which lay ready, pointing over the
bow in a raised fork of wood called the "crutch."

All of a sudden, at a motion of the chief's hand, the peak of
our mainsail was dropped, and the boat swung up into the
wind, laying "hove to," almost stationary. The center-board
was lowered to stop her drifting to leeward, although I cannot
say it made much difference that ever I saw. *Now* what's the
matter, I thought, when to my amazement the chief addressing
me said, "Wonder why we've hauled up, don't ye?" "Yes, sir, I
do," said I. "Wall," said he, "the fish hev sounded, an' 'ef we
run over 'em, we've seen the last ov'em. So we wait awhile till
they rise agin, 'n then we'll prob'ly git thar' 'r thareabouts
before they sound agin." With this explanation I had to be
content, although if it be no clearer to my readers than it then
was to me, I shall have to explain myself more fully later on.
Silently we lay, rocking lazily upon the gentle swell, no other
word being spoken by anyone. At last Louis, the harpooner,

gently breathed "blo-o-o-w"; and there, sure enough, not half a mile away on the lee beam, was a little bushy cloud of steam apparently rising from the sea. At almost the same time as we kept away all the other boats did likewise, and just then, catching sight of the ship, the reason for this apparently concerted action was explained. At the main-mast head of the ship was a square blue flag, and the ensign at the peak was being dipped. These were signals well understood and promptly acted upon by those in charge of the boats, who were thus guided from a point of view at least one hundred feet above the sea.

"Stand up, Louey," the mate murmured softly. I only just stopped myself in time from turning my head to see why the order was given. Suddenly there was a bump, at the same moment the mate yelled, "Give't to him, Louey, give't to him!" and to me, "Haul that main-sheet, naow haul, why don't ye?" I hauled it flat aft, and the boat shot up into the wind, rubbing sides as she did so with what to my troubled sight seemed an enormous mass of black india-rubber floating. As we *crawled* up into the wind, the whale went into convulsions befitting his size and energy. He raised a gigantic tail on high, threshing the water with deafening blows, rolling at the same time from side to side until the surrounding sea was white with froth. I felt in an agony lest we should be crushed under one of those fearful strokes, for Mr. Count appeared to be oblivious of possible danger, although we seemed to be now drifting back on to the writhing leviathan. In the agitated condition of the sea, it was a task of no ordinary difficulty to unship the tall mast, which was of course the first thing to be done. After a desperate struggle, and a narrow escape from falling overboard of one of the men, we got the long "stick," with the sail bundled around it, down and "fleeted" aft, where it was secured by the simple means of sticking the "heel" under the after thwart, two-thirds of the mast extending out over the stern. Meanwhile, we had certainly been in a position of the greatest danger, our immunity from damage being unquestionably due to anything but precaution taken to avoid it.

By the time the oars were handled, and the mate had exchanged places with the harpooner, our friend the enemy had "sounded," that is, he had gone below for a change of scene, marveling no doubt what strange thing had befallen him. Agreeably to the accounts which I, like most boys, had read of the whale fishery, I looked for the rushing of the line round the loggerhead (a stout wooden post built into the boat aft), to raise a cloud of smoke with occasional bursts of flame; so as it began to slowly surge round the post, I timidly asked the harpooner whether I should throw any water on it. "Wot for?" growled he, as he took a couple more turns with it. Not knowing "what for," and hardly liking to quote my authorities here, I said no more, but waited events. "Hold him up, Louey, hold him up, cain't ye?" shouted the mate, and to my horror, down went the nose of the boat almost under water, while at the mate's order everybody scrambled aft into the elevated stern sheets.

The line sang quite a tune as it was grudgingly allowed to surge round the loggerhead, filling one with admiration at the strength shown by such a small rope. This sort of thing went on for about twenty minutes, in which time we quite emptied the large tub and began on the small one. As there was nothing whatever for us to do while this was going on, I had ample leisure for observing the little game that was being played about a quarter of a mile away. Mr. Cruce, the second mate, had got a whale and was doing his best to kill it; but he was severely handicapped by his crew, or rather had been, for two of them were now temporarily incapable of either good or harm. They had gone quite "batchy" with fright, requiring a not too gentle application of the tiller to their heads in order to keep them quiet. The remedy, if rough, was effectual, for "the subsequent proceedings interested them no more." Consequently his maneuvers were not so well or rapidly executed as he, doubtless, could have wished, although his energy in lancing that whale was something to admire and remember. Hatless, his shirt tail out of the waist of his trousers streaming behind him like a banner, he lunged and thrust at the whale alongside of him, as if possessed of a destroying devil, while his half articulate yells of rage and blasphemy were audible even to us.

Suddenly our boat fell backward from her "slantindicular" position with a jerk, and the mate immediately shouted, "Haul line, there! look lively, now! you—so on, etcetera, etcetera" (he seemed to invent new epithets on every occasion). The line came in hand over hand, and was coiled in a wide heap in the stern sheets, for silky as it was, it could not be expected in its wet state to lie very close. As it came flying in the mate kept a close gaze upon the water immediately beneath us, apparently for the first glimpse of our antagonist. When the whale broke water, however, he was some distance off, and apparently as quiet as a lamb. Now, had Mr. Count been a prudent or less ambitious man, our task would doubtless have been an easy one, or comparatively so; but, being a little over-grasping, he got us all into serious trouble. We were hauling up to our whale in order to lance it, and the mate was standing, lance in hand, only waiting to get near enough, when up comes a large whale right alongside of our boat, so close, indeed, that I might have poked my finger in his little eye, if I had chosen. The sight of that whale at liberty, and calmly taking stock of us like that, was too much for the mate. He lifted his lance and hurled it at the visitor, in whose broad flank it sank, like a knife into butter, right up to the pole-hitches. The recipient disappeared like a flash, but before one had time to think, there was an awful crash beneath us, and the mate shot up into the air like a bomb from a mortar. He came down in a sitting posture on the mast-thwart; but as he fell, the whole framework of the boat collapsed like a derelict umbrella. Louis quietly chopped the line and severed our connection with the other whale, while in accordance with our instructions we drew each man his oar across the boat and lashed it firmly down with a piece of line spliced to each thwart for the purpose. This simple operation took but a minute, but before it was completed we were all up to our necks in the sea. Still in the boat, it is true, and therefore not in such danger of drowning as if we were quite adrift; but, considering that the boat was reduced to a mere bundle of loose planks, I, at any rate, was none too comfortable. Now, had he known it, was the whale's golden opportunity; but he, poor wretch, had had quite enough of our company, and cleared off without any delay, wondering, no doubt, what fortunate accident had rid him of our very unpleasant attentions.

I was assured that we were all as safe as if we were on board the ship, to which I answered nothing; but, like Jack's parrot, I did some powerful thinking. Every little wave that came along swept clean over our heads, sometimes coming so suddenly as to cut a breath in half. If the wind should increase— but no—I wouldn't face the possibility of such a disagreeable thing. I was cool enough now in a double sense, for although we were in the tropics, we soon got thoroughly chilled.

By the position of the sun it must have been between ten a.m. and noon, and we, of the crew, had eaten nothing since the previous day at supper, when, as usual, the meal was very light. Therefore, I suppose we felt the chill sooner than the better-nourished mate and harpooner, who looked rather scornfully at our blue faces and chattering teeth.

In spite of all assurances to the contrary, I have not the least doubt in my own mind that a very little longer would have relieved us of *all* our burdens finally. Because the heave of the sea had so loosened the shattered planks upon which we stood that they were on the verge of falling all asunder. Had they done so we must have drowned, for we were cramped and stiff with cold and our constrained position. However, unknown to us, a bright look-out upon our movements had been kept from the crow's-nest the whole time. We should have been relieved long before, but that the whale killed by the second mate was being secured, and another boat, the fourth mate's being picked up, having a hole in her bilge you could put your head through. With all these hindrances, especially securing the whale, we were fortunate to be rescued as soon as we were, since it is well known that whales are of much higher commercial value than men.

However, help came at last, and we were hauled alongside. Long exposure had weakened us to such an extent that it was necessary to hoist us on board, especially the mate, whose "sudden stop," when he returned to us after his little aerial excursion, had shaken his sturdy frame considerably, a state of body which the subsequent soaking had by no means improved. In my innocence I imagined that we should be commiserated for our misfortunes by Captain Slocum, and certainly be relieved from further duties until we were a little recovered from the rough treatment we had just undergone. But I never made a greater mistake. The skipper cursed us all (except the mate, whose sole fault the accident undoubtedly was) with a fluency and vigor that was, to put it mildly, discouraging. Moreover, we were informed that he "wouldn't have no adjective skulking"; we must "turn to" and do something after wasting the ship's time and property in such a blank manner. There was a limit, however, to our obedience, so although we could not move at all for awhile, his threats were not proceeded with farther than theory.

A couple of slings were passed around the boat, by means of which she was carefully hoisted on board, a mere dilapidated bundle of sticks and raffle of gear. She was at once removed aft out of the way, the business of cutting in the whale claiming precedence over everything else just then. The preliminary proceedings consisted of rigging the "cutting stage." This was composed of two stout planks a foot wide and ten feet long, the inner ends of which were suspended by strong ropes over the ship's side about four feet from the water, while the outer extremities were upheld by tackles from the main rigging, and a small crane abreast the try-works.

These planks were about thirty feet apart, their two outer ends being connected by a massive plank which was securely bolted to them. A handrail about as high as a man's waist, supported by light iron stanchions, ran the full length of this plank on the side nearest the ship, the whole fabric forming an admirable standing-place from whence the officers might, standing in comparative comfort, cut and carve at the great mass below to their heart's content.

So far the prize had been simply held alongside by the whale-line, which at death had been "rove" through a hole cut in the solid gristle of the tail; but now it became necessary to secure the carcass to the ship in some more permanent fashion. Therefore, a massive chain like a small ship's cable was brought forward, and in a very ingenious way, by means of a tiny buoy and a hand-lead, passed round the body, one end brought through a ring in the other, and hauled upon until it fitted tight round the "small" part of the whale next the broad spread of the tail. The free end of the fluke-chain was then passed in through a mooring-pipe forward, firmly secured to a massive bitt at the heel of the bowsprit (the fluke-chain-bitt), and all was ready.

In an Open Boat

SIR ERNEST SHACKLETON

One of the most famous open boat journeys in all of literature was made by Sir Ernest Shackleton after his ship, the Endurance, *in an attempt to reach the South Pole, was torn to bits by ice on the Weddell Sea.*

For a while his party was desperate, as they were marooned on Elephant Island with little food and wounded crew. They decided to gamble and a group of them set sail for South Georgia over 800 miles away in an open boat, the James Caird, *a twenty-foot ordinary ship's whaler. Shackleton has told the story of this Subantarctic Ocean voyage with chilling immediacy.*

*T*he tale of the next sixteen days is one of supreme strife amid heaving waters. The Subantarctic Ocean lived up to its evil winter reputation. I decided to run north for at least two days while the wind held and so get into warmer weather before turning to the east and laying a course for South Georgia. We took two-hourly spells at the tiller. The men who were not on watch crawled into the sodden sleeping bags and tried to forget their troubles for a period; but there was no comfort in the boat. The bags and cases seemed to be alive in the unfailing knack of presenting their most uncomfortable angles to our rest-seeking bodies. A man might imagine for a moment that he had found a position of ease, but always discovered quickly that some unyielding point was impinging on muscle or bone. The first night aboard the boat was one of acute discomfort for us all, and we were heartily glad when the dawn came and we could set about the preparation of a hot breakfast.

This record of the voyage to South Georgia is based upon

scanty notes made day by day. The notes dealt usually with the bare facts of distances, positions, and weather, but our memories retained the incidents of the passing days in a period never to be forgotten. By running north for the first two days I hoped to get warmer weather and also to avoid lines of pack that might be extending beyond the main body. We needed all the advantage that we could obtain from the higher latitude for sailing on the great circle, but we had to be cautious regarding possible ice streams. Cramped in our narrow quarters and continually wet by the spray, we suffered severely from cold throughout the journey. We fought the seas and the winds and at the same time had a daily struggle to keep ourselves alive. At times we were in dire peril. Generally we were upheld by the knowledge that we were making progress toward the land where we would be, but there were days and nights when we lay hove to, drifting across the storm-whitened seas and watching, with eyes interested rather than apprehensive, the uprearing masses of water, flung to and fro by Nature in the pride of her strength. Deep seemed the valleys when we lay between the reeling seas. High were the hills when we perched momentarily on the tops of giant combers. Nearly always there were gales. So small was our boat and so great were the seas that often our sail flapped idly in the calm between the crests of two waves. Then we would climb the next slope and catch the full fury of the gale where the wool-like whiteness of the breaking water surged around us. We had our moments of laughter—rare, it is true, but hearty enough. Even when cracked lips and swollen mouths checked the outward and visible signs of amusement we could see a joke of the primitive kind. Man's sense of humor is always most easily stirred by the petty misfortunes of his neighbors, and I shall never forget Worsley's efforts on one occasion to place the hot aluminum stand on top of the Primus stove after it had fallen off in an extra heavy roll. With his frostbitten fingers he picked it up, dropped it, picked it up again, and toyed with it gingerly as though it were some fragile article of lady's wear. We laughed, or rather gurgled with laughter.

The wind came up strong and worked into a gale from the northwest on the third day out. We stood away to the east. The increasing seas discovered the weaknesses of our decking.

The continuous blows shifted to box lids and sledge runners so that the canvas sagged down and accumulated water. Then icy trickles, distinct from the driving sprays, poured fore and aft into the boat. The nails that the carpenter had extracted from cases at Elephant Island and used to fasten down the battens were too short to make firm the decking. We did what we could to secure it, but our means were very limited, and the water continued to enter the boat at a dozen points. Much bailing was necessary, and nothing that we could do prevented our gear from becoming sodden. The searching runnels from the canvas were really more unpleasant than the sudden definite douches of the sprays. Lying under the thwarts during watches below, we tried vainly to avoid them. There were no dry places in the boat, and at last we simply covered our heads with our Burberrys and endured the all-pervading water. The bailing was work for the watch. Real rest we had none. The perpetual motion of the boat made repose impossible; we were cold, sore, and anxious. We moved on hands and knees in the semidarkness of the day under the decking. The darkness was complete by 6 P.M., and not until 7 A.M. of the following day could we see one another under the thwarts. We had a few scraps of candle, and they were preserved carefully in order that we might have light at mealtimes. There was one fairly dry spot in the boat, under the solid original decking at the bows, and we managed to protect some of our biscuit from the salt water; but I do not think any of us got the taste of salt out of our mouths during the voyage.

The difficulty of movement in the boat would have had its humorous side if it had not involved us in so many aches and pains. We had to crawl under the thwarts in order to move along the boat, and our knees suffered considerably. When a watch turned out it was necessary for me to direct each man by name when and where to move, since if all hands had crawled about at the same time the result would have been dire confusion and many bruises. Then there was the trim of the boat to be considered. The order of the watch was four hours on and four hours off, three men to the watch. One man had the tiller ropes, the second man attended to the sail, and the third bailed for all he was worth. Sometimes when the water in the boat had been reduced to reasonable proportions, our pump could be used. This pump, which Hurley had made from the Flinders bar case of our ship's standard compass, was quite effective, though its capacity was not large. The man who was attending the sail could pump into the big outer cooker, which was lifted and emptied overboard when filled. We had a device by which the water could go direct from the pump into the sea through a hole in the gunwale, but this hole had to be blocked at an early stage of the voyage, since we found that it admitted water when the boat rolled.

While a new watch was shivering in the wind and spray, the men who had been relieved groped hurriedly among the soaked sleeping bags and tried to steal a little of the warmth created by the last occupants; but it was not always possible for us to find even this comfort when we went off watch. The boulders that we had taken aboard for ballast had to be shifted continually in order to trim the boat and give access of the pump, which became choked with hairs from the moulting sleeping bags and finnesko. The four reindeer-skin sleeping bags shed their hair freely owing to the continuous wetting, and soon became quite bald in appearance. The moving of the boulders was weary and painful work. We came to know every one of the stones by sight and touch, and I have vivid memories of their angular peculiarities even today. They might have been of considerable interest as geological specimens to a scientific man under happier conditions. As ballast they were useful. As weights to be moved about in cramped quarters they were simply appalling. They spared no portion of our poor bodies. Another of our troubles, worth mention here, was the chafing of our legs by our wet clothes, which had not been changed now for seven months. The insides of our thighs were rubbed raw, and the one tube of Hazeline cream in our medicine chest did not go far in alleviating our pain, which was increased by the bite of the salt water. We thought at the time that we never slept. The fact was that we would doze off uncomfortably, to be aroused quickly by some new ache or another call to effort. My own share of the general unpleasantness was accentuated by a finely developed bout of sciatica. I had become possessor of this originally on the floe several months earlier.

Our meals were regular in spite of the gales. Attention to this point was essential, since the conditions of the voyage made increasing calls upon our vitality. Breakfast, at 8 A.M., consisted of a pannikin of hot hoosh made from Bovril sledging ration, two biscuits, and some lumps of sugar. Lunch came at 1 P.M., and comprised Bovril sledging ration, eaten raw, and a pannikin of hot milk for each man. Tea, at 5 P.M., had the same menu. Then during the night we had a hot drink, generally of milk. The meals were the bright beacons in those cold and stormy days. The glow of warmth and comfort produced by the food and drink made optimists of us all. We had two tins of Virol, which we were keeping for an emergency; but, finding ourselves in need of an oil lamp to eke out our supply of candles, we emptied one of the tins in the manner that most appealed to us, and fitted it with a wick made by shredding a bit of canvas. When this lamp was filled with oil it gave a certain amount of light, though it was easily blown out, and was of great assistance to us at night. We were fairly well off as regarded fuel, since we had 6½ gallons of petroleum.

A severe southwesterly gale on the fourth day out forced us to heave to. I would have liked to have run before the wind, but the sea was very high and the *James Caird* was in danger of broaching to and swamping. The delay was vexatious, since up to that time we had been making sixty or seventy miles a day; good going with our limited sail area. We hove to under double-reefed mainsail and our little jigger, and waited for the gale to blow itself out. During that afternoon we saw bits of wreckage, the remains probably of some unfortunate vessel that had failed to weather the strong gales south of Cape Horn. The weather conditions did not improve, and on the fifth day out the gale was so fierce that we were compelled to take in the double-reefed mainsail and hoist our small jib instead. We put out a sea anchor to keep the *James Caird's* head up to the sea. This anchor consisted of a triangular canvas bag fastened to the end of the painter and allowed to stream out from the bows. The boat was high enough to catch the wind, and, as she drifted to leeward, the drag of the anchor kept her head to windward. Thus our boat took most of the seas more or less end on. Even then the crests of the waves often would curl right over us and we shipped a great deal of water, which necessitated unceasing bailing and pumping. Looking out abeam, we would see a hollow like a tunnel formed as the crest of a big wave toppled over onto the swelling body of water. A thousand times it appeared as though the *James Caird* must be engulfed; but the boat lived. The southwesterly gale had its birthplace above the Antarctic Continent, and its freezing breath lowered the temperature far toward zero. The sprays froze upon the boat and gave bows, sides, and decking a heavy coat of mail. This accumulation of ice reduced the buoyancy of the boat, and to that extent was an added peril; but it possessed a notable advantage from one point of view. The water ceased to drop and trickle from the canvas, and the spray came in solely at the well in the after part of the boat. We could not allow the load of ice to grow beyond a certain point, and in turns we crawled about the decking forward, chipping and picking at it with the available tools.

When daylight came on the morning of the sixth day out we saw and felt that the *James Caird* had lost her resiliency. She was not rising to the oncoming seas. The weight of the ice that had formed in her and upon her during the night was having its effect, and she was becoming more like a log than a boat. The situation called for immediate action. We first broke away the spare oars, which were encased in ice and frozen to the sides of the boat, and threw them overboard. We retained two oars for use when we got inshore. Two of the fur sleeping bags went over the side; they were thoroughly wet, weighing probably forty pounds each, and they had frozen stiff during the night. Three men constituted the watch below, and when a man went down it was better to turn into the wet bag just vacated by another man than to thaw out a frozen bag with the heat of his unfortunate body. We now had four bags, three in use and one for emergency use in case a member of the party should break down permanently. The reduction of weight relieved the boat to some extent, and vigorous chipping and scraping did more. We had to be very careful not to put ax or knife through the frozen canvas of the decking as we crawled over it, but gradually we got rid of a lot of ice. The *James Caird* lifted to the endless waves as though she lived again.

About 11 A.M. the boat suddenly fell off into the trough of the sea. The painter had parted and the sea anchor had gone. This was serious. The *James Caird* went away to leeward, and we had no chance at all of recovering the anchor and our valuable rope, which had been our only means of keeping the boat's head up to the seas without the risk of hoisting sail in a gale. Now we had to set the sail and trust to its holding. When the *James Caird* rolled heavily in the trough, we beat the frozen canvas until the bulk of the ice had cracked off it and then hoisted it. The frozen gear worked protestingly, but after a struggle our little craft came up to the wind again, and we breathed more freely. Skin frostbites were troubling us, and we had developed large blisters on our fingers and hands. I shall always carry the scar of one of these frostbites on my left hand, which became badly inflamed after the skin had burst and the cold had bitten deeply.

We held the boat up to the gale during that day, enduring as best we could discomforts that amounted to pain. The boat tossed interminably on the big waves under gray, threatening skies. Our thoughts did not embrace much more than the necessities of the hour. Every surge of the sea was an enemy to be watched and circumvented. We ate our scanty meals, treated our frostbites, and hoped for the improved conditions that the morrow might bring. Night fell early, and in the lagging hours of darkness we were cheered by a change for the better in the weather. The wind dropped, the snow squalls became less frequent, and the sea moderated. When the morning of the seventh day dawned there was not much wind. We shook the reef out of the sail and laid our course once more for South Georgia. The sun came out bright and clear, and presently Worsley got a snap for longitude. We hoped that the sky would remain clear until noon, so that we could get the latitude. We had been six days out without an observation, and our dead reckoning naturally was uncertain. The boat must have presented a strange appearance that morning. All hands basked in the sun. We hung our sleeping bags to the mast and spread our socks and other gear all over the deck. Some of the ice had melted off the *James Caird* in the early morning after the gale began to slacken, and dry patches were appearing in the decking. Porpoises came blowing round the boat, and Cape pigeons wheeled and swooped within a few feet of us. These little black-and-white birds have an air of friendliness that is not possessed by the great circling albatross. They had looked gray against the swaying sea during the storm as they darted about over our heads and uttered their plaintive cries. The albatrosses, of the black or sooty variety, had watched with hard, bright eyes, and seemed to have a quite impersonal interest in our struggle to keep afloat amid the battering seas. In addition to Cape pigeons an occasional stormy petrel flashed overhead. Then there was a small bird, unknown to me, that appeared always to be in a fussy, bustling state, quite out of keeping with the surroundings. It irritated me. It had practically no tail, and it flitted about vaguely as though in search of the lost member. I used to find myself wishing it would find its tail and have done with the silly fluttering.

We reveled in the warmth of the sun that day. Life was not so bad, after all. We felt we were well on our way. Our gear was drying, and we could have a hot meal in comparative comfort. The swell was still heavy, but it was not breaking and the boat rode easily. At noon Worsley balanced himself on the gunwale and clung with one hand to the stay of the mainmast while he got a snap of the sun. The result was more than encouraging. We had done over 380 miles and were getting on for halfway to South Georgia. It looked as though we were going to get through.

The wind freshened to a good stiff breeze during the afternoon, and the *James Caird* made satisfactory progress. I had not realized until the sunlight came how small our boat really was. There was some influence in the light and warmth, some hint of happier days, that made us revive memories of other voyages, when we had stout decks beneath our feet, unlimited food at our command, and pleasant cabins for our ease. Now we clung to a battered little boat, "alone, alone, all, all alone, alone on a wide, wide sea." So low in the water were we that each succeeding swell cut off our view of the skyline. We were a tiny speck in the vast vista of the sea—the ocean that is open to all and merciful to none, that threatens even when it seems to yield, and that is pitiless always to weakness. For a moment the consciousness of the forces arrayed against us would be almost overwhelming. Then hope and confidence would rise again as our boat rose to a wave and tossed aside the crest in a sparkling shower like the play of prismatic colors at the foot of a waterfall. My double-barreled gun and some cartridges had been stowed aboard the boat as an emergency precaution against a shortage of food, but we were not disposed to destroy our little neighbors, the Cape pigeons, even for the sake of fresh meat. We might have shot an albatross, but the wandering king of the ocean aroused in us something of the feeling that inspired, too late, the Ancient Mariner. So the gun remained among the stores and sleeping bags in the narrow quarters beneath our leaking deck, and the birds followed us unmolested.

The eighth, ninth, and tenth days of the voyage had few features worthy of special note. The wind blew hard during those days, and the strain of navigating the boat was unceasing, but always we made some advance toward our goal. No bergs showed on our horizon, and we knew that we were clear of the ice fields. Each day brought its little round of troubles, but also compensation in the form of food and growing hope. We felt that we were going to succeed. The odds against us had been great, but we were winning through. We still suffered severely from the cold, for, though the temperature was rising, our vitality was declining owing to shortage of food, exposure, and the necessity of maintaining our cramped positions day and night. I found that it was now absolutely necessary to prepare hot milk for all hands during the night, in order to sustain life till dawn. This meant lighting the Primus lamp in the darkness and involved an increased drain on our small store of matches. It was the rule that one match must serve when the Primus was being lit. We had no lamp for the compass and during the early days of the voyage we would strike a match when the steersman wanted to see the course at night; but later the necessity for strict economy impressed itself upon us, and the practice of striking matches at night was stopped. We had one watertight tin of matches. I had stowed away in a pocket, in readiness for a sunny day, a lens from one of the telescopes, but this was of no use during the voyage. The sun seldom shone upon us. The glass of the compass got broken one night, and we contrived to mend it with adhesive tape from the medicine chest. One of the memories that comes to me from those days is of Crean singing at the tiller. He always sang while he was steering, and nobody ever discovered what the song was. It was devoid of tune and as monotonous as the chanting of a Buddhist monk at his prayers; yet somehow it was cheerful. In moments of inspiration Crean would attempt "The Wearing of the Green."

On the tenth night Worsley could not straighten his body after his spell at the tiller. He was thoroughly cramped, and we had to drag him beneath the decking and massage him before he could unbend himself and get into a sleeping bag. A hard northwesterly gale came up on the eleventh day (May 5) and shifted to the southwest in the late afternoon. The sky was overcast and occasional snow squalls added to the discomfort produced by a tremendous cross sea—the worst, I thought, that we had experienced. At midnight I was at the tiller and suddenly noticed a line of clear sky between the south and southwest. I called to the other men that the sky was clearing, and then a moment later I realized that what I had seen was not a rift in the clouds but the white crest of an enormous wave. During twenty-six years' experience of the ocean in all its moods I had not encountered a wave so gigantic. It was a mighty upheaval of the ocean, a thing quite apart from the big white-capped seas that had been our tireless enemies for many days. I shouted, "For God's sake, hold on! It's got us!" Then came a moment of suspense that seemed drawn out into hours. White surged the foam of the breaking sea around us. We felt our boat lifted and flung forward like a cork in breaking surf. We were in a seething chaos of tortured water; but somehow the boat lived through it, half full of water, sagging to the dead weight and shuddering under the blow. We bailed with the energy of men fighting for life, flinging the water over the sides with every receptacle that came to our hands, and after ten minutes of uncertainty we felt the boat renew her life beneath us. She floated again and ceased to lurch drunkenly as though dazed by the attack of the sea. Earnestly we hoped that never again would we encounter such a wave.

The conditions in the boat, uncomfortable before, had been made worse by the deluge of water. All our gear was thoroughly wet again. Our cooking stove had been floating about in the bottom of the boat, and portions of our last hoosh seemed to have permeated everything. Not until 3 A.M., when we were all chilled almost to the limit of endurance, did we manage to get the stove alight and make ourselves hot drinks. The carpenter was suffering particularly, but he showed grit and spirit. Vincent had for the past week ceased to be an active member of the crew, and I could not easily account for his collapse. Physically he was one of the strongest men in the boat. He was a young man, he had served on North Sea trawlers, and he should have been able to bear hardships better than McCarthy, who, not so strong, was always happy.

The weather was better on the following day (May 6), and we got a glimpse of the sun. Worsley's observation showed that we were not more than a hundred miles from the northwest corner of South Georgia. Two more days with a favorable wind and we would sight the promised land. I hoped that there would be no delay, for our supply of water was running very low. The hot drink at night was essential, but I decided that the daily allowance of water must be cut down to half a pint per man. The lumps of ice we had taken aboard had gone long ago. We were dependent upon the water we had brought from Elephant Island, and our thirst was increased by the fact that we were now using the brackish water in the beaker that had been slightly stove in in the surf when the boat was being loaded. Some sea water had entered at that time.

Thirst took possession of us. I dared not permit the allowance of water to be increased since an unfavorable wind might drive us away from the island and lengthen our voyage by many days. Lack of water is always the most severe privation that men can be condemned to endure, and we found, as during our earlier boat voyage, that the salt water in our clothing and the salt spray that lashed our faces made our thirst grow quickly to a burning pain. I had to be very firm in refusing to allow anyone to anticipate the morrow's allowance, which I was sometimes begged to do. We did the necessary work dully and hoped for the land. I had altered the course to the east so as to make sure of our striking the island, which would have been impossible to regain if we had run past the northern end. The course was laid on our scrap of chart for a point some thirty miles down the coast. That day and the following day passed for us in a sort of nightmare. Our mouths were dry and our tongues were swollen. The wind was still strong and heavy sea forced us to navigate carefully, but any thought of our peril from the waves was buried beneath the consciousness of our raging thirst. The bright moments were those when we each received our one mug of hot milk during the long, bitter watches of the night. Things were bad for us in those days, but the end was coming. The morning of May 8 broke thick and stormy, with squalls from the northwest. We searched the waters ahead for a sign of land, and though we could see nothing more than had met our eyes for many days, we were cheered by a sense that the goal was near at hand. About ten o'clock that morning we passed a little bit of kelp, a glad signal of the proximity of land. An hour later we saw two shags sitting on a big mass of kelp, and knew then that we must be within ten or fifteen miles of the shore. These birds are as sure an indication of the proximity of land as a lighthouse is, for they never venture far to sea. We gazed ahead with increasing eagerness, and at 12:30 P.M., through a rift in the clouds, McCarthy caught a glimpse of the black cliffs of South Georgia, just fourteen days after our departure from Elephant Island. It was a glad moment. Thirst-ridden, chilled, and weak as we were, happiness irradiated us. The job was nearly done.

We stood in toward the shore to look for a landing place, and presently we could see the green tussock grass on the ledges above the surf-beaten rocks. Ahead of us and to the south, blind rollers showed the presence of uncharted reefs along the coast. Here and there the hungry rocks were close to the surface, and over them the great waves broke, swirling viciously and spouting thirty and forty feet into the air. The rocky coast appeared to descend sheer to the sea. Our need of water and rest was well-nigh desperate, but to have attempted a landing at that time would have been suicidal. Night was drawing near, and the weather indications were not favorable. There was nothing for it but to haul off till the following morning, so we stood away on the starboard tack until we had made what appeared to be a safe offing. Then we hove to in the high westerly swell. The hours passed slowly as we awaited the dawn, which would herald, we fondly hoped, the last stage of our journey. Our thirst was a torment and we could scarcely touch our food; the cold seemed to strike right through our weakened bodies. At 5 A.M. the wind shifted to the northwest and quickly increased to one of the worst hurricanes any of us had ever experienced. A great cross sea was running, and the wind simply shrieked as it tore the tops off the waves and converted the whole seascape into a haze of driving spray. Down into valleys, up to tossing heights, straining until her seams opened, swung our little boat, brave still but laboring heavily. We knew that the wind and set of the sea was driving us ashore, but we could do nothing. The dawn showed us a storm-torn ocean, and the morning passed without bringing us a sight of the land, but at 1 p.m., through a rift in the flying mists, we got a glimpse of the huge crags of the island and realized that our position had become desperate. We were on a dead lee shore, and we could gauge our approach to the unseen cliffs by the roar of the breakers against the sheer walls of rock. I ordered the double-reefed mainsail to be set in the hope that we might claw off, and this attempt increased the strain upon the boat. The *James Caird* was bumping heavily, and the water was pouring in everywhere. Our thirst was forgotten in the realization of our imminent danger, as we bailed unceasingly, and adjusted our weights from time to time; occasional glimpses showed that the shore was nearer. I knew that Annewkow Island lay to the south of us, but our small and badly marked chart showed uncertain reefs in the passage between the island and the mainland, and I dared not trust it, though as a last resort we could try to lie under the lee of the island. The afternoon wore away as we edged down the coast, with the thunder of the breakers in our ears. The approach of evening found us still some distance from Annewkow Island, and dimly in the twilight, we could see a snowcapped mountain looming above us. The chance of surviving the night, with the driving gale and the implacable sea forcing us onto the lee shore, seemed small. I think most of us had a feeling that the end was very near. Just after 6 p.m., in the dark, as the boat was in the yeasty backwash from the seas flung from this iron-bound coast, then, just when things looked their worst, they changed for the best. I have marveled often at the thin line that divides success from failure and the sudden turn that leads from apparently certain disaster to comparative safety. The wind suddenly shifted, and we were free once more to make an offing. Almost as soon as the gale eased, the pin that locked the mast to the thwart fell out. It must have been on the point of doing this throughout the hurricane, and if it had gone nothing could have saved us; the mast would have snapped like a carrot. Our backstays had carried away once before when iced up and were not too strongly fastened now. We were thankful indeed for the mercy that had held that pin in its place throughout the hurricane.

We stood off shore again, tired almost to the point of apathy. Our water had long been finished. The last was about a pint of hairy liquid, which we strained through a bit of gauze from the medicine chest. The pangs of thirst attacked us with redoubled intensity, and I felt that we must make a landing on the following day at almost any hazard. The night wore on. We were very tired. We longed for day. When at last the dawn came on the morning of May 10 there was practically no wind, but a high cross sea was running. We made slow progress toward the shore. About 8 A.M. the wind backed to the northwest and threatened another blow. We had sighted in the meantime a big indentation which I thought must be King Haakon Bay, and I decided that we must land there. We set the bows of the boat toward the bay and ran before the freshening gale. Soon we had angry reefs on either side. Great glaciers came down to the sea and offered no landing place. The sea spouted on the reefs and thundered against the shore. About noon we sighted a line of jagged reef, like blackened teeth, that seemed to bar the entrance to the bay. Inside, comparatively smooth water stretched eight or nine miles to the head of the bay. A gap in the reef appeared, and we made for it. But the fates had another rebuff for us. The wind shifted and blew from the east right out of the bay. We could see the way through the reef, but we could not approach it directly. That afternoon we bore up, tacking five times in the strong wind. The last tack enabled us to get through, and at last we were in the wide mouth of the bay. Dusk was approaching. A small cove, with a boulder-strewn beach guarded by a reef, made a break in the cliffs on the south side of the bay, and we turned in that direction. I stood in the bows directing the steering as we ran through the kelp and made the passage of the reef. The entrance was so narrow that we had to take in the oars, and the swell was piling itself right over the reef into the cove; but in a minute or two we were inside, and in the gathering darkness the *James Caird* ran in on a swell and touched the beach. I sprang ashore with the short painter and held on when the boat went out with the backward surge. When the *James Caird* came in again three of the men got ashore, and they held the painter while I climbed some rocks with another line. A slip on the wet rocks twenty feet up nearly closed my part of the story just at the moment when we were achieving safety. A jagged piece of rock held me and at the same time bruised me sorely. However, I made fast the line, and in a few minutes we were all safe on the beach, with the boat floating in the surging water just off the shore. We heard a gurgling sound that was sweet music in our ears, and, peering around, found a stream of fresh water almost at our feet. A moment later we were down on our knees drinking the pure, ice-cold water in long drafts that put new life into us. It was a splendid moment.

Typhoon

HANSON W. BALDWIN

Some of the greatest writing about the ocean has been done by men who have observed war at sea. In the glorious tradition of fighting words, Hanson W. Baldwin recounts here the story of a storm that lost a battle. This was the storm that was to be immortalized later in Herman Wouk's The Caine Mutiny.

It was a disaster that led to many changes in seagoing vessels: new ship designs emerged; new pumps were established for fuel and ballast; new protections were made against floodwater; finally, the system of hurricane hunters was developed. As Baldwin says, it put the emphasis in the Navy back where it should be—on seamanship.

*I*t was the greatest fleet that had ever sailed the seas, and it was fresh from its greatest triumph. But the hand of God was laid upon it and a great wind blew, and it was scattered and broken upon the ocean. The inexorable law of storms— the Bible of all seamen since the days of astrolabe and sail— was neglected, and the Third Fleet, proud in its might, paid the penalty—more men lost, more ships sunk and damaged than in many of the engagements of the Pacific War.

Storms have intervened before in history, and Nature has adjudicated the small affairs of Man. A great wind, as well as Drake of Devon, saved England from the Spanish Armada. Dampier the Navigator noted in his log book in 1687—the first Westerner to record the phenomenon—the violent ravages of a typhoon, which he called a "tuffoon." And at Apia harbor, Samoa, in 1889, wind and sea with catholic impartiality wrecked the men-of-war of two nations. But in five hundred years of naval history there had been no wind the like of that which struck the Third Fleet, Admiral William F. Halsey, commanding, and humbled it in its hour of victory, on December 17 and 18, 1944.

In mid-December the Battle for Leyte Gulf was history; the Japanese Empire only a few weeks before had been dealt a fatal blow. The invasion of Mindoro started on December 15, and the Third Fleet was weary from three days of wide-ranging strikes against the island of Luzon in the Philippines. As the fleet retired to the east to refuel, the beginning of the end was in sight; enemy land-based air power in the Philippines had been neutralized or destroyed, and MacArthur's "I have returned" was already loud upon the lips of the world.

Admiral Halsey, flying his flag in the battleship *New Jersey*, was tired after 36,000 miles of steaming and ninety-five days of action (eighty-five of them at sea), and was trying to relax from the "constant threat of air attack" and the "burden of responsibility."

". . . it took me a long time to unwind," he records in his book, *Admiral Halsey's Story*. "Other men may have done it with the help of noble literature; I used to read *The Police Gazette*."

New Jersey dispatched the refueling rendezvous—14 degrees, 50 minutes north, 129 degrees, 57 minutes east, about five hundred miles east of Luzon—to the oilers and to Task Force 38—the carriers—Vice Admiral John S. ("Slew") McCain, commanding. Halsey started his *Police Gazette*, his deck tennis, and his movies—trying to relax. But it was not to be. On the night of December 16–17 the sea made up, and there was the queasiness of impending storm. Rear Admiral ("Mick") Carney, Chief of Staff to Halsey, noted a "tropical disturbance of some sort to the east of us," but nobody thought the storm would curve across the fleet's course. The enemy was the Japanese—not the cruel sea; this great fleet, unmatched in history, could disdain the elements.

Sunday, December 17 This day dawns dark and brooding, the sea choppy, the wind brisk but fickle, the ships fretful. Across hundreds of miles of ocean, the Third Fleet steams—the masts, the flight decks bowing and dipping, swinging in wide arcs across the horizon. Here, in all its panoply and power, is the fleet that has humbled Japan—a score of carriers, big and little; eight "battlewagons"; numerous cruisers; dozens of destroyers—spread wide in three great task groups across the ocean. The refueling rendezvous is changed three times in search of calmer seas; Third Fleet makes contact with the twenty-four big fleet oilers and their escort of Task Group 30.8, and despite the querulous swells refueling starts. The rigorous demands of combat, the support needed by those "G.I.'s" back on Mindoro permit no concession to Nature.

The destroyers—the little ships that dance in any sea, the ships with empty maws from their days of high-speed steaming —come alongside the tankers and the battleships in the morning. But the ocean will have none of it; this is a job for superseamen. There's nothing but a mad swatch of white water between oilers and "tin cans" as the hungry little ships try to gulp their food through hoses leading from the oilers' tanks. Some get aboard hundreds of gallons before the lines break and the ships swing wildly apart, but most part line after line as boatswains curse and the water boils aboard the well decks and the steel plates run with oil. Destroyer *Hull,* a name soon to be on the lips of all the fleet, from the ASW (anti-submarine warfare) group of a fueling unit, puts forty bags of mail aboard battleship *South Dakota* with "much difficulty," but mail for thirty other ships of the fleet is undelivered; the sea is wild.

"*1107.* Spence *alongside* New Jersey, *starboard side, to fuel.*

1128. Both for'd and after hoses to Spence *parted.*"

U.S.S. *Buchanan* tries to transfer pilots by a swaying boatswain's chair to CVE-18—escort carrier *Altamaha*—but the sea's too rough. *San Jacinto,* light carrier, gets aboard 172,000 gallons from tanker *Monongahela* before the log noted at 1331 "discontinued fueling because of adverse weather."

Wind—Force 26 knots. Barometer, 29.74. Temperature, 82. Visibility—5 miles. Sea—Force 4.

In early afternoon Com. Third Fleet orders fueling suspended, sets course to northwest, then later to southwest to escape storm center not clearly located. The barometer drops, the winds moan; there's the uneasy leaden feeling of a hand across the heavens, but the Third Fleet steams on in cruising formation—the destroyers screening the "big boys," the AA guns alert, the sonars "pinging," the radars . . . searching, searching. . . .

Monday, December 18 Third Fleet moves through troubled waters, the compulsion of combat dictating its movements. But the storm, with the catholic impartiality of Nature, sweeps across the war, puts in puny framework the efforts of Man. The night is haggard; aboard the destroyers the sideboards are around the wardroom tables, the sleepers are braced in their bunks, but the sharp motion of the aroused ocean shakes and pounds the ships, makes sleep fitful and despairing. Barometers drop steadily, rain squalls and flung spray and spume reduce visibility; station-keeping is difficult—at times almost impossible. The seas make up; the winds beat and buffet; the fleet is battened down.

"But no estimates of the storm center were in agreement"; and not until dawn did Third Fleet realize it lay in the path of the grand-daddy of all typhoons. And units of Task Group 30.8—the fleet oilers, and their escorting destroyers and escort carriers—somewhat to the north and east of the main body, are directly athwart the "eye" of the approaching typhoon. Fleet course is ordered changed to 180 degrees—due south— but it is too late; the fury is upon them.

0400 to 0800 *The Morning Watch*

Nantahala (Oiler)—". . . this ship pitching deeply and heavily."

Altamaha (Escort Carrier)—". . . heavy weather making station-keeping only approximate."

Aboard *Dewey,* DD (destroyer) 349, the officer-of-the-deck reports to the captain that the barometer has dropped seven points between 7 and 8 A.M. Seas are so violent, winds so strong, *Dewey* finds it "impossible," when fleet course is changed, to countermarch to new station.

Morning fuel reports from many of the destroyers are ominous. All were low the day before; some had de-ballasted (pumped salt water out of their tanks) to prepare to refuel. They are riding light and high; stability is reduced. And their crews know that topside weight has been greatly increased since commissioning by more AA guns, fire control gear, and radar. *Yarnall* reports 20 per cent of fuel remaining; *Wedder-burn*, 15 per cent; *Maddox, Hickox* and *Spence* 10 to 15 per cent.

0800 to 1200 *The Forenoon Watch*

The forenoon watch opens, in the words of an old seagoing term, "with hell to pay and no pitch hot."

The moaning violence of the wind is terrible; it shrieks and whinnies, roars and shudders, beats and clutches. The sea is convulsed, diabolic; the ships are laboring deeply—laid over by the wind, rolling rigidly through tremendous arcs with sharp violent jerks, pounding and pitching, buried deep beneath tons of water, rising heavily streaming foam and salt from gunnels and hawse pipes. Violent rain gusts, spindrift blown with the sting of hail, a rack of scud blot out visibility. Third Fleet is scattered; few ships see others; only on the radar scopes do the pips of light loom up to show in wild confusion Man's panoply of power.

The deeply-laden oilers, the heavy battleships, the larger carriers, roll and plunge deeply and work violently but not dangerously through the towering seas, but for the escort carriers, the light carriers and the destroyers, the struggle is to live; the war now is against Nature, not the Japanese; no man in all the fleet had ever felt before the full fury of such a howling, demonic wind. Some of the fleet is in the "dangerous semicircle" of the typhoon where no seaman ought to be; a few ships—though rocked and tossed like chips—are on the fringes of the terrible vortex, but at least one task unit is directly in the center, where the funnel of wind and the boiling ocean leap to climax.

Ship after ship falls away into the terrible troughs and will not answer her helm.

At 0820 the destroyer *Dewey*—DD 349—loses bridge steering control; at 0825 the SG radar, short-circuited by the flying scud, is out of operation.

At 0845 escort carrier *Altamaha* records in her deck log: "Mobile crane on hangar deck tore loose from moorings and damaged three aircraft," and, a few minutes later: "Wind and sea approaching hurricane violence. Ship laboring heavily and rolling violently as much as twenty-five to thirty degrees on either side."

The barometer drops as no seaman there had ever seen it fall before; the wind is up.

Aboard U.S.S. *Cowpens,* an F6F5 airplane, triple-lashed on the flight deck, breaks loose on a 45-degree roll, and smashes into the catwalk, starting a fire. Men fight it, as the wind howls and the roll indicator registers 45 degrees with the small bubble of the ship's inclinometer (roll indicator) "two-blocked and off the scale." Men fight it, as a bomb-handling truck breaks free on the hangar deck and smashes the belly tank of a fighter. Men fight it as a wall of solid green water rips open —like a can opener—the steel roller curtains on the port side of the hangar deck. Men fight it as the anemometer, with one of its cups gone, registers a wind velocity of more than one hundred knots. Men fight it as the wind and sea pull out of its steel roots the forward port 20 mm. guns sponsor and leave it hanging, and tear loose the radar antenna screen from the foremast and fling it into the boiling sea. And men fight it as the motor whaleboat is carried away by a wall of water, as bombs break their battens in the magazine and skitter about the deck, as jeeps and tractors, a kerry crane, and seven planes are flung and blown off the flight deck into the writhing sea. But in the end it is the sea which extinguishes the fire as it was the sea which started it; the F6F5 breaks clear of the catwalk and falls into the tumult of water.

As the day wears on the log books run out of the language of nautical superlatives. Several ships record the barometer at a flat 28 inches, an awesome low; *Dewey* reads hers at 27.30—possibly the world's lowest recorded reading. Oiler *Nantahala,* with other ships of a fueling unit to the northeast of the main body near the storm center, records a wind velocity of 124 knots. The wind shifts rapidly in direction as the typhoon circles, blowing from north and south and east and west— backing and filling as do all circular storms—and increasing in intensity to Force 17, far beyond that ancient nautical measuring-stick of mariners—the Beaufort scale—which defines Force 12, its maximum—"that which no canvas could withstand"— as a "hurricane above 65 knots."

Third Fleet is scattered now, station-keeping impossible,

visibility five hundred yards to zero, only the radars—when operative—preventing collisions. Com. Third Fleet in *New Jersey*, his plan to refuel this day long since abandoned, his immediate commitment to MacArthur regretfully canceled, records in his war diary the reports of disaster:

0841. The Wasp *reported a life raft to her port, which appeared to have three persons on it.*

0907. The Independence *reported man overboard.*

0911. The Monterey *reported that, due to excessive roll, planes on her hangar deck had broken loose and caught fire.*

0942. The Kwajalein *reported she had lost steering control.*

1012. The Wisconsin *reported 1 Kingfisher [plane] overboard.*

1017. The Rudyerd Bay *reported she was dead in the water.*

1128. The Cape Esperance *reported fire on her flight deck. . . .*

The ships—the big and little—are racked and strained, punished and pommeled. The men are dazed; all hands are in lifejackets; none stand topside in exposed positions; muscles are sore and bodies bruised from clinging to stanchions, pounding against bulkheads; a miserable many retch from seasickness, but for hundreds terror calms the queasiness of the stomach. The violent rolls and the terrible mountains of water —seventy feet from trough to crest—are frightening, even to the experienced; some are plain scared, but most have confidence in the stoutness of their vessels.

But this is "one-hand-for-your-ship-and-one-for-yourself" weather; the business is to survive.

The voice of the storm drowns all other voices; the wind has a thousand notes—the bass of growling menace, the soprano of stays so tautly strained they hum like bowstrings. The tops of the wave crests are flattened off by the wind and hurled straight before its violence; rain and spindrift mix in a horizontal sheet of water; one cannot tell where ocean stops and sky begins. . . .

. . . And over all is the cacophony of the ships—the racked and groaning ships, the creaking of the bulkheads, the working of the stanchions, the play of rivets, the hum of blowers, the slide and tear and roar of chairs and books adrift, of wreckage slipping from bulkhead to bulkhead. . . .

Low fuel, attempts to keep station, or to change course to ease pounding spell havoc for some. The seas are so great, the wind so strong, that some of the lighter destroyers are derelicts; all possible combinations of rudders and screws fail to take them out of the troughs; they are sloughed and rolled and roughed far on their sides by wind and water—and drift, out of control, downwind.

The light and escort carriers fare little better; aboard *San Jacinto, Monterey, Altamaha* and others, planes slide and slip; wreckage crashes groaning from bulkhead to bulkhead; the hangar decks are infernos of flame and crashing metal, of fire and wind and sea.

Early in the morning watch *San Jacinto*, Captain Michael H. Kernodle, commanding, tries to "swing to new course to ease her." The skipper backs the starboard engines, goes ahead twenty knots on the port, but the howling wind will have none of it; *San Jacinto* falls off into the trough, rolls 42 degrees. A plane breaks loose on the hangar deck, skids into other planes —each lashed to steel deck pad eyes with fourteen turns of wire and rope—tears them loose, and the whole deckload crash from side to side with each roll, "rupturing and tearing away all air intakes and vent ducts passing through the hangar decks." Engine spares and other heavy material stowed on the hangar deck break loose and smash and tear into the bulkheads; oily water greases the deck; steam hisses from the ruptured exhausts; the fire sprinkling system, damaged by the wreckage, sprays water indiscriminately over the deck spaces; general flooding results through the broken ventilation vents in fire rooms and engine rooms; the evaporators are out of commission; the galley ovens out; the after gyro compass inoperative; electrical leads severed.

It is Man against the sea, but Man wins; personnel of the damage control and fire-fighting parties lash themselves to lines suspended from the overhead of the hangar deck, and swinging and slithering like pendulums across the slippery deck, risk their lives to secure the mass of sliding, groaning wreckage.

Aboard *Altamaha*—all 14,000 tons of her, planing like a surfboard on the tremendous rollers—the planes she mothers turn against her; fire mains burst; wreckage litters the elevator pit; heavy seas break over the fantail; damage repair parties shore the bulkheads.

In *Monterey*, Nos. 1 and 2 firerooms are abandoned at 0914 because of heavy smoke from a hangar deck fire; ready ammunition is jettisoned; the boilers are manned by skeleton crews using rescue breathing masks; a gasoline vapor explosion kills one seaman; another, trapped by the flames, is burned to death, a third asphyxiated; many injured.

Destroyer *Dewey* labors almost to the death. Throughout the morning watch, with the storm howling like a banshee, the quartermaster on watch scribbles painfully in the deck log, as casualty reports funnel to the bridge:

0950. . . . Dewey *reported to CTG 30.8 she was out of control and passed through formation from starboard to port. Heavy rolling caused loss of lube oil suction repeatedly. . . .*

1006. *Captain ordered all port fuel tanks filled to capacity. 30,000 gallons of oil pumped to port side. Rolling through 40 to 50 degrees.*

1020. *Lost bridge steering control; steering aft. Telephone circuits began to go. Lost radar and TBS [radio—"Talk Between Ships"] contact with rest of formation. . . . Wind and sea rising, barometer falling.*

1102. *Doctor reported many men had been injured by falling.*

1130. *Main engines stopped—main switchboard shorted from salt water. Secured main generator. Electrical power and lights all gone. 500 to 1,000 gallons of water entering ⋕ 2 main forced draft intake on every big roll. Bucket brigade in mess hall and one aft kept water down.*

1130. *All control and communication lost from bridge. Dead in the water. The air . . . continually filled with salt spray 200 feet in the air or higher. Visibility zero. This blast of salt spray penetrated everything and grounded all electrical connections. . . . 8 inches of water in all living spaces produced undesirable "free surface effect." All hands told to remain on port side. Rolling and pounding worse. Inclinometer to 73 degrees to starboard and stopped for a few seconds. Engine room [indicated] 75 degrees. The masts and stacks . . . swinging and expected to carry away at any time. Tops of 3 ready ammo lockers torn off and 80 rounds of 5 inch spilled over the side. . . . All thin shielding of ship stove in—by water on starboard side—by wind on port.*

1145. The wind . . . estimated to be more than 110 knots. All hands performed in a commendable manner, especially the engineers . . . no panic.

But *Dewey*, as the morning dies, still lives.

Not so destroyers *Monaghan* and *Spence*.

Monaghan, DD 354, with twelve battle stars on her bridge and a veteran of combat from Pearl Harbor to Leyte, lunges to her doom—the fleet unknowing—late in that wild wind-swept morning.

She's last heard and dimly seen when the morning is but half spent:

0936. Monaghan to *Com. T.G. 30.8*—"I am unable to come to the base course. Have tried full speed, but it will not work."

1006. Monaghan to *unknown ship*—"You are 1,200 yards off my port quarter. Am dead in water. Sheer off if possible."

1007. Monaghan to *Hobby*—"Bearing is 225, 1,400 yards . . ."

Then . . . silence . . .

Monaghan's 1,500 tons of steel are racked and strained; her starboard whaleboat drinks the sea as the davits dip into green water. But there's little intimation of disaster. About eight bells—as the Wagnerian dirge of the typhoon drowns the lesser noises of the laboring ship—the wind pushes *Monaghan* far on her starboard side. She struggles to rise again—and makes it, but sluggishly. In the after deck house forty or fifty men cling to stanchions and pray—silently, or aloud:

"Don't let us down now, Dear Lord. Bring it back, Oh God! bring it back!"

Slowly the ship recovers:

"Thanks, Dear Lord."

But the lights go out; again the deep roll to starboard, again and again she struggles back, shudderingly, from disaster.

Then, about noon, the wind brutalizes her; heavily *Mona-*

ghan rolls to starboard—30, 40, 60, 70 degrees—tiredly she settles down flat on her side to die amid a welter of white waters and the screaming Valkyries of the storm. And there go with her eighteen officers and 238 men. . . .

Spence, DD 512, goes about the same time, but again the fleet unknowing. *Spence* is de-ballasted, light in fuel; she rides like a cork in the terrible canyon-like troughs. Power fails; the electrical board is shorted from the driven spray; the ship goes over 72 degrees to port—and stays there. The lights are out; the pumps are stopped—the ship's heart dead before the body dies; she drifts derelict. Sometime before noon, the Supply Officer—Lt. Alphonso Stephen Krauchunas, United States Naval Reserve, one-time of Kalamazoo, destined to be *Spence's* only officer survivor—sits on the edge of the bunk in the captain's cabin talking tensely with the ship's doctor. An awful roll throws Krauchunas on his back against the bulkhead "in a shower of books and whatnot." Crawling on hands and knees on the bulkheads (walls) of the passageway, Krauchunas gets topside just before the entering ocean seeks him out. He fights clear along with seventy others—but *Spence*, 2,000 tons of steel with the power of 60,000 horse, is done.

1200 *to* 1600 *The Afternoon Watch*

The afternoon watch brings some slight surcease to some ships, climax and desperation to others. The fleet is widely dispersed across a raging ocean; some ships have felt the full fury of the storm; others are still to feel it. Between 1100 and 1400 of that day the peak is reached; "mountainous seas . . . confused by backing winds made the vessels roll to unprecedented angles."

For *Hull*, Destroyer ⚓350, with much of the mail of the fleet still aboard, the afternoon watch of December 18, 1944, is to be her last. The quartermaster has hardly turned the log page before it happens.

Small and old as destroyers go, *Hull* had made heavy weather of it in the morning; the driven spray had shorted everything; in the CIC (Combat Information Center) leaky seams admitted the sea and "sparks were jumping back and forth among the electrical cables."

Hull's tanks are 70 per cent full of fuel oil; she's better off than her lighter sisters, though she has no water ballast. But the storm brooks no objections; gradually *Hull* loses the fight. Her radar is out; her TBS inoperative; the whaleboat smashed and torn loose; depth charges wrenched from the K-guns, and to "every possible combination of rudder and engines" the ship will not respond, and is blown "bodily before wind and sea, yawing between headings of 100 and 080 true."

Shortly after noon, as the seas tower into toppling mountains, the ship lies over on her side in terrible sickening rolls, and the junior officer of the watch is "catapulted completely through the air from the port side of the pilot house to the upper portion of the starboard side."

But still Lieutenant Commander James Alexander Marks, the young skipper, has hope. . . .

". . . the ship had withstood the worst punishment any storm could offer."

("I had served in destroyers," he later noted, "in some of the worst storms of the North Atlantic and believed that no wind could be worse than that I had just witnessed.")

But the wind increases to an estimated 110 knots; "the force of the wind . . . [lays] the ship steadily over on her starboard side and holds her down in the water until the seas come flowing into the pilot house itself."

Early in the afternoon—probably before 1300—the leaping sea hurtled up into the port wing of the bridge and young Lieutenant Commander James Alexander Marks steps off his capsized ship—his first command—into a sea "whipped to a froth," a sea so wildly angry, so ravening for life that life-jackets are torn from the backs of the few survivors. . . .

Destroyer *Dewey*, battered and racked in the morning watch, makes it—though hurt almost mortally.

At 1230 No. 1 stack carries away and falls over the side in a clutter of wreckage, leaving a gaping wound in the main deck and four hundred pounds of steam escaping from the ruptured whistle line in a shuddering roar that mingles with the berserk voice of the typhoon. The falling funnel carries away the whaleboat davits; this easing of the topside weight —and the skipper's prescience in the morning watch in counter-ballasting the high side—the port side—with most of his fuel, probably save the ship. Nevertheless, green water slops over the starboard wing of the bridge as the ship lies over an estimated 80 degrees to starboard—and lives to tell about it —perhaps the first vessel in the history of the sea to survive such a roll.

At 1300 the barometer drops to an estimated 27.30 inches —the needle off the scale—one of the lowest readings in the long narrative of storms.

But the typhoon has done its worst; at 1340 the barometer registers a slight rise, and at 1439 the wind slackens to about eighty knots.

The storm curves on into the wide open spaces of the Pacific the rest of that day—the eighteenth. The winds still howl; the ships still heave, the ocean is confused, and even on the nineteenth the seas are huge and horrid, but the great typhoon is over. Behind it, it leaves the fleet scattered and broken, with more unrequited damage, as Admiral Halsey later noted, than at any time since the First Battle of Savo Island. Survivors of *Monaghan* and *Hull* and *Spence* are pitifully few; destroyer escort *Tabberer*, herself demasted, picks up the first survivors from *Hull* at ten that night, and others—including Lieutenant Commander Marks—who had lost his first command—the next day. *Tabberer* also rescues ten survivors from *Spence* aboard a liferaft on the twentieth; other ships—scouring the ocean now that news of the sinkings is widely disseminated—find a handful of spent and injured sailors, who will forever comprehend, more fully than any living men, the meaning of the fury of the sea.

The great typhoon of December 17 and 18, 1944, cost 790 dead or missing—202 from the *Hull*, about 256 from the *Monaghan* (only six were saved), 317 from the *Spence*, three dead in the *Monterey*, others killed or missing from other ships. More than eighty men were injured; 146 planes were blown overboard or damaged beyond repair. The battleships lost planes and gear, but sustained no major damage; the large carriers suffered damage to radars and to the hangar deck roller curtains. But the small ships were battered and spent. Of the light carriers, *San Jacinto*, *Monterey*, *Cowpens*, *Cabot*, and *Langley* suffered badly; the list of *Monterey*'s damages covered nine closely-typed legal pages. The cruisers *Miami* and *Baltimore;* the escort carriers *Cape Esperance, Anzio* and *Altamaha,* and the destroyers and destroyer escorts *Aylwin, Dewey, Buchanan, Hickox, Benham, Donaldson, Melvin R. Nawman,* and *Dyson* required major repair, while nine other vessels sustained more minor damage. The strikes against Luzon were canceled and the Third Fleet straggled—cockbilled and askew—into the atoll of Ulithi.

A Navy Court of Inquiry, summoned to solemn postmortem, found that "large errors [had been] made in predicting the location and path" of the typhoon. Admiral Halsey called the typhoon a "disaster." Admiral Chester W. Nimitz pointed out that the damage done "represented a more crippling blow to the Third Fleet than it might be expected to suffer in anything less than a major action"; and the Commander-in-Chief of the Pacific Fleet noted his determination to inculcate his officers with "the necessity of understanding the Law of Storms. . . ."

The damaged ships were repaired; the typhoon warning service and meteorological forecasts were improved; the war continued toward its triumphant finale.

Yet on June 5, 1945—just six months later, with the end not far off—Third Fleet was again lashed, though with no ships lost and lesser damage, by a typhoon. Fleet Admiral "Ernie" King, the hard-bitten "sun-downer," who chivvied and harried the Navy to global victory from his Washington command post, was caustic; he noted the Third Fleet had been "involved" in a similar situation during the great typhoon of December 1944, and declared that "on each occasion," there had been sufficient information to avoid the worst damages, had officers "reacted to the situation as it developed with the weather-wise skill to be expected of professional seamen."

And . . . from Commander Service Force, a sobering comment from Man—arrogant in his victory against Man:

". . . there is no ship afloat that cannot be capsized in a seaway."

NOTES The great typhoon of 1944 was the real-life genesis for the fictional typhoon which formed the climactic denouement of *The Caine Mutiny.*

David J. Woodland of Atlantic City, N.J., writes that "I was serving aboard the De 415, *Lawrence C. Taylor,* flagship of the division containing the destroyer escorts *Tabberer* and *Melvin R. Nawman* . . . our ship remained on station with the escort carrier *Anzio* throughout the typhoon. With the exception of severe weathering, we emerged mostly undamaged and steamed continuously for another thirteen months with no further attention. We attributed this achievement to the excellent maintenance of the ship before the storm and seamanship under the command of Lt. Commander Ralph Cullihan."

Responsibility for the damages and losses sustained in the typhoon of December, 1944, was placed squarely upon the Commander Third Fleet (Admiral William F. Halsey), and to a "lesser degree" upon some of his subordinate commanders, but in "view of the valuable services rendered by these officers in prosecution of the war against our enemies" no action was taken. The mistakes made were "errors in judgment resulting from insufficient information committed under stress of war operations and stemmed from the firm determination to meet military commitments."

The second typhoon of June 5, 1945, which caught the fleet committed to support of the Okinawa battle, did less damage but caused even more ire in Washington, since to Admiral Ernest King it was redundant evidence of the lack of a seaman's "weather eye." Actually, the fleet's commitment to Okinawa permitted somewhat less discretion and gave it less maneuvering flexibility than it had had in December, 1944. Nevertheless, the records and endorsements of the second Naval Court of Inquiry show that Admiral King was quite angry and rightly so. Some of his remarks singed even three-star and four-star admirals.

The June 5, 1945 (Okinawa) typhoon caused serious damage to the carriers *Hornet, Bennington, Windham Bay,* and *Salamaua;* the cruisers *Pittsburgh* (which lost her bow), *Baltimore,* and *Duluth* were seriously damaged, and twenty-six other vessels sustained minor damage. Seventy-six planes were destroyed, seventy damaged, six officers and men were killed or lost overboard and four were seriously hurt.

Admiral King noted that the "gravity of the occurrence was accentuated by the fact that the senior officers concerned were also involved in a similar and poorly handled situation during the typhoon of Dec. 1944." But Admiral Chester W. Nimitz, Commander-in-Chief of the Pacific Fleet, noted that Admiral Halsey and other officers concerned had "rendered invaluable service to [their] country. . . . [Their] skill and determination have been demonstrated time and again in combat with the enemy."

The destroyers lost in the December, 1944, typhoon were not, by any means, the only ships that have capsized in a seaway.

The destroyer *Warrington* was lost in an Atlantic hurricane in 1944 and other smaller ships have similarly foundered. A few of our prewar destroyers had bad names as "top-heavy," a criticism that was oversimplified but that contained a definite kernel of truth. The addition of heavy top-side weights in the form of radar and anti-aircraft armament after the war started made it imperative that fuel tanks be ballasted as fuel was used.

The two typhoons led to improvements in ship design, particularly in quick-pumping arrangements for fuel and ballast tanks, in electrical panels more protected against floodwater, and in the lightening of top-side weights. They also speeded the development of the modern system of "hurricane-hunters" and storm forecasting, and renewed the traditional emphasis of the Navy—too much neglected during the war and, indeed, minimized in the age of steam and plane—on seamanship.

An August Day's Sail

SAMUEL ELIOT MORISON

The oceans can rage with typhoons, but then they can change dramatically. They can become so placid that they are an invitation to all sailors. Such day sailors are given a voice by Samuel Eliot Morison.

Samuel Eliot Morison was recently awarded the Medal of Freedom by the President of the United States. The highest civilian honor our country bestows, it is of course appropriate for a man of such diverse talents. A Rear Admiral, the Historian of United States Naval Operation in World War II, an authority on Columbus (and on all phases of our country's history), Morison can sail all types of craft from the ship of Columbus to a contemporary sailing dinghy. It seems particularly fitting to award the Medal of Freedom to a man who sails small boats—one of the last adventures in freedom left in our mechanical world. Here Admiral Morison and his son experience one of the greatest joys of the sea—an August day's sail.

A light, caressing southerly breeze is blowing; just enough to heel the yawl and give her momentum. The boy and I get under way from the mooring by the usual ritual. I take in the ensign, hoist the mizzen, cast off main sheet and slack the backstays; he helps me hoist the mainsail, sway the halyards and neatly coil them. I take the wheel and the main sheet in hand, the boy casts off the mooring rode and hoists the jib, and off she goes like a lively dog let off the leash.

We make a long, leisurely beat to windward out of the Western Way, with tide almost dead low; the reefs, sprayed with brown rockweed, show up clearly. We pass the bell buoy and leave to starboard the naked reef known to chart makers as South Bunkers Ledge.

Now we are in the open sea, nothing between us and Nova Scotia. The day is pleasantly cool and bright, with gathering cirrus clouds that sometimes obscure the sun. Old ocean today is green, heaving with a surge farflung from a blow somewhere between us and Europe. Visibility is so high that the horizon is a clean-cut line over which one can see the masts of fishing draggers whose hulls are concealed by the earth's bulge. Seaward, the Duck Islands seem to float on the emerald waters. Landward, the rocky shores of Great Cranberry Island are misty with the spray from a line of white breakers. One thinks of Heredia's line about Britanny: "Du Raz jusqu'à Penmarc'h la côte entière fume"—the entire coast is smoky. Ocean swell makes the yawl roll and pitch, not unpleasantly but in harmonious cadence with the sea, the motion starting little snaps and whistles among the cordage, and the tapping of reef-points on the mainsail.

This is the time for the lunch that Priscilla prepared for us— jellied eggs and baby carrots as hors d'oeuvres; mushroom soup in a thermos; succulent ham sandwiches freshly made with lettuce and mayonnaise; chilled beer from the icebox; homemade doughnuts, crisp outside and flaky-soft inside, as you find them only when made by a master hand in Maine.

Now we are off Bakers Island where the long, flat granite ledges, washed clean by winter gales, hang over a reddish-brown apron of kelp and dulse, whirling in the breakers that roar in past the Thumper ledge. We round the groaner, the perpetually whistling buoy, haul our wind and turn northward.

Here we face the superb panorama of Mount Desert Island and Frenchmans Bay. The westering sun kindles the granite summits of Sargent, Green and Newport mountains to rose color; and the ocean between us and them is cobalt blue. Spruce-dark Otter Cliff and bare, brown Great Head thrust out into Frenchmans Bay. Under this luminous northern sky, distant Schoodic stands out bold and clear; miles beyond, the summit of Pigeon Hill appears, and Petit Manan lighthouse tower, entrance post to the Bay of Fundy, pricks the eastern horizon.

We close-haul our sails, round the black can buoy and glide out of the ocean swell into the smooth, sheltered anchorage of Bakers Island. Flood tide is only one hour old; and my quest

is for fresh mussels in that clear, unpolluted water. We shoot
into the wind, avoiding the numerous lobster-pot buoys, hand
the jib and mainsail, drop the anchor and pay out scope on
the cable. I pull the skiff alongside and row ashore. Spicy late
summer fragrance wells out from the sundrenched island—
sweet grasses, goldenrod, aster; even some of the white and
pink *Rosa rugosa* for which this place is famous are still in
bloom. The colorful sea bottom appears; gray sand studded
with big smooth pebbles tumbled and polished by millennia
of winter gales, when the great combers at high water rip over
the reef barrier that now makes this spot a sheltered harbor.
Two more strokes of the oars, and the skiff grounds on a rock;
bucket in one hand and boat painter in the other, I make a
wobbly landing, unlike the fishermen who splash boldly ashore
in their rubber boots. Mussels are there in great plenty, their
dark blue shells with brown "beards" clinging in clusters to
barnacled rocks and to the wooden ways laid years ago for
the lighthouse keeper's skiff. In ten minutes' time I have
gathered a pailful, then shove the skiff off the rock where she
grounded, and row back to the yawl, facing forward to admire her perfect proportions, and the backdrop of mountains.

We make sail once more, weigh anchor, and the yawl
pirouettes on her keel to head toward home. My young sailor,
blond and lithe as one imagines ancient Greek sailors to have
been in the Ægean, gazes, speechless, at sea and mountains.
What is he, at nineteen, thinking of it all? Does the beauty of
sunwashed shore and granite mountains mean the same to him
as to me, four times his age? I respect the youth's right to his
own thoughts and do not ask, fearing perhaps to break the
spell by some offhand or discordant reply.

Now we close-haul the sails again to pass between Suttons
Island and the two Cranberries. I turn my back on the Isles-
ford shore where the summer houses are pretentiously in-
appropriate, but linger lovingly on the south shore of Suttons, its little cottages built in the good simple taste of a
century ago, when Maine men knew how to create as beautiful a house as a ship. Suttons, with its memories of John
Gilley and Mary Wheelwright, of picnics long ago, of clumps
of blue harebell growing like weeds from the wild grass. In
this bight of the Bay we encounter the inevitable spell of

calm. The yawl holds her headway for two or three hundred yards, her sails full although the surface of the sea has become a wavy mirror; the ripples from her bows making sweet music. Finally her headway ceases, the sails gently flap, the booms swing from side to side, and the reef points play a tattoo on the mainsail.

What makes this particular day so memorable is its freedom from the mutter of motors. All power yachts are following the annual race in Blue Hill Bay, no snarling outboards are about. The lobstermen have finished hauling their traps and are at home eating supper. There is no sound but the lapping of waves on the shore, the lazy clang of Spurlings Ledge bell buoy, and the distant bark of a dog.

After a breathless calm of a quarter hour, the breeze returns, limp sheets stretch out taut with a clatter of blocks, sails fill, and the yawl heels to the last of the west wind.

Around the western point of Suttons, Bear Island makes out. Its white lighthouse tower and pyramidical bell house seem to look down like benign parents on three tiny sloops that flutter past, having a little race of their own as they did not rate the big cruise. How many thousands of sailing craft have passed that sea mark since 1839 when, at the suggestion of a naval captain, the government built the light station? How many seamen have blessed that winking white eye guiding them through Eastern or Western Way to the snug harbors within, or strained their ears to catch the deep-throated note of the fog bell?

Leaving the cliffs of Bear Island astern on the starboard quarter, we enter Northeast Harbor with the dying breeze, avoiding the ever present "Kimball's Calms" on the port hand. My boy lowers and neatly furls the jib, then stands with boat hook, poised like a classic harpooner, to spear the mooring buoy. Main and mizzen sheets are hauled flat to give the yawl one last graceful curvet before her way is checked in the wind's eye. Then the mooring rode is secured to the forward bitts, and the yacht's white wings are folded for the night.

ABOUT THE CONTRIBUTORS

Rachel Carson was born in Springdale, Pennsylvania, in 1907. She began her study of biology at Pennsylvania College for Women and continued it at Johns Hopkins University and the Marine Biological Laboratory at Woods Hole. While working on *The Sea Around Us* Miss Carson consulted leading oceanographers in this and other countries and literally made the sea her laboratory, taking part in an oceanographic expedition in North Atlantic waters, and diving among the Florida coral reefs. She died in 1964.

John Griffith London was born in San Francisco in 1876. In 1897 he took part in the Klondike gold rush, and from his experiences wrote *The Call of the Wild*. His book *The Cruise of the Snark* relates his experiences on a world cruise. At this time he was reckoned the best paid and most popular writer in America. He died in 1916.

Lafcadio Hearn was born on the Ionian island of Santa Maura in 1850, son of a British surgeon-major and his Greek wife. He was educated in England and France, and then went to America where he took up journalism. He went to Japan in 1890, became a Japanese citizen, and held the Chair of English Literature at Tokyo University. He died in 1904.

Edward Rowe Snow was born in Winthrop, Massachusetts, in 1902. He received his A.B. from Harvard University in 1932, and his M.A. from Boston University in 1939. A former high school teacher, daily columnist for a Massachusetts newspaper, and lecturer, Mr. Snow's numerous publications all deal with the sea.

Archie Carr, Professor of Biological Sciences at the University of Florida, was born in Mobile, Alabama, in 1909. Five years in Honduras and travels to all the other Central American countries, the northern part of South America, Mexico, and the West Indies have made him thoroughly familiar with all the shores of the Caribbean.

Henry Beston was born in Quincy, Massachusetts, in 1888. He is the author of many books, including *White Pine and Blue Water, Northern Farm,* and *St. Lawrence.* He has also written many articles for periodicals and is an honorary editor of the national *Audubon Magazine.*

William Beebe, an eminent naturalist, was born in Brooklyn in 1877, and was educated at Columbia University. He became curator of ornithology at the Bronx Zoo, and many of his books are accounts of expeditions he made to Mexico and British Guiana. Beebe was the first man to descend more than 3000 feet into the depths of the ocean, and *Half Mile Down* tells of descents in his bathysphere off Bermuda. He died in 1962.

Henry David Thoreau was born in Concord, Massachusetts, in 1817. After graduation from Harvard, he tried to undertake a teaching career, but he considered himself a failure. He lived for two years in a cabin on Walden Pond, an experiment he recorded in *Walden, or Life in the Woods.* It was published in 1854 and is a world-famous contribution to the literature of nature. He died in 1862.

Gilbert C. Klingel, author, naturalist, and businessman, was born in Baltimore, Maryland, where he now resides, and was educated at Baltimore Polytech Institute. He has undertaken several scientific expeditions, and has made underwater explorations in Chesapeake Bay, in co-operation with the Chesapeake Biological Laboratory. Mr. Klingel is the author of *The Bay,* which won him the John Burroughs Medal in 1953 for excellence in nature writing.

Jacques-Yves Cousteau was born at St. André de Cubzac, France, in 1910 and was educated at the Brest Naval Academy. He is the director of the Oceanographic Museum of Monaco and the president of the World Underwater Confederation. His movie *The Silent World* won a Hollywood Oscar and the Grand Prize of the Cannes International Film Festival.

Eugenie Clark was born in New York City in 1922 and attended Hunter College and New York University. She specialized in ichthyology and oceanography at the University of Michigan Biological Station, at Scripps Institute of Oceanography at the University of California, at the Woods Hole Marine Biological Laboratory, and at the Lerner Marine Laboratory in the West Indies. She has had three science fellowships: from the Pacific Science Board to study poisonous fishes in Micronesia, from the Atomic Energy Commission to study reproductive behavior and physiology of fishes, and as a Fulbright Research Scholar in Egypt to study the fishes of the Red Sea. In private life, Dr. Clark is the wife of Dr. Ilias Konstantinu and the mother of two daughters.

Arthur C. Clarke was born in Somerset, England, in 1917. A well-known authority on space, he is a founder of the British Interplanetary Society. He went underwater in 1951 and has been diving constantly since. He and his cameraman-partner, Michael Wilson, work out of Colombo, Ceylon.

Captain Edward L. Beach was born in Mystic, Connecticut, in 1918. A 1939 Annapolis graduate and son of a naval officer, he fought in submarines all through World War II and commanded the U.S.S. *Trigger II* during the Korean War. From 1953 to 1957 he was Naval Aide to the President. He is the author of a novel of submarine warfare, *Run Silent, Run Deep.*

William Lay of Saybrook, Connecticut, and *Cyrus Hussey* of Nantucket, Massachusetts, were the only survivors of the 1824 mutiny on the *Globe.*

Frank R. Stockton was born in Philadelphia in 1834. He was well known as a wood engraver before he became an important editor of the famous *St. Nicholas* magazine. He wrote many novels and a very famous short story, "The Lady or the Tiger?". He died in 1902.

Frank Thomas Bullen was born in England in 1857. He went to sea as a boy and became in his later years one of England's foremost writers and lecturers on ocean life. *Told in the Dog Watches* and *The Cruise of the Cachalot* are two of his best-known works. He died in 1915.

Sir Ernest Shackleton was born in 1874 in Ireland. He trained to be a merchant service officer while still a young boy. By the time he was sixteen he was an apprentice aboard a full-rigged ship. He served as a junior officer on the Robert Scott "Discovery" expedition. He died at South Georgia Island on his third Antarctic expedition in 1922.

Hanson W. Baldwin was born in Baltimore in 1913. He graduated

from the United States Naval Academy and served aboard battleships and destroyers. He was awarded a Pulitzer Prize in 1942.
He is military editor of the New York *Times*.

Samuel Eliot Morison lives in the same house in Boston in which
he was born seventy-eight years ago. In that time he has sailed
the world. He was the first recipient of the Balzan Foundation
award in history (a prize comparable to a Nobel Prize). He is
the author of many books including the brilliant *Oxford History of
the United States*. He taught at Harvard University for forty years.

ABOUT THE EDITORS

Seon Manley (Mrs. Robert R. Manley) and *Gogo Lewis* (Mrs. William W. Lewis), who are sisters, have collaborated on many books. Their interest in the oceans started early, as they have always lived part of each year on the shores of the Atlantic. Professionally, Mrs. Manley and Mrs. Lewis have also collaborated on several ocean technology projects for Robert Manley Associates, Inc., an engineering management firm which has worked on outer space and on inner space—the oceans.